Jossey-Bass Teacher

Jossey-Bass Teacher provides K–12 teachers with essential knowledge and tools to create a positive and life-long impact on student learning. Trusted and experienced educational mentors offer practical classroom-tested and theory-based teaching resources for improving teaching practice in a broad range of grade levels and subject areas. From one educator to another, we want to be your first source to make every day your best day in teaching. *Jossey-Bass Teacher* resources serve two types of informational needs—essential knowledge and essential tools.

Essential knowledge resources provide the foundation, strategies, and methods from which teachers may design curriculum and instruction to challenge and excite their students. Connecting theory to practice, essential knowledge books rely on a solid research base and time-tested methods, offering the best ideas and guidance from many of the most experienced and well-respected experts in the field.

Essential tools save teachers time and effort by offering proven, ready-to-use materials for in-class use. Our publications include activities, assessments, exercises, instruments, games, ready reference, and more. They enhance an entire course of study, a weekly lesson, or a daily plan. These essential tools provide insightful, practical, and comprehensive materials on topics that matter most to K–12 teachers.

A Teacher's Guide to Classroom Assessment

A Teacher's Guide to Classroom Assessment

Understanding and Using Assessment to Improve Student Learning

Susan M. Butler
Nancy D. McMunn

SERVE Regional
Educational Laboratory
Greensboro, North Carolina

JOSSEY-BASS
A Wiley Imprint
www.josseybass.com

Published by Jossey-Bass
A Wiley Imprint
989 Market Street, San Francisco, CA 94103-1741   www.josseybass.com

ISBN-10 0-7879-7877-9
ISBN-13 978-0-7879-7877-8

Page 247 constitutes a continuation of this copyright page.

The content of this publication does not necessarily reflect the view or policies of the Institute of Education Sciences, U.S. Department of Education, nor does mention of trade names, commercial products, or organizations imply endorsement by the U.S. Government. This document was produced with funding from the Institute of Education Sciences, U.S. Department of Education, under contract no. ED-01-CO-0015.

Readers should be aware that Internet Web sites offered as citations and/or sources for further information may have changed or disappeared between the time this was written and when it is read.

Jossey-Bass books and products are available through most bookstores. To contact Jossey-Bass directly call our Customer Care Department within the U.S. at 800-956-7739, outside the U.S. at 317-572-3986, or fax 317-572-4002.

Jossey-Bass also publishes its books in a variety of electronic formats. Some content that appears in print may not be available in electronic books.

Printed in the United States of America
FIRST EDITION
PB Printing   10 9 8 7 6

Contents

Figures, Tables, and Exhibits

Figures

Tables

Exhibits

Foreword

Anticipating the pleasant task of writing this foreword, I began to reflect on my personal assessment experiences and those of my children. Unfortunately, the experiences that I remember most clearly were negative events, in particular, concerning my son. Two such experiences that really stick in my mind are reflective of the assessment practices my son was exposed to in high school.

Throughout his high school career, my son had great difficulty completing tests within the set time limit, often leaving unfinished work that lowered his grade. I will never forget one year when his English teacher came up to me in the local supermarket and said, "You know your son's grades don't accurately reflect what he knows and understands in English." My response was that if she was confident in this judgment, she should make the appropriate changes in his grade to reflect her belief. She replied, however, that she could not do this because all his scores had to be averaged to determine the report card grade. To me, this teacher had a misconception of what a grade represented.

Another experience that comes to mind was during my son's junior year, when he missed a chemistry test because he was playing football for the school and, although he said that he had told the teacher, his teacher claimed that he had not let him know in advance. My son received a zero on the test, which resulted in a poor grade on his interim report card. He had twelve other scores, besides the zero, that were A's and B's. When I suggested to the teacher that my son was actually achieving well, he was genuinely surprised because all he had looked at was the summary (averaged) grade.

I am sure that many teachers—and their children—have had poor assessment experiences like these, but unfortunately in most cases those experiences do not cause many teachers to reflect and change their own practice. The above examples represent varying aspects of poor quality assessment, as well as a lack of thinking about the rationale and effects of the practices used. Teachers would benefit greatly from reading this book because it does two things superbly: (1) it comprehensively addresses the *how* of quality classroom assessment and, more important, (2) it highlights the need for teachers to think reflectively about their assessment practices. Both achievements are particularly important in this area of assessment because, as the authors point out, most teachers have had little formal training in assessment and so tend to do in their classes what was done to them as students.

I believe that the most common inadequacies in classroom assessment are

- Lack of clarity with regard to learning goals and performance standards

- Failure to distinguish between the various purposes for assessment (diagnostic, formative, and summative)

- Overreliance on selected-response (especially multiple choice) tests that often do not match the nature of the learning goals

- Failure to recognize that assessment is a sampling procedure so teachers "count" everything rather than judiciously deciding how much and what evidence is necessary for each learner

- Insufficient control of factors that distort achievement, such as time, setting, and student characteristics

The Classroom Assessment Cycle that is the basis for this book provides a framework for overcoming all these failings. Topics covered include the design of good performance tasks and rubrics, and the communication challenge involved in grading and reporting. Using information such as this, teachers can develop into competent, confident assessors who use their professional knowledge and skills to help children learn. Ultimately, this is what this book is about—the use of assessment to support learning. In the standards-based systems in which we are now operating, this is a critical professional responsibility.

Many books have been written about assessment in the last few years, but what sets this book apart is its comprehensiveness and clarity, its emphasis on reflective thinking, and the experience of the authors as teachers, researchers, and staff developers, which has clearly informed the book's content and focus.

This book will be of interest and great value to teachers and students in a variety of settings: as a guide for all practicing teachers (K–16) and students and teachers in faculties of education, as a resource for teachers in learning teams and professional learning communities, and as a textbook for college courses on assessment. It would also be a valuable book for teachers to read on their own and use to reflect on their personal practices.

What stood out for me as I read this book is its clarity of focus and how true it is to the helpful template of the Classroom Assessment Cycle that is the basis for the book. The ultimate significance of this book will come from this laser-like focus on the authors' goal—"we wanted this text to encompass all of the topics needed for teacher understanding of assessment"—and from their adherence to the "bottom line" litmus test in decision making: *Does it promote learning, and is it what is best for our students?* Their goal is met by providing comprehensive theoretical knowledge and many practical examples, together with an emphasis on making readers think reflectively about their own practice. Other features of the book that make it so valuable are the emphasis on clear terminology, the useful and novel examples, and the ways in which the authors reveal their own thinking. This book will make a significant contribution to the body of works on classroom assessment. It will be equally valuable to new teachers and veterans. I am very glad that Susan and Nancy put their time and effort into producing this book. They are to be be commended for the excellent result.

January 2006

Ken O'Connor
Toronto and Panama City Beach

To our mothers, Dorothy and Janie, who have given us the love, wisdom, and courage to believe in ourselves and to value the work we do.

To our husbands, Lennie and Don, who have listened to us, supported us, and given up a lot of their personal time with us over the past few years, we love you.

To our children, Kerensa, Melody, Melissa, and Ryan, who have shown extreme patience with our lack of time to spend with them (we intend to make that up).

And to our boss, colleague, and friend, Wendy McColskey, who has pushed us beyond our limits, constantly provided the foundation of research we needed, and given us the freedom to write, as we wanted.

Thanks to all, you all!

Preface

This book, *A Teacher's Guide to Classroom Assessment: Understanding and Using Assessment to Improve Student Learning,* is appropriate for both beginning and veteran teachers who are searching for an understanding of quality classroom assessment practices. With practical information that also explores assessment theories and research studies, this text will aid readers in developing assessment skills and strategies, building their assessment literacy, and ultimately improving student learning. The guide may also be used by teacher educators, professional developers, and school administrators who are interested in preparing teachers to improve the use of classroom assessment practices to drive student learning.

In addition, this guide encourages readers to think about, reflect upon, and explore the power of classroom assessment to improve learning. The book presents many detailed, practical examples of how classroom assessment works in classrooms where assessment drives the instruction. As you read, we ask you to reflect on the many components of high-quality assessment practices and how these components interact, and to think seriously about the quality of the practices used in your own classroom or the classrooms in your school.

One impetus for this book is the lack of teacher preparation for designing and implementing high-quality classroom assessment practices. When interviewed, very few teachers report discussing classroom assessment issues during their preservice training. These teacher interviews, a research investigation of teacher preparation programs (which revealed that only two of sixteen such programs in North Carolina included any information on classroom assessment), our own experiences as teachers, and observations of colleagues have led us to believe that teachers are not getting the classroom assessment information they need to implement good assessment strategies (ones that emphasize using assessment to improve learning).

In preparing this manuscript, we have drawn upon personal experiences as students, parents, teachers, and professional developers to shape the topics presented here. We also examined many of the excellent existing publications on classroom practice (including those by Ken O'Connor, Grant Wiggins, Richard Stiggins, Robert Marzano, Tom Guskey, Sue Brookhart, Dylan Wiliam, and Jay McTighe). From these sources, we have tried to collate and organize the plethora of assessment information currently available. We feel that this text encompasses all the topics needed to promote teacher understanding of classroom assessment. We have organized these topics into one summarizing template, the Classroom Assessment Cycle, to help teachers visualize how one assessment action must flow into the next. These actions include

- Clarifying learning targets
- Collecting assessment evidence
- Analyzing assessment data
- Modifying instruction based upon assessment data

We present these topics and this guide because we believe that good assessment practices can greatly enhance student achievement.

Organization of the Text

The Introduction and Chapter One provide an overview of topics and introduce important assessment terms. Following these introductory sections, the book is then organized into five separate parts: Part One, "Clarifying Learning Targets"; Part Two, "Gathering Assessment Evidence"; Part Three, "Making Sense of Assessment Data"; Part Four, "Linking Assessment to Instruction"; and Part Five, "Related Assessment Factors." Within each part, chapters help explicate the four Classroom Assessment Cycle actions listed above and further explore factors of assessment that are interwoven internally and externally to these four quadrants of the cycle, such as

- Teacher beliefs and practices
- Classroom environments that promote learning
- Grading and reporting of student achievement
- High-stakes testing

The chapters, organized around key questions, provide the background knowledge and the practical examples teachers need to identify key learning targets from mandated curricula and to construct quality assessments aimed at measuring student performance against these targets. The chapters detail the kinds of assessment evidence that are the most useful in determining student achievement and provide instruction in the analysis of assessment data. They also explore the four factors listed above that may exist more externally to the Classroom Assessment Cycle, but which greatly influence it.

In addition, readers will find a wealth of material from and examples situated in the work of teachers. Such materials include examples of classroom dialogue between teachers and students, actual samples of student work, teacher-constructed classroom assessment instruments, sample scoring guides, rubrics and checklists, and design guides for planning classroom assessment tools and instruments.

All the concepts, chapters, and materials here are derived from the actual classroom experiences of over seven thousand teachers and other educators within the southeastern United States who participated in assessment enhancement professional development sessions with the authors. Therefore, the information presented in this book has been previously field tested by these seven thousand teachers, as well as used by teacher educators at North Carolina State University, the University of Georgia, and the North Georgia State College and University. In addition, the materials from this text have been filtered and distilled from use within the state departments of education in North Carolina and Mississippi.

We now share this distilled classroom assessment knowledge with you. We hope our readers will take this information, use it, and share it with other educators so quality assessment practices can grow throughout our educational system.

January 2006

Susan M. Butler
Lynn Haven, Florida

Nancy D. McMunn
Charlotte, North Carolina

Acknowledgments

What are the chances that two former chemistry teachers, each living in different states, would find each other and realize how similar their backgrounds were and decide that their futures would evolve together? It was fate!

Throughout the evolution of our careers in classroom assessment, we have had the privilege of meeting and working with exemplary colleagues, educators, and friends. We would like to acknowledge all the input into our thinking we garnered from this special group of people. First, our friends working in schools who have given us input, data, and characters for our work: educator Patricia Schenck with Bay District Schools in Panama City, Florida, and Hope Reagan, formerly working in the Winston-Salem Forsyth County Schools in North Carolina. They have given us ongoing availability and encouraged us to finish this book.

We also want to acknowledge readers who have provided feedback to us on drafts of this text, such as the University of Georgia (Athens) English Teachers Group directed by Sally Ross, Peg Graham, and Patti McWhoriter. College professors who have used written portions of this book in their course work include India Podsen and Susan Galloway at the North Georgia College and State University in Dahlonega.

Reviewers who have offered feedback, extensive editing, and honest input to help us improve this book include Carla Lovett, Panama City, Florida; Jan Williamson, Greensboro, North Carolina; and Ken O'Connor, Toronto, Canada. They stimulated our thinking, served as a sounding board for ideas, and encouraged the completion of the text.

We also want to acknowledge other assessment professionals: Dylan Wiliam, Rick Stiggins, Judy Arter, Ken O'Connor, Tom Guskey, Sue Brookhart, and others who have not only helped shape our thinking but who also continue working to spread the message about the importance of classroom assessment.

We have also benefited greatly from our SERVE colleagues and the work we have done in the area of classroom assessment at the SERVE Regional Educational Laboratory housed at the University of North Carolina in Greensboro. SERVE's mission is to promote and support the continuous improvement of educational opportunities for all learners in the Southeast, with a strong focus on research and development. Without the SERVE work, this book would not have been possible.

About the Authors

Nancy D. McMunn is an experienced project director for classroom assessment for the Assessment, Accountability, and Standards program at the SERVE Regional Education Laboratory housed at the University of North Carolina, Greensboro. She has substantial experience in translating research into practice for educators in all curriculum and classroom areas. She has developed and delivered professional development opportunities related specifically to classroom assessment to over 7,000 educators. Her most recent work at SERVE is directing the development of the Competent Assessment of Reading Toolkit and professional development program and other supplemental resources as a result of her research and development work with reading teachers in grades three through eight. She is a former high school chemistry and biology teacher in the North Carolina public school system. During her classroom-teaching career she received numerous educational awards such as the Ben Craig Award, WBTV Thanks to Teachers Award, and the AT&T Teachers and Technology Governor's Fellow appointment for North Carolina. Since leaving the classroom she has coauthored over fourteen articles and training resources, including working with the other national regional laboratories to produce the *Toolkit98, Improving Classroom Assessment,* available online at (www.nwrel.org). Two publications have received Outstanding Awards from the American Educational Research Association (AERA) in the area of building capacity in classroom assessment. She is further distinguished through more than forty national and international conference presentations for organizations such as NSDC, ASCD, and AERA. She received her BS in science, her teaching certification, and master's degree at the University of North Carolina in Charlotte. She may be contacted at 8530 Brookings Drive, in Charlotte, North Carolina, 28269. E-mail: donmcmunn@bellsouth.net.

Susan M. Butler is presently a faculty member in teacher education at Gulf Coast Community College in Panama City, Florida. While coauthoring this book, she was employed as the Senior Program Specialist in Classroom Assessment for the Assessment, Accountability, and Standards program at SERVE, a regional education laboratory housed at UNCG. Susan has conducted and published educational research since 1995, contributed chapters to educational texts, and offered workshops and presentations to educators across the country. Her most recent work at SERVE has been in leading the development of a training manual for the Mississippi Department of Public Instruction, *Creating a Complete Instructional Experience for Students: Putting All the Pieces Together,* and in creating an interactive online course in assessment in conjunction with the Cisco Learning Institute. She is a former high school chemistry and biology teacher in the Florida public school system. During her classroom-teaching career, she received numerous educational awards, such as the prestigious 1995 Presidential Award for Excellence in Secondary Science Teaching, as well as the Outstanding High School Science Teacher for the State of Florida. In 1994, Susan was selected as a National Science Teachers Association/Dow Chemical Company Fellow. Since leaving the classroom she has authored and coauthored over thirty articles, publications, and papers. From 1998 to 2003 she was a teacher educator at North Carolina State University, in Raleigh, first serving as assistant professor and program coordinator, health occupations education, Department of Curriculum and Instruction, and then as assistant professor, science education, Department of Mathematics, Science, and Technology. While at North Carolina State she was inducted into the 2000 class of the Academy of Outstanding Faculty Engaged in Extension at North Carolina State University and received the 1998–1999 Outstanding Extension Service Award for service to North Carolina State University's extension students. She also garnered the 1999 VIP Award for service to the North Carolina Health Occupations Students of America organization. Other distinctions in her career include the development and implementation of over forty workshops and presentations on topics such as problem-based learning, classroom assessment, and unit development. She received her doctorate in science education and master's in science education from Florida State University. She may be contacted at 113 Landings Drive, in Lynn Haven, Florida, 32444. E-mail: smbutler@knology.net.

Introduction: Assessment for Classroom Learning

Classroom assessment is of vital importance to student learning. Research demonstrates that student achievement is increased (particularly for low student achievers) by the use of classroom assessment when such assessment features good feedback to students about their performance, sets clear standards for learning, is ongoing so it can be used to monitor student growth and progress, and is used to modify instruction to meet the needs of the student (see, for example, Black and Wiliam, 1998). Such classroom assessment promotes assessment *for* learning rather than assessment *of* learning. Assessment *for* learning (a term coined by Black and Wiliam) requires that assessment occur regularly and that the information gained is used to mold teaching and learning. Assessment *for* learning is assessment that helps students identify the strengths and weaknesses of their performance so that they can improve their achievement. It is differentiated from assessment of learning, which simply provides a means of rating students, or comparing them one to another. Assessment *of* learning, unlike assessment *for* learning, does not focus on feedback for improvement.

Why Classroom Assessment Matters

What really matters in assessment is what is happening or not happening in the classroom on a daily basis. For most teachers, unfortunately, implementing assessments that have the power to positively affect student learning is difficult. Difficulty arises due to a lack of direct support for classroom assessment activities, (Black and Wiliam, 1998), the complicated nature of such assessments, and conflicts between classroom assessment practices and current policy or professional development precepts (Martin-Kniep, 1998). As a result (for those looking in from outside classroom walls), teachers have seemed slow to change. In order to change and make improvements in the classroom, teachers need a clear understanding of classroom assessment, examples and models to emulate, feedback on their efforts, and support along the way.

Therefore, much of what we do in this book is designed to give classroom teachers the knowledge and tools they need to enhance the quality of classroom interactions and to implement ongoing assessment so as to make a difference in how students learn. We primarily focus on formative assessment (assessment that occurs during the learning process) rather than on summative assessment (assessment that occurs at the end of the learning process). We provide teachers with the support necessary for translating state standards into classroom practice, with the aim that classroom assessments (*formative* processes) prepare students well for high-stakes evaluations (*summative* processes).

So, the purpose of formative assessment (often referred to as *monitoring*) is to provide feedback to students as they progress toward a learning goal. If this feedback is of high quality, improvement in student performance can result. As Rick Stiggins reminds us,

> We have centered so heavily on the development of ever-more-sophisticated psychometrics and test development tactics for our high stakes tests that we have almost completely ignored the other 99.9% of the [formative] assessments that happen in a student's life. These are the assessments developed and used by their teachers in the classroom. If we seek excellence in education, then the time has come to invest whatever it takes to assure that every teacher is gathering dependable information about student learning, day-to-day and week-to-week, and knows how to use it to benefit students.
>
> This action must be central to all future school improvement efforts, because if assessment is not working effectively in our classrooms everyday, then assessment at all other levels (district, state, national or international) represents a complete waste of time and money [Stiggins, 1999, p. 193].

In this book, we offer instruction on a great variety of assessment styles and techniques, including rubrics for scoring. We also address the knowledge versus implementation gap that has resulted from the research on assessment and evaluation having outpaced classroom applications of that knowledge. We aim in this book to help teachers apply these new understandings of assessment and new methods in the classroom. Finally, we address the complexity of ongoing assessment by presenting the Classroom Assessment Cycle, an approach that guides teachers to improve their assessment practice systematically over time and to refine how they use assessment results to inform instruction and engage students more actively. We attempt to equip teachers with the knowledge, understanding, and habits of mind to deal competently with these complexities in everyday practice. By studying this cycle, we hope teachers learn to plan with the end in mind.

We ourselves have had the experience of learning through trial and error about the power of classroom assessment. Here, for example, is one of Nancy's personal learning experiences:

One year Nancy taught a young football star named Len. Len did not pass the first quarter of chemistry and was in danger of failing the second quarter. At this time, Nancy was using the multiple-choice "pullout tests" that accompanied the textbook to assess her students' understanding of chemical concepts. However, during the second quarter, she decided that too many of her students were failing her class and showing a lack of motivation toward learning the concepts. She decided that her students needed an opportunity to view and appreciate chemistry as a lifelong learning experience, and she began to think that maybe her teaching strategies did not match the way her students were assessed. She wanted to make chemistry enjoyable for her students, and at the same time she wanted them to understand the basic concepts.

Nancy decided to change her assessment strategy as students were beginning their study of the gas laws. She began her instruction on this topic with the end in mind—the assessment. Instead of taking a test, the students' assessment experience would be to present one of the gas laws. In this presentation, the student had to show his or her classmates the following: an authentic use of the gas law, a real-world application of the law through a demonstration, and an explanation by example of the formula for determining some relevant factor, using the gas law. She felt that if her students could hit those three targets, they would understand the basic concepts, and their presentations would show what they knew and were able to do.

Although not all Nancy's students were supportive of this change, she soon realized that many of the students, including Len, were excited about the possibility of viewing chemistry as it related to their "real" world. After several days of facilitated classroom work, she asked her students to help in creating a rubric for scoring their presentations. The students responded to this session with a good attitude but at the same time showed some hesitancy because they had never been asked to do this. They did want to know how they would be assessed, since this assessment was not their typical paper and pencil test.

The day for the presentations arrived, and Len came to class carrying a bicycle tire, an air pump, soda pop cans, and posters. He stood in front of his classmates and demonstrated how his gas law related to their world and how to calculate pressure differences by using the formulas from their text. He made a tremendous mess in the classroom with the soda pop under pressure, and for weeks afterward his classmates teased him about the sticky pop on their chairs. However, he responded well to such teasing because he knew he had understood his assignment and he had become more confident and comfortable in the chemistry class. He was actually ready for the next assignment.

Nancy also learned a few things that day. The most depressing was that it had taken her almost two quarters of the school year to realize Len's strengths and talents. Len understood some areas of chemistry even better than his teacher, but the earlier assessments had not revealed his understanding, and Nancy realized Len was not able to express his knowledge through tests. Nancy was depressed about failing to meet the needs of this student, but she also felt he might still have time to succeed in her class, and she began to work on that.

She began to change her assessment and instructional strategies in the classroom to meet the needs of all her multitalented students. Nancy could not do everything but she focused on a few things she could accomplish the rest of the year. She learned to use multiple types of assessments, created rubrics for labs and projects, and provided ways for more student involvement in assessment through peer and self-assessment activities. And she began to build more instructional strategies that would involve students in thinking about what they were doing by relating their assignments to the real world. That year changed Nancy's ideas about teaching. This was the "aha" that changed her perspective on what good teaching was about.

This story illustrates the transformative power of thoughtful classroom assessment: accurate assessments lead to better learning. At the same time, it also reveals how poor assessments can result in poor evaluations of students. Nancy was using one type of assessment, a multiple-choice test, repeatedly in her classroom. Obviously, this assessment process did not reveal Len's understanding of chemistry. It was only through changing her assessment methods that Nancy came to realize Len's grasp of some chemical concepts. This led her to a further exploration of assessment techniques that require students to construct rather than simply select answers (and eventually led her to coauthor this book).

What the Research and the Experts Say

In the 1980s, educational researchers such as Benjamin Bloom (1984) were busy looking at classroom activities that improved student learning. One attribute that evolved from the experimental groups in his study, "The Search for Methods of Group Instruction as Effective as One-to-One Tutoring," was the power of formative assessment.

As Protheroe (2001) tells us, "There is a growing body of evidence that the use of high-quality, targeted assessment data, in the hands of school staff trained to use it effectively, can improve instruction" (p. 2). For example, the North Carolina Department of Public Instruction (NCDPI) profiled a study on schools that demonstrated success with "closing the gap." "Closing the (achievement) gap" is a target of the North Carolina Department of Public Instruction's School Improvement Division, in which staff work to improve student achievement (reduce the gap) among various populations of public school students and also challenge all students to achieve higher standards. The 2000 study *Closing the Achievement Gap: Views from Nine Schools*, "focused specifically on such schools where Black student achievement is exceptionally high, where Black students have made strong gains, or where the achievement gap between white and Black students is closing faster than the state average" (p. 1). One of the eight common themes that contributed to gains in "closing the gap" showed that these high-performing schools often diagnostically assessed students and then analyzed the resulting data to learn how to help students (North Carolina Department of Public Instruction, 2000a).

Niyogi, too, finds that high-quality classroom-based assessments can tell teachers much more about student learning than they can gather from other testing: "Assessment should be used not simply to judge how much kids know but to illuminate the nature of their knowledge and understandings in order to help kids learn. . . . Common sense tells us that on-going, classroom-based assessment can serve this purpose. Teachers interacting with students will observe the nuances of their cognitive growth and development over time, their individual strengths and weaknesses in ways that would be extremely difficult, if not impossible, to capture through standardized or conventional testing alone" (Niyogi, 1995, p. 3).

An example of illuminating knowledge of students comes from Ms. Reagan, a middle school reading coach who often reads with a huge number of low-ability readers during the day. When she asks her students whether they think they are good readers, most of them tell her, "yes," they read well. What her middle school students do not realize is that they only read on a second grade level. This could explain why these students do not do well in their academic classes. The lesson here is that the teacher has an obligation to let students know what a good reader looks like in middle school and then plan instruction to help them get there.

Formative classroom assessment can uncover individual student learning needs while most standardized testing results simply reveal the tip of the assessment iceberg of student achievement (see Figure I.1). Classroom assessment from day-to-day student interactions with curriculum provides data that are far more varied, and this information forms the base of the assessment iceberg. As we learned from the Titanic, it can be very dangerous to ignore the massive base of the iceberg and focus only on the smaller, more visible tip.

Of course the object of identifying students who are not mastering particular objectives—or who are just generally below grade level—should be to provide support for these students. In their study of "high-performance districts," Cawelti and Protheroe revealed some common characteristics among the ways these districts organized and then used classroom assessment. They supported "instructional processes that enable teachers to accomplish three things on a daily and weekly basis: (1) organizing instruction to regularly administer interim assessments of skills taught before moving on to new material, (2) providing tutoring or extra help for those students who fail to master the skills taught and enrichment learning activities for those who have mastered the skills, and (3) providing frequent practice throughout the year to ensure retention for students who have initially mastered the skills needed" (Cawelti and Protheroe, 2001, p. 98).

It has been our experience, too, that using the data from assessment is important for teachers, schools, and districts; nevertheless, we find that the use of classroom assessment data as a powerful means of linking assessment to instruction is often overlooked. Our observation is in accord with the findings in an award-winning paper from the American Educational Research Association. In "Districts Building Teacher Assessment

FIGURE I.1. ASSESSMENT ICEBERG.

Evidence of Student Learning

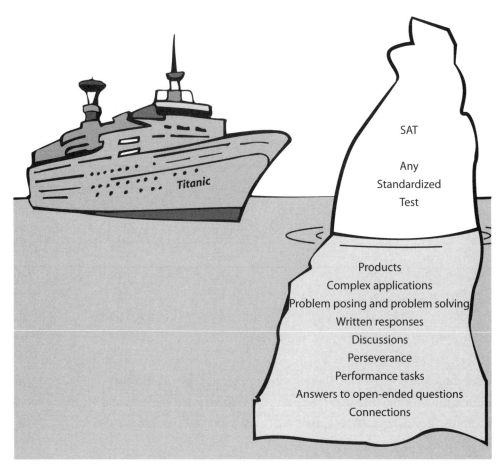

Source: Jeane Joyner and Jan Williamson. Developed for classroom assessment training for the North Carolina Department of Public Instruction, 1999.

Capacity in Classroom Assessment," McMunn, McColskey, and O'Connor (2000, p. 8) listed the lessons learned in a study of thirteen school districts (twelve in the United States and one in Canada) to determine what these districts were doing to build teachers' assessment capacity. These districts did many excellent things. They

1. Had a vision or plan that supported standards-based assessment

2. Took on the challenge of change in secondary schools

3. Defined standards-based assessment, especially as it related to large-scale (state) assessments

4. Involved district leadership

5. Created time

6. Included school leaders (early)

7. Ensured adequate financial resources

8. Organized resources, especially staff, to support change

9. Provided assessment workshops—started with volunteers but at some point made it a requirement for all teachers

10. Required classroom application and follow-up

11. Developed models—units, assessments, etc.

12. Provided a flexible approach/examples

13. Collected evidence (to help look at student and teacher work)

14. Encouraged action research

However, the lessons learned did not include using classroom assessment data in order to change instructional strategies and improve student learning. The above list does emphasize the collection of student evidence, but often the use of the data collected did not necessarily affect the instructional strategies used to improve the learning.

Stiggins (2001b) shares two conditions necessary to integrate assessment into the teaching and learning process. First, "to assess student achievement accurately, teachers and administrators must understand the achievement targets their students are to master. They cannot assess (let alone teach) achievement that has not been defined" (2001b, p. 19). The second condition Stiggins describes is an assessment-literate faculty. "Assessment literacy comprises two skills: first is the ability to gather dependable and quality information about student achievement; the ability to use that information effectively to maximize student achievement" (Stiggins, 2001b, p. 20).

However, research also shows that assessment literacy is not a routine part of teacher education:

> Even though teachers can spend as much as a third to a half of their professional time involved in assessment related activities (Herman and Dorr-Bremme, 1982; Crooks, 1988; Stiggins and Conklin, 1991), study after study shows that K–12 teachers lack skill in assessing their students (Impara, et al., 1993; Plake, et al., 1993; Hills, 1991) and that they feel unprepared and uncomfortable in their own knowledge of assessment practices (Shafer, 1993; Wise et al., 1991; Zhang, 1997). Due to current emphasis on standards-based education teachers will probably be expected to be even more assessment literate in the future than they are today (Stiggins, 1998) [Arter, 2000, p. 6].

Our Classroom Assessment Cycle guides teachers in acquiring both of these assessment literacy skills.

The Classroom Assessment Cycle

Figure I.2 outlines the central portion of the Classroom Assessment Cycle, the elements of assessment that are under the teacher's direct control. This cyclic guide to classroom action synthesizes our research and development over a number of years. We have been systematically developing and reviewing the ideas that underlie the Classroom Assessment Cycle since 1998. As described later in this book, the elements of the Classroom Assessment Cycle, like current educational trends and legislation (data-driven instruction, differentiated learning, No Child Left Behind), are derived from recent educational research studies.

Figure I.2 is an aid intended to help teachers visualize the use of high-quality assessment practices. The cycle forms a working design upon which teachers can build their assessment knowledge, and it illustrates a thinking process that gets at the heart of formative assessment. It is a vision of assessment *for* student learning (not *of* student learning), and it illustrates the key assessment components a teacher should reflect upon and use in the classroom in an ongoing, recursive cycle that has four parts, or quadrants:

1. *Learning targets are clarified.* This quadrant involves defining learning targets clearly so that students understand them.

2. *Evidence is gathered in a variety of ways.* This quadrant asks teachers to use multiple and diverse assessments in order to produce a fuller and clearer view of how well students met the learning targets: that is, what students really know.

3. *Inferences, analyses of data, and interpretations are made.* In this quadrant teachers determine what the assessment results mean: what they say about how students are learning and how that learning might be improved.

4. *Instructional plans and modifications are carried out.* In this quadrant new or modified instructional plans are designed to meet student needs revealed by the inferences and interpretations made in quadrant 3.

Parts One through Four of this book focus on a holistic explanation of the Classroom Assessment Cycle as an interactive process that concentrates on improving student performance, not merely giving grades. Each quadrant is explained separately and in considerable detail, with many examples. Teachers can enter the cycle in

FIGURE I.2. CLASSROOM ASSESSMENT CYCLE.

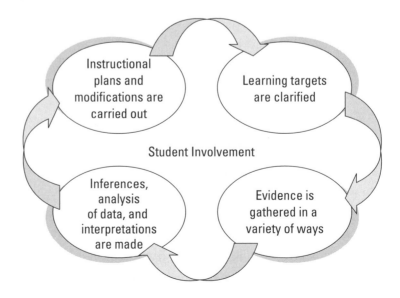

any quadrant. We feel that setting learning targets is a good entry point, so Part One of this book, "Clarifying Learning Targets," begins with this quadrant of the Classroom Assessment Cycle. This portion of the book focuses on helping teachers outline the key learning targets for students and design strategies and methods to assess these learning targets. It discusses relating these targets to standards, benchmarks, and curricular guidelines and defining student expectations for learning.

In Part Two, "Gathering Assessment Evidence," we move to the next quadrant of the cycle. This part explores many of the assessment methods that will measure student achievement of the targets. It offers approaches to designing tasks to assess student performance, creating useful scoring guides, or rubrics, using portfolios, and assessing through teacher questions and observations.

Part Three, "Making Sense of Assessment Data," presents ideas from the section of the Classroom Assessment Cycle in which inferences, analysis of data, and interpretations are made. This section introduces teachers to methods of analyzing assessment data to uncover information of practical significance to classroom instruction.

Part Four, "Linking Assessment to Instruction," completes the Classroom Assessment Cycle by exploring the quadrant in which assessment and instructional modifications are carried out. This portion of the book guides teachers to integrate lessons, assessment activities, and rubrics; motivate students; give students feedback that they can act on; and engage in reflection on their own beliefs about assessment and how those beliefs might be affecting their classroom practice.

Assessment occurs in a context, of course. Four factors that the internal Classroom Assessment Cycle is immersed in, which are very important to understanding assessment, are shown in Figure I.3. These factors influence teacher actions in each of the four quadrants and include what teachers believe about assessment and learning, how learning is communicated to others, how the classroom environment promotes learning, and issues of high-stakes assessment and accountability.

It is essential for teachers to be aware of these factors and to manage them as much as possible, because they affect how assessment is managed and used in the classroom. They are addressed throughout this book. In addition, the chapters in Part Five, "Related Assessment Factors," look closely at communication of assessment evidence, including examining grading practices and issues raised by high-stakes testing, especially large-scale testing.

Teachers and Change

Earlier we described one of Nancy's experiences with using assessment. Perhaps the most important word in this story is *change.* Nancy's decision to change her assessment practice brought about deep and complex changes in Nancy's classroom practice.

One of our purposes in writing this book is to invoke change in teaching practices related to assessment. Throughout, we encourage readers to reflect on and critically assess their present practices with the goal of making essential changes. While you are

FIGURE I.3. CLASSROOM ASSESSMENT CYCLE SHOWING EXTERNAL AND INTERNAL FACTORS.

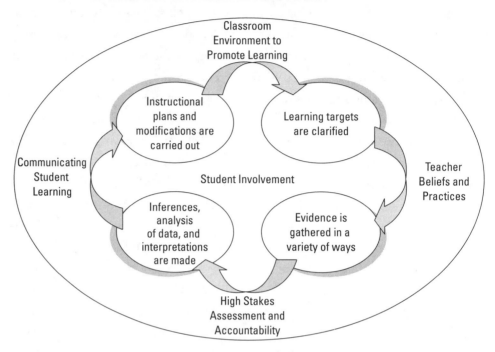

experiencing this process, it is important to remember that resistance to change is natural and that only by seeing a need for alteration is change evoked. Kuhn (1970) states that scientists never reject a previously accepted theory without accepting a new one. Moreover, the reason for accepting the new theory has to be compelling. Usually individuals need extrinsic or intrinsic motivation, often in the form of tension or frustration with what they are currently doing, before they decide to alter behavior or thinking. Reading this text may plant that first niggling seed of doubt, allowing you to question what is currently perceived as the "normal" way to assess students.

However, just seeing the need for change is not enough. Recent research into teacher change (Tobin & LaMaster, 1995; Davis & Helly, 1995) has revealed three necessary factors: commitment, vision, and reflection. Commitment to the change is of course necessary because it is so much easier not to change. Once the commitment to change is made, however, it is important that participants in the change perceive a vision of the anticipated alteration. This occurs when teachers are allowed to raise questions for themselves about their teaching and figure out for themselves how to answer the questions. In this manner, teachers envision a role for themselves in the planned change, feel empowered to act, and formulate a plan of action by reflecting on their own actions in the classroom. Reflection is what a teacher does when he looks back at the teaching and learning that has occurred and reconstructs, reenacts, or recaptures the events, emotions, and accomplishments. It is through this process that a teacher learns from experience. Such reflection can lead to a change in the beliefs that teachers hold about teaching and learning. Once such beliefs are changed, change in practice becomes inevitable.

Not all researchers, however, feel that changes in belief must come before a change in practice. For example, Guskey (2000), in his book *Evaluating Professional Development,* examines the process of effective change. He implies that educators usually do not change their own attitudes and beliefs from most professional development opportunities but that a change in practice occurs when the change positively affects student learning.

In fact, often teachers walk away from rich staff development on classroom assessment frustrated, overwhelmed, and doubtful. However, in workshops that require teachers to experiment with the concepts they have learned and to report on the success of these experiments, teachers have the opportunity to see for themselves that change in assessment practice positively affects student learning. For example, in one effort to increase assessment capacity, in which one of us was involved, veteran teachers, mandated to attend, were openly displeased at an assignment that asked them to design and conduct an "alternative assessment" in their classrooms and to bring in evidence that they had done so. One of them said: "I've tested kids for years and some of them get it, some of them don't, and that won't ever change."

To the surprise of the session leaders, these same sour-faced teachers were the first ones through the door to the returning session. They had their arms loaded with student work they wanted the leaders to review. Their students' work was very good, and they all shared assessment stories. Leaders critiqued the work and offered comments on how to improve it next time. The rubrics the teachers had created and used with their students were a good start, but they admitted that knowing what they valued in good work was the hardest part for them to express to students. Several teachers brought in samples of before and after work to show how much better their students performed when they were given the judging criteria up-front. The best part was hearing several of these teachers say, "I thought I did a good job assessing my students, but now I wish I could go back these thirty years and undo some of the damage I've done by being unclear about my expectations for learning."

It is the increase in student learning that causes change in teacher attitudes and beliefs about assessment. This change in belief mandates changes in the ways they use assessment to help their students learn. Teachers who report such positive impacts are then encouraged to reflect on current practices and to question what they do in the classroom. Frequently, in our training sessions, we ask teachers to *try* a new assessment practice, hoping that enhanced student achievement will help teachers change their old assessment beliefs and practices.

While reading through the scenarios presented in this book, examining, through reflection, your understanding of classroom assessment and working though the accompanying activities, you may begin to question assessment practices you have experienced or promulgated. This perturbation should lead to a search for alternatives. We urge you to engage in the Classroom Assessment Cycle and discover where it leads you.

A Teacher's Guide to Classroom Assessment

Understanding the Varieties of Assessment

In this chapter, we examine the purposes of assessment and describe assessment language. In the course of doing so we establish an assessment vocabulary for this book, so authors and readers will speak the same language. The definitions we present have been developed from our assessment research with districts, schools, and teachers, as well as from our work with the SERVE Regional Educational Laboratory.

Another, more essential, purpose of this chapter is to begin the process of increasing your assessment repertoire by looking at the diverse functions of various assessments. The more you know about what each kind of assessment seeks to assess, the better able you will be to select the assessment that tells you what you need to know about students' levels of knowledge and ability. In turn, you will be able to create assessments that will be most relevant to your students.

One can view assessment from many different perspectives: its purpose, it methods, its processes, its objects, its data results, its measurement accuracy, its relationship to activities outside of school. Moreover, because they consider different things, these perspectives are not mutually exclusive. There is much overlapping, and any given assessment activity may fall into several of the groupings we discuss here.

Moreover, from this discussion of assessment terms one should not infer that one type of assessment is "good" while another is "bad" or that one type of assessment stimulates higher-order thinking more than another. There is a place for *all types of assessment* in the classroom; the key is to use a *variety* of assessment types to assess student learning. This chapter will give you an overview of the kinds of things you will be considering as you design or select assessments to meet particular classroom goals.

Assessment Purposes

Assessment is the act of collecting information about individuals or groups of individuals in order to better understand them. The twin purposes of assessment are to provide feedback to students and to serve as a diagnostic and monitoring tool for instruction. The definition of *classroom assessment* expands on these purposes: "Classroom assessment is an ongoing process through which teachers and students interact to promote greater learning. The assessment process involves using a range of strategies to make decisions regarding instruction and gathering information about student performance or behavior in order to diagnose students' problems, monitor their progress, or give feedback for improvement. The classroom assessment process also involves using multiple methods of obtaining student information through a variety of assessment strategies such as written tests, interviews, observations, and performance tasks" (McMunn, 2000, p. 6).

Assessment is not a thing that is done to students but a process that can lead to improved learning. In essence, assessment raises or answers the following questions:

> Did the students achieve the intended standards?
>
> If the student did not achieve the intended standards, will the feedback she received help improve the student's performance?
>
> Was the instruction effective?
>
> If the instruction was *not* effective, how can the teacher improve instruction to meet the needs of all students?

The results of the assessment are shared with both the students and the teacher. If the assessment indicates a need for improvement, students can explore new study strategies, and teachers can search out and implement new instructional techniques that target the student's strengths and weaknesses.

Many texts use the terms *assessment* and *evaluation* interchangeably. However, in our view the two terms are not synonymous. *Evaluation* is a judgment regarding the quality or worth of the assessment results. This judgment is based on multiple sources of assessment information. Envision each classroom assessment as a snapshot of what students know and are able to do. A number of these snapshots can be collected into an album and used as evidence in an evaluation. This evaluation process goes beyond just collecting information, however; evaluation is concerned with making judgments about the collection. Evaluation thus involves placing a "value" on the collection. Assume for a moment that the album contains real photographs and belongs to a professional photographer. When she applies for a job, she brings her photo album (her portfolio of her best work [assessments]) along. She has performed a personal evaluation of each snapshot in the album (judging which individual pieces to include), and has made a decision about whether or not to include each one. Now, her future employer (she hopes) can use the multiple examples of her work presented in the album to make an informed judgment of the overall proficiency of her photography work (judging all the pieces as a whole). The photographer *assesses and evaluates* her ongoing work, and the future employer *evaluates* her worth as a photographer based upon multiple examples of good evidence. Similarly, grades given to students are also based upon the *evaluation* of *assessment* information. (That is why, as we will discuss later, a student's final grade should also be a result of quality, best-work data from the assessment process in the classroom, not the compendium of grades on everything the student has done or attempted in the classroom.)

Evaluation, then, is mostly a *summative* process whereas assessment, if done correctly, is both *formative* and *summative*. Formative assessment sets targets for students and provides feedback on progress toward those targets in ways that foster *more* progress. In the classroom, teachers use formative assessment on a daily basis and then use summative assessments as a culminating experience, which give information on students' mastery of content, knowledge, or skills. Summative assessments would be scored events that are placed in a teacher's grade book. These grades are evaluated into final grades for the end of a marking period, course of study, or mastery of standards, and are reported for student achievement.

Such summative assessments may include teacher-made tests or large-scale assessments. Unfortunately, the final evaluation, the "grade," can only be as good as the assessment information collected. If a teacher is producing or collecting poor assessment snapshots, the grade given for the full photo album will be of little use in determining what the students really know or are able to do. Nancy's story about Len, in the Introduction, illustrates this possibility.

One other purpose for assessment in addition to formative and summative processes not mentioned previously is *diagnostic* assessment. The purpose for this assessment is designed to determine student's knowledge, skills, or misconceptions prior to planning instruction. An example of this type of assessment would be when a middle school social studies teacher gives students a map and asks students to locate places, interpret the legend, and calculate distances prior to a unit on mapping. This would help a teacher know what vocabulary or skills needed to be taught.

Assessment Language

Formative, diagnostic, and *summative* are terms that relate to the overall purposes for which assessment is being carried out. However, over the years, numerous other terms, such as "traditional," "non-traditional," "alternative," "authentic," "performance," and "sound assessment," have filled books and journals. The key to using assessment well is to understand the terminology. We describe below key terms and provide examples to help you understand the importance of this language of assessment.

Selected Versus Constructed Response

Assessments may be considered from the point of view of the methods or techniques they employ. Some assessments ask students to choose a response from a given list. Both classroom and larger-scale assessments have traditionally relied heavily on this assessment type. Such *selected-response* (more traditional, or paper-and-pencil tests) assessments include the standard true-false quiz and the multiple-choice test so familiar to students. However, matching exercises also fall under this category, as do fill-in-the-blank activities when students are given a "word bank" from which to choose answers. In these assessments, students are expected to recognize that one particular choice or best answer to the question asked is sought. A selected response example is the following:

An acid[*]

   a. Turns red litmus paper to yellow

   b. Releases hydroxide ions in solution

   c. Tastes sour

   d. Feels slippery to touch

[*] The correct answer is c.

Of course, this can have limiting effects on students with creative minds, those who can think of reasons that many of the choices would work. These assessments can also be detrimental when test questions are written that may unintentionally trick students with an answer choice such as "(e) I don't know." This choice is counted as a wrong answer if it is chosen, although it might be a true answer in that the student really does not know the answer. In addition, on selected-response items, students can guess at the answers and often do well on the assessment even without a true understanding of the concepts covered. Assessments seeking selected responses have a place, especially in assessing certain types of understanding, but they should not be the only measure of student achievement of learning targets.

In contrast, assessments may also be designed so that students must create, or *construct,* a response to a question or prompt. In the past we sometimes called these constructed responses *alternative* (nontraditional) assessments because they were alternative to the more traditional, selected-response assessments just described.

Assessments requiring a constructed response include stock classroom assessments such as short-answer and essay questions, in which students are called upon to respond to a question by using their own ideas and their own words. Thus, formats for assessments include either selected or constructed responses where the "information is presented in one form, and students are asked either to construct or to select the same information in a different form" (Anderson, Krathwohl, Airasian, Cruikshank, Mayer, Pintrich, Raths, & Wittrock, 2001, p. 71). A constructed response example follows:

Differentiate between an acid and a base.

Of course many other activities require student creativity in the classroom. Also included in this category are musical recitals, theme papers, drama performances, student-made posters, art projects, and models, among many others. It should be evident, then, that using constructed response forms of assessment does not necessarily require inventing new ways of assessing students because many assessments that ask students to construct responses are already in use in classrooms around the country. We simply encourage *more* teachers to use this type of assessment *more* often. However, teachers must be careful to use and design assessments that measure targets or skills that have been made clear to students. Without clear targets, these assessments can simply become activities that go nowhere. Teachers must think about the purpose for the assessment in terms of how it will be judged and what instructional strategies will help students achieve the assessed targets.

Performance and Product Assessment Methods

As mentioned previously, constructed responses can include both performances (musical recitals and dramas, for instance) and products (essays and posters). Both of these assessment methods require that students obtain mastery of learning targets outlined in the curriculum. Products are student creations and performances that show what students can do; however, both assessment methods must align to the learning targets. These assessment methods will be explored more in Chapters Four and Five. Here we try to differentiate between literal or true assessment methods and basic activities that teachers sometimes use that may not lead to assessing student learning.

The word *performance* often elicits a vision of a musical recital, a dance, a concert, or a play. However, an understanding of the influence performance assessment has on the learning process requires a broader view of this type of assessment. Using performance assessment methods, student expectations for learning may take a variety of forms and are not limited to the arts. Making a speech, performing a laboratory experiment, demonstrating the construction of a birdhouse to specifications, or driving a car in driver's education class may all be construed as types of performance assessments.

Teachers are sometimes confused about the difference between products or performances used as assessment methods and those that are simply classroom activities. Often teachers have students engage in very enjoyable activities that are, however, not aligned with the standards for the course and therefore do little to forward the curriculum for the course. A true performance or product assessment, conversely, *demonstrates student mastery of a portion of the curriculum.* Therefore, in using a true performance or product assessment method, the targeted curriculum is linked directly to the result because the curricular standards are used to define the student expectations for learning, and the instructional strategies are selected to aid students in achieving the targets. Thus, when teachers plan lessons and units, it is important that curriculum, assessment, and instruction be considered together in order to ensure a quality learning experience for students.

Differentiation between classroom activities and these assessment methods is one of the harder concepts to convey to teachers—perhaps because teachers may enjoy doing a particular activity with their students and believe the lesson has merit simply because it is so enjoyable. For example, a chemistry teacher made peanut brittle with her students at Christmas. The scientific-sounding title of this activity was "Partial Degradation of a Six Carbon Sugar, Utilizing Protein Inclusions." Although it sounded scientific, the activity was not effective in forwarding the curriculum because very little learning about science occurred. Therefore, the construction of the peanut brittle in this activity could not be classified as a true assessment method, since it did not forward the curriculum for the course.

Authentic Assessment

Some assessments elicit demonstrations of knowledge and skills in ways that prepare students for life, not just to take a test. These assessments may resemble "real life" as closely as possible. For example, being able to subtract $1.57 from $5.00 on paper does not mean that the student could make change in the real world. Making change is authentic; subtraction on paper may not be. *Authentic* types of assessment may be perceived as realistic and relevant to the student's needs and interests if these assessments are meaningful, challenging, performance driven, and if they integrate rather than fragment knowledge for students. An authentic response example follows:

> Your mother took a TUMS™ tablet last night for acid indigestion. Why? Trace the TUMS through her system, describing the correct chemical reactions. Why did she burp?

When students participate in politically oriented debates, write for the school newspaper, conduct student government, club, or research group meetings, or perform scientific research, they are engaging in tasks that are authentic. Students appear to learn best when they have a personal reason (see relevance) for learning and when the learning environment is familiar to them. Authentic assessments provide this environment and relevance for students. For example, one way to implement such assessments is to strive to assess students as they would be assessed in the workplace or when carrying out some task that is especially meaningful to them now. Speaking (not just reading) a foreign language, developing paintings for educational offices to use, seeking out information on why cast iron frying pans are good sources of iron, and determining what brand of bubble gum has the highest percentage of sugar are all engaging assessments for students.

Exhibit 1.1 illustrates a sampling of selected-response, constructed-response, and authentic assessments in an elementary classroom.

Quality Assessment

Another term, prevalent in recent literature, is *quality assessment*. When teachers are clear in their expectations for students regarding an assessment, consider bias and purposes of the assessment, and share those expectations in advance of the assessment, they are

---

EXHIBIT 1.1. SAMPLE ASSESSMENTS FROM AN ELEMENTARY CLASSROOM.

Selected response: Noelle wishes to buy three apples. If each apple costs 11 cents, how much money must she spend?

    a) 31 cents
    b) 22 cents
    c) 33 cents
    d) $1.33

Constructed response: Noelle has $1.00 to spend on candy. She wants to buy a lollipop for herself and one for each of the other ten players on her softball team. Will Noelle have enough money to buy these lollipops? Explain your answer.

Authentic: (Teacher's instructions) Jesse, take a $5.00 bill from your practice (play) money to the "classroom store." Choose one of the items in the store (nothing in the store costs over $3.00) and pay the storekeeper. Noelle, as the storekeeper, you are responsible for giving Jesse his correct change.

---

practicing quality assessment. Quality assessment also necessitates providing good feedback to students, using assessment data to improve instruction, and using a variety of assessment methods. One key to understanding quality classroom assessment is to view assessment as an ongoing, student-participatory activity, not just as something the teacher "does" to students. Teachers must strive to give students quality work to do if they want students to do quality work for them.

Tests

Testing involves using a method or instrument to measure skills, knowledge, performance, capacities, intelligence, or aptitude of an individual or group. Tests are generally only one piece of classroom assessment information. Tests are constructed to meet a specific need or purpose, such as individual diagnosis, summative assessment of individual achievement, or school accountability for teaching a curriculum.

Standardized and High-Stakes Tests

The various tests the states administer are sometimes referred to as "standardized" tests or "high-stakes" tests. These large-scale tests are used to collect information about student learning and are administered in the same way across many classrooms so that the data can be used for making comparisons.

The U.S. Congress, Office of Technology Assessment (1992), defines a standardized test as one that uses uniform procedures for administration and scoring. Therefore, any test can be standardized if the conditions under which it is given are controlled and if identical scoring mechanisms are used for each group who takes the test. This means that standardized tests can include multiple choice tests, oral examinations, essay writing, and performance-based assessments. However, in general use, the term *standardized test* usually refers to a multiple-choice type of exam. Standardized tests are of "high stakes" when the results are used to mandate actions that affect stakeholders in education or simply when the public perceives the tests to be of high importance. Examples of actions that may follow from high-stakes tests include evaluation and rewarding of teachers or administrators, allocation of resources to the school or school districts, school or school system accreditation, and graduation, promotion, or placement of students. For example, a competency test given to students in high school can mandate who will graduate and who will not receive diplomas. This example is high stakes because the results mandate a particular action: graduation from high school. The SAT (Scholastic Aptitude Test) does not mandate any action, but is still perceived as high stakes because of the importance the public places on this test. The public believes that SAT scores are of the highest importance in gaining admission to universities. In fact some universities may view such results as secondary in importance to factors such as high school grade point average, admissions essays, and references from teachers. However, regardless of whether the SAT is the deciding factor for admission or not, the public perceives it to be. Therefore, the SAT is classified as a high-stakes test. (In Chapter Twelve we discuss a number of important issues in standardized, high-stakes testing.)

Conventional Classroom Tests

Conventional tests are typical tests used or created by teachers. For example, teacher-created tests can be quizzes, multiple choice, true or false, and writing prompts for essays or literature readings. Many ready-made tests can also be found online or in textbook resources. Problems with alignment to instructional learning targets may arise, however, if such ready-made tests are used.

Norm-Referenced Versus Criterion-Referenced Tests

All tests, like other assessments, may be further classified into two categories: norm-referenced and criterion-referenced. *Criterion-referenced* assessment tells the teacher how well students are performing in terms of specific goals or standards. *Norm-referenced* assessment compares student performance to the performance of a normal group of students, either national or local. In order to understand and make use of the information that tests reveal about student achievement, it is essential to understand the differences between these two test types.

Norm-referenced and criterion-referenced tests basically differ in the method by which content is chosen and how a score is determined. Norm-referenced tests are used primarily to classify students. Therefore, the content of a norm-referenced exam is chosen according to how well it discriminates among student achievement levels. To this end, the test uses achievement differences between students to establish rank ordering from high achievers to low achievers. In standardized testing, the scores of the "norm" group of students that takes such a test before it is published for general use are the standard by which subsequent test-takers are measured. Once "norm" scores for standardized tests are established, it is not unusual to continue to use these scores for seven years (Bond, 1996).

Criterion-referenced tests, as opposed to norm-referenced ones, are designed to share what and how much a student has learned. Criterion-referenced tests, then, measure how well a student did compared to some predetermined standard of performance. The content for these exams is selected based upon the extent to which such content matches the learning outcomes of the curriculum. In standardized and high-stakes testing, these tests are primarily used to measure student achievement relative to educational goals or objectives set by a school, district, or state curriculum. The test scores are used to determine how well a student is progressing through the curriculum or how well the school is teaching the curriculum (Bond, 1996).

Since norm- and criterion-referenced tests have different purposes, the scoring for these tests is also differentiated. Mehrens & Lehmann (1987, p. 15) summarize these scoring differences as follows:

> If we interpret a score of an individual by comparing that score with those of other individuals (called a norm group), this would be norm referencing. If we interpret a person's performance by comparing it with some specified behavioral domain or criterion of proficiency, this would be criterion referencing. To polarize the distinction, we could say that the focus of a normative score is on how many of Johnny's peers perform (score) less well than he does; the focus of a criterion-referenced score is on what it is that Johnny can do. . . . In norm referencing we might make a statement that "Johnny did better than 80 percent of the students in a test on addition of whole numbers." In criterion referencing we might say that "Johnny got 70 percent of the items correct on a test on addition of whole numbers." Usually we would add further "meaning" to this statement by stating whether or not we thought 70 percent was inadequate, minimally adequate, excellent, or whatever.

It is important to remember that both norm- and criterion-referenced tests can be standardized and can be high-stakes.

Aptitude Versus Achievement

Tests can be further classified by whether they measure aptitude or achievement. Again, the proper label for a test and, more important, the proper subsequent use of test scores is influenced by the test's purpose and content. For example, the purpose of an aptitude test appears to be related to the U.S. Army slogan, "Be all that you can be." How can capacity, potential, or ability be determined? An aptitude test strives to do this by measuring or predicting various kinds of behavior related to these concepts. Among standardized tests, the SAT and the ACT, for example, are used to predict a student's success in college. Intelligence tests, like the Stanford-Binet or Wechsler Intelligence Scale for Children, are further exemplars of this classification. Therefore, aptitude tests "tend to measure or predict (a) the effects of the cumulative influence of experiences, (b) the effects of learning under relatively uncontrolled and unknown conditions, and (c) the future behavior, achievements, or performance of individuals or groups" (Payne, 1997, p. 380). Aptitude tests are primarily norm-referenced exams, as the aptitude of an individual is compared to those of a norm group.

Conversely, as Payne states, achievement tests "measure (a) the effects of special programs, (b) the effects of a relatively standardized set of experiences, (c) the effects of learning that occur under partially known and controlled conditions, and (d) what the individual student can do at a given point in time" (Payne, 1997, p. 380). Further, "aptitude measures (including readiness tests) are administered before the learning program, and achievement tests are administered after the fact" (Payne, 1997, p. 380).

One particular type of achievement test, introduced in Florida (Beard, 1986), has created a storm of controversy. This type of achievement test is the test of minimum competency. In 1976, Florida mandated by law that all high school students had to pass a minimum competency exam in order to receive a diploma. "Whether such a diploma sanction applies or not, minimum competency testing is precisely what the name implies: a program to test students in terms of, and only in terms of, whatever competencies state or local authorities have decided are the minimally acceptable result of an education" (Lazarus, 1981, p. 2). A minimum competency test, therefore, is a special subset of the achievement test classification, in that it is given after the learning experience, and measures what the student can actually do at a particular point in time. Minimum competency exams, like all achievement tests, may be either norm-referenced or criterion-referenced. Therefore, student performance on these tests may be compared to norm groups or to curriculum standards.

Relevance, Reliability, and Validity

Whether we are examining tests or other assessments, relevance, reliability, and validity are important terms in the assessment language. When assessments are *relevant* they are closely tied to classroom instruction. Teacher-made assessments may fail to be relevant because the teacher is attempting either to assess skills not taught or to assess those not included in the curriculum. For example, one student in an assessment class reported on going to Back to School Night at her daughter's school:

> I was particularly anxious to meet my daughter's science teacher, Ms. Church, as my daughter was reporting academic difficulty in this class. . . . Ms. Church explained her grading practices and revealed that many of her students currently had low marks in science. . . . According to her, most of the low cumulative grades could be attributed to the low scores earned on the pre-test for the current unit. When I questioned Ms. Church about WHY she would "count" scores earned on a PRE-test, she was unable to answer my question. In fact, she seemed to believe that ALL work should "count." That night, when I got home, I talked with my daughter about her grade on this pre-test and she showed me the huge red "53" scrawled across the top of this paper. We celebrated with a trip to Dairy Queen, after I explained to my daughter that she ALREADY KNEW 53 percent of the material Ms. Church had not yet taught! [Butler, 1999].

This experience is not, alas, unique or uncommon. It is, however, a perfect example of irrelevant, misused assessment.

When assessments are *reliable* they show consistency of scores across evaluators, over time, or across different versions of a test. An assessment is reliable when (1) the same answers receive the same score no matter when the assessment occurs or who does the scoring or (2) students receive the same scores no matter which version of the test they take.

When assessments are *valid,* they measure what they are intended to measure, rather than extraneous features. An example of an invalid assessment of the ability to use a microscope correctly would be to give a pencil and paper test on the parts of the microscope. A more valid assessment would be to hand the student a slide and have him or her focus the slide under low and high power.

Conclusion

As we will show throughout the following chapters, the usefulness of classroom assessment depends on understanding what each assessment does and does not reveal about student learning, using multiple and varied assessments to produce a rounded picture, and applying all that assessment information to the design of future classroom instruction and assessment.

We focus mainly on the formative assessment process but realize that there are many factors inside and outside the classroom that affect how we view and use classroom assessment.

Chapter One has laid the groundwork for our thinking about formative assessment and provided some of the language pertinent to understanding the vast concept of assessment.

To continue our study of formative assessment, Part One, Clarifying Learning Targets, begins by outlining the Classroom Assessment Cycle. Chapters Two and Three explore unpacking the targets and defining our expectations for student learning. To understand what we mean by "unpacking," just think about a suitcase full of clothes. Suppose the suitcase is lost and a claim must be made for the items to be replaced. You would certainly want the most important or most essential items to be on this replacement list. When we "unpack the targets," we are taking a standard course of study and determining the most important learning targets embedded in these standards. Chapters Two and Three provide insights into identifying these most important learning targets.

Clarifying Learning Targets

Learning targets
are clarified

Part One focuses on the quadrant of the Classroom Assessment Cycle that deals with learning targets. Chapters Two and Three describe how teachers can work to clarify learning targets, identifying in detail what students are expected to learn.

Chapter Two, "Unpacking Standards and Benchmarks," explains the significance of knowing and understanding the learning targets. The chapter defines learning targets as what we want students to know and be able to do, and states that these arise from standards and benchmarks within mandated curricula. Also discussed in this chapter are global transitions that support and impel changes in curriculum. A discussion of how teachers "unpack" (analyze to discern embedded learning targets) state standards is also highlighted.

Chapter Three, "Defining Student Expectations," focuses on clarifying teacher expectations for student learning. Learning targets include knowledge and understanding, reasoning, performance skill, product development, and dispositions (Stiggins, 2001a). The chapter emphasizes that the assessment method selected by a teacher should align with the instruction delivered and with the target being assessed. For example, if the target of learning is for students to successfully operate a microscope, the instructional strategies should support that target. Activities such as teacher demonstrations, teacher modeling, and student practice would prepare students for this skill. The assessment of the target should be a student demonstration of the skill, rather than a paper and pencil test.

Unpacking Standards and Benchmarks

2

This chapter begins our exploration of the quadrant of the Classroom Assessment Cycle in which the teacher clarifies learning targets prior to actually gathering assessment information. We examine the following questions:

- What are learning targets?
- How do teachers "unpack," or analyze and reflect on, learning targets?

Consider this scenario. A science teacher performed a demonstration for students. First she placed a 400-milliliter beaker on the table. Then she proceeded to add large rocks to this container. When the beaker could hold no more large rocks, she asked the class, "Is the beaker full?" In unison, they answered, "Yes." The teacher then said, "No, it's not full. Watch." She then began to add gravel to the beaker, shaking the beaker to distribute the gravel around the rocks. "Now," she asked, "is the beaker full?" The class hesitated to answer. Some wanted to say "yes," but they suspected the answer was "no." The teacher again said, "No, it's not full. Watch." She brought out a bag of sand, and poured it into the beaker, again shaking the container to help distribute the sand. When the beaker was filled to the top with sand, she asked the class, "Is the beaker full?" By this time, the whole class had caught on, and they all answered, "No!" "That's right," the teacher said, as she poured water into the beaker. "Now," she continued, "what was the point of this demonstration?" One student answered, "You wanted to show us that there's always room for the little stuff, if you fit it in around the big stuff." The teacher replied, "Not quite! That is a good explanation but my reason was the opposite. What I showed you was that unless you start with the big rocks, you'll never get them all in!" Sometimes we must start with the big pieces in order to make them fit, and then the little pieces will fall into place.

FIGURE 2.1. BEAKER WITH BIG ROCKS.

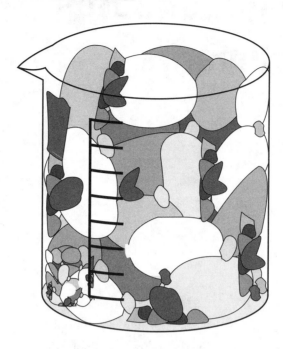

This is also an important lesson to bear in mind when planning classroom assessment. Curricular guidelines, standards, and benchmarks are the big rocks, the concepts and skills essential to a subject or discipline. Teachers must ensure that these big rocks, the most valuable concepts and skills, are included in their instructional plans. Then they must devise methods for assessing the level of student achievement relative to the standards and benchmarks. To this end, teachers should plan the assessment before planning for instruction. If teachers know which standards and benchmarks they are going to teach and how they are going to assess student achievement of these standards and benchmarks, then they can plan their lessons accordingly to allow these components to complement and agree. In other words, the instruction should help match assessment back to the original learning target (the standards and benchmarks).

Learning Targets

To begin classroom planning with the assessment cycle in mind, teachers first must be clear about what they are trying to get their students to learn. What are the "big rocks"? Ask a reading teacher, for example, what his goals are for his students and he will probably say he wants his students to be able to demonstrate oral fluency, comprehend the meaning of what they have read, use appropriate reading strategies, demonstrate higher-order thinking skills, and be motivated to read. In this stage of the assessment cycle, then, teachers identify the learning targets for students and then unpack these targets so they can discuss them with their students, clearly articulating and modeling exactly what they want students to learn.

Similarly, a language arts teacher might know that her students should be able to write a comparative paragraph. The teacher knows that the assessment of this *benchmark* will entail the writing of a comparative paragraph by students. However, before she can plan a lesson on comparative paragraphs, it is important for her to devise the criteria for assessing the student paragraphs. She must ask: What are the integral parts that all comparative paragraphs must contain? What components are found in exemplary comparative paragraphs? This assessment design process forces the teacher to define, explicitly, the task students will be asked to complete. Then she needs to plan the lesson accordingly, in order to impart to students all the concepts and skills generated in this analytical process.

All assessments help answer the query, Did students achieve the intended *standard?* Do they know the things that, according to the curriculum, should be taught? Frequently assessments also answer the question, Did the students achieve a standard's accompanying *benchmark;* can they do a specific task that shows that they meet the standard? It is these standards and benchmarks that teachers need to analyze and reflect on (*unpack*) to identify explicit learning targets. Standards and benchmarks derive from the curriculum, so in this section we will unpack today's curriculum expectations before getting down to the standards and benchmarks.

Curriculum

Curriculum, instruction, and assessment are equally important components that are woven throughout education. However, the curriculum serves as an entry point that can provide a foundation for the other two.

Holistically, curriculum may be considered a plan that outlines a process for instruction and learning. It may be presented as a conceptual framework outlining specific learning goals and expectations. It is the curriculum that defines what students should know and be able to do after they have experienced instruction and before they are assessed. The curriculum is made up of "big rocks" of concepts that constitute the foundation of a course. Within a curriculum course of study, the standards and benchmarks set the parameters of student achievement.

Understanding why the curriculum emphasizes what it does and the influences that make the curriculum what it is today may help teachers formulate their coursework to facilitate greater student learning.

How and Why Curriculum Is Changing

As all classroom teachers know, the standards and benchmarks currently being selected by curriculum developers show a marked difference from those selected in the past. Such an alteration in valued concepts and skills necessitates a corresponding transformation in teachers' thinking about teaching and learning.

Curriculum is changing because the world, the global community, is changing. In essence, teaching and learning must change in order to prepare students for a future

TABLE 2.1. GLOBAL TRANSITIONS.

Global Shift	Curriculum Change Needed
From an industrial to an information society	Focus on finding, evaluating, and using knowledge more than on understanding known information
From simple to complex technology	Add technology to the curriculum as a new domain of knowledge
From work that requires a traditional set of knowledge and skills to work that requires knowledge and skills appropriate to an information society with complex technology	Add new content to the curriculum to address these new needs
From work that requires relatively narrow abilities to work that requires interdisciplinary knowledge and the ability to work in teams	Integrate subject areas, disciplines, and fields of study, and increase the real-world relevance of the curriculum
From local marketplaces to global marketplaces with increasing economic competition	Alter the curriculum in order to create workers able to compete in the world market; emphasize problem-solving and cognitive abilities
From homogeneous workforces to diverse workforces, reflecting social and demographic changes in society	Encourage achievement by underrepresented groups

Source: Adapted from Howe, 1990, and Butler, 2004.

that will be vastly different from the past. What has caused these sweeping changes in society? Howe (1990) identifies six global shifts that are demanding the restructuring of classroom content and delivery. These transitions are summarized in Table 2.1.

It is informative to look a little more closely at the educational significance of each shift, beginning with the shift from an industrial society to an information society.

The task of traditional teaching in an industrial society, said Marx (1989), was the reproduction of the existing society. To this end, experts identified the specific content considered necessary for all citizens, textbook authors wrote texts describing these bits of information, teachers lectured to transmit the information to students, and pupils memorized and reproduced the knowledge on written exams.

However, in the information age, the overall amount of known information has expanded exponentially. Schools have yet to catch up with this change, causing many observers to realize that, as Corrigan puts it, "Our schools are failing to educate students for a world that depends more and more on sophisticated and rapidly changing science and technology" (Corrigan, 1993, p. 8).

At the same time this increase in knowledge has clearly made it impossible to include all knowledge within school curricula. What information should then be included? Exactly how much information should be taught? These content-related questions continue to challenge curriculum designers. Westheimer (1994, p. 204) suggests that "we need to teach enough so that our students are able to cope with the books that have yet to be written (and the ones that exist but have not yet been read), with the economic principles that have not yet been formulated, and of course, with the science that has yet to be discovered." In this vision, the curriculum would shift from a focus on understanding known information to a focus on finding, evaluating, and using new information.

An added complication is that this increasing amount of information is available to all world citizens through the continuing advances in technology (such as the transistor, magnetic tape, microprocessors, and the Internet). Technology, the driver of the second global shift identified by Howe, contributes to the need to reform curricula in two ways: it ensures that the ever-expanding scope of information is available to all citizens who understand how to access and interpret it, and it introduces into the curriculum a whole new domain of knowledge that students must become skillful in using.

The global shift to an information society and a society more and more dependent on technology is spawning the third global transition, a change in the knowledge and skills required of the workforce. The changing requirements for jobs certainly substantiate the need for changes in the education of the workforce and again brings into question the content that should be taught. Moreover, the manner in which workers interact is also being transformed. Because their work requires sharing knowledge, workers must be prepared to become part of an interdisciplinary, team-based, cooperative workforce. This means expanding the educational experience not only of upper-level students specializing in particular fields but also of K–12 students. It suggests that traditional school subjects should no longer be taught as separate, stand-alone disciplines but should assimilate information from other disciplines in order to prepare students to meet the challenges they will face on the job.

This interdisciplinary approach may also help to address lack of relevance between concepts taught in schools and the ordinary, everyday life of students (Krieger, 1989; see also Yager and Lutz, 1994). Prather (1993) found that curriculum designers give little attention to planning for relevance in the curriculum, pointing out that subject-specific content and instructional materials are written by experts in the field, who overemphasize factual data and underemphasize understanding of concepts, with the result that students may memorize the information yet not know how to use it. Teachers should be prepared for changes in this area as interdisciplinary teaching makes connections between facts and students' daily lives more obvious to the students and asks them to integrate concepts from other disciplines into classroom activities.

In addition to these first four shifts, Howe (1990) maintains that a significant shift in economic competition among the world's nations has occurred. Many countries have been able to develop educational and economic programs that are better able to produce an educated workforce than the educational programs currently used in the United States. For example, activities including such critical thinking skills as problem solving, application of knowledge, and troubleshooting are currently more highly valued (and assessed) in nations outside the United States. Some see this as "an economic and ideological crisis. Profits and production are not high enough. Workers are not disciplined, as they should be. We are not [economically] competitive enough" (Apple, 1992, p. 781). The current education system must change if it hopes to produce workers who will enable the U.S. to compete successfully in a global market. One modification may be a change in the delivery system of concepts (Yager and Lutz, 1994).

When education is viewed within economic parameters, it becomes even more evident that *all* workers must receive an education that will aid them in reaching their fullest potential.

The sixth global transition that is requiring curriculum change involves demographic change in the workforce (at least in developed countries), which now includes an increasing percentage of minorities and women. Unfortunately, the increasing percentage of women and minorities in the workforce is not yet reflected in some academic disciplines. There is gross underrepresentation of these groups in math, science, and engineering courses, for example (Krieger, 1989). High curriculum standards must not be optional for women and minorities.

In review, education needs to reflect the transition in the global community toward a more interdisciplinary, team mode of learning. It also needs to prepare and encourage all employees, including minorities and women, to face challenges within the marketplace, thereby enhancing the competitiveness of the United States within the world economy. The implication is that the present delivery system is not accomplishing these goals and is due for restructuring. The delivery of educational information should respond to and model new economic and societal practices in order to prepare students to cope with an increasingly competitive, multicultural, and complex workplace.

With these goals in mind, Besvinick (1988, p. 52) suggests that students be taught to "develop the ability to think rationally, to grapple with and solve problems." Such teaching will not be "fact-bound," but will educate students to become creative problem solvers by applying basic information. Marx (1989, p. 143) also advocates the teaching of problem solving. He sees the traditional school "offering unique instructions, giving closed-ended problems, preferring children who give expected answers" in contrast to the creative school of the future, "presenting alternative models, giving open-ended problems, tolerating children who ask unexpected questions." Prather (1993, p. 58), like Marx, sees the retention of "traditional textbook-oriented, teacher-centered teaching methods" as problematic in preparing students for the future. He believes that advances in research on learning have demonstrated the need to instruct students in nontraditional methods. The problem-solving approach suggested by both Besvinick (1988) and Marx (1989) is one such nontraditional method. Open-ended (Marx, 1989) and student-centered, as opposed to teacher-centered, activities (Prather, 1993) are two further examples of alternative teaching methods.

The global transitions described here are impelling modifications in curriculum design. Curriculum standards are addressing students' abilities to problem solve and use information but are also focusing on necessary facts of content pertinent to promoting this type of informational use. Delivery systems in education must undergo restructuring in response to changing workforce demographics, global economic competition, and advances in research on learning. These global transitions are important considerations for educators as they plan for student instruction and assessment.

How Curriculum Orientation Affects What Is Taught

In addition to reflecting current social needs, every curriculum (and hence instruction and assessment) reflects various *orientations* (Eisner & Vallance, 1974) in varying degrees. These curriculum orientations are philosophically or theoretically based systems of approaching education. Elliott Eisner (1979) identified five curriculum orientations that have an impact on what is taught in schools. These orientations are cognitive processes, academic rationalism, social adaptation and reconstruction, personal relevance, and technology. These can influence the way that curriculum is developed at both the state and district or school levels. Glatthorn and Jailall (2000) analyzed Eisner's following orientations, which they refer as "curriculum streams," when they sought to look at the past and sum up future needs for curriculum in the new millennium.

Cognitive Process. This orientation or stream focuses on helping students learn to think and to solve problems. This stream originated in the nineteenth century, when psychologists began studying mental development. The modern curriculum innovation that supports this stream is *constructivism,* which began in the 1990s and continues to thrive today. Problem-based learning is another current approach that reflects this stream.

Academic Rationalism. This orientation or stream is subject centered, with *academics* as its basis. "Back to basics" movements in the teaching of reading, writing, and math show this stream's influence today. The current prominent innovation that supports this stream is the *standards-based* curriculum, an approach begun around 1992 and still very powerful. It emphasizes teaching the standards and benchmarks established on the national or state level.

Personal Relevance. This orientation or stream is student centered, designed to meet student needs. It seeks to help students find personal meaning in what is studied (self-actualization). The broad array of electives and course offerings now present in schools result from this orientation, as does project-based education.

Social Adaptation and Social Reconstruction. This orientation or stream seeks to prepare students for adult living. Based on the needs of society, it works toward improving society. Today this stream is present largely in school-to-work programs.

Technology. This means-end (setting goals and determining how to accomplish them) orientation or stream adopts technical processes for mastery learning. Several curriculum innovations (adopted from 1980 to the present) are presently strong in this stream. Computer innovation, for example, employs computer programs for drill and practice exercises and uses computers as instructional tools to store, monitor, and enrich the curriculum. Total quality education (TQE) (1985–present) is an innovation that uses technology to achieve quality.

Presently, the cognitive processes (constructivist innovation) and academic rationalism (standards-based) streams seem to have the strongest influence on curriculum. However, the technology stream is also prevalent (both in the computer and TQE innovations) (Glatthorn & Jailall, 2000).

Curriculum Change at the Local Level

Because the local level is where the actual implementation of curriculum takes place, it is also where curriculum change, or reform, succeeds or fails. Curriculum change, like all change, is difficult to achieve and faces many barriers. One of these barriers can be the beliefs and values (acknowledged or unacknowledged) of the people involved in the curriculum revision, including their beliefs about preferable orientations. Preparing teachers for teaching the new curriculum, reeducating the students, introducing new assessment approaches that must reflect the change, initiating new curriculum while using the old system or resources, and finding time to perform all the necessary tasks are all challenges in curriculum change. The complexities involved in revising the curriculum can create frustration for those who must use it or for those who are closely influenced by the curriculum, namely school administrators, teachers, students, and parents.

Nevertheless, changes in the world are resulting in changes in curriculum design. On the most practical level, this is important to classroom assessment because the curriculum defined by the state or the school system contains the standards and benchmarks against which student achievement will be measured. Therefore, if a teacher does not use the state or district curriculum, his students will not fare well on state or district measures of achievement since most states assess the curriculum through high-stakes testing of students, using tests that are aligned to the state standards and benchmarks. Poor performance by students on such high-stakes tests has negative ramifications for the district, the school, and the teacher. These ramifications may include loss of prestige for the district or school and loss of a job by the teacher.

Since the implemented curriculum and measures of student achievement are so closely allied, it is important that the school or district develop a quality curriculum. Considerations for building a good curriculum at the district or school level should include the following:

- Make it meaningful for students and teachers.
- Make it include unity and diversity issues.
- Make it connect to important entities.
- Make it reflect sound human values.
- Make it emphasize student responsibility.

Glatthorn and Jailall (2000, p. 110) suggest a curriculum, based upon the above criteria, that has the power to make a difference in student achievement. Table 2.2 summarizes their comparisons of what this new curriculum should reflect as compared to the traditional curriculum.

Standards and Benchmarks

Whichever curriculum is chosen by a district or school, it is important for the teacher to be cognizant of the standards and benchmarks that will be used to measure student achievement. Therefore it is important to understand what these pieces of the curriculum encompass.

Standards are, simply, statements of what should be taught. They establish a level of achievement, quality of performance, or degree of proficiency expected from students. Standard statements, on the one hand, are generally rather broad in scope. *Benchmarks,* on the other hand, are used to explicate the standards. Benchmarks explain what students must do to meet the standards; they focus on explicit behaviors or particular products. In some school districts, *standards* may be referred to as *competencies, objectives,* or *goals. Benchmarks* may be referred to as *objectives, competencies,* or *targets.* The important thing is not the exact terms that are used but that the definitions of the chosen terms are clear so that everyone in the district speaks the same language and can identify what it is that students are expected to learn.

State departments of education usually establish standards and benchmarks for courses taught in their public schools. However, there are also national standards and benchmarks for many subject areas, such as science, foreign language, English language arts, history, art, health, civics, economics, geography, physical education, mathematics, and social studies (Marzano & Kendall, 1996). Some states also use the term

TABLE 2.2. A COMPARISON BETWEEN NEW AND TRADITIONAL CURRICULA.

| | *Emphasis* | |
Area	*New Curriculum*	*Traditional Curriculum*
Primary parameters emphasized	Depth of understanding	Coverage of topics
Problems	Authentic, contextualized; learning strategies in context	Contrived, thinking skills isolated
Skills and knowledge	Both emphasized in solving problems	Overemphasis on knowledge
Individual differences	Provided for	Ignored
Common core or curriculum tracks	Common core	Curriculum tracks
Coordination	Closely coordinated	Fragmented
Integration	Selectively integrated	All subjects separated
Focus	Focus on results	Focus on activities
Streams	Emphasis on personal relevance with other streams	Emphasis on academic rationalism

Source: Glatthorn and Jailall, 2000, p. 110. Reprinted by permission. The Association for Supervision and Curriculum Development is a worldwide community of educators advocating sound policies and sharing best practices to achieve the success of each learner. To learn more, visit ASCD at (www.ascd.org).

"accountability standards," which refers to the specific standards that districts, schools, and students must meet in order for students to be promoted to the next grade.

The following examples from diverse curricula help differentiate between standards and benchmarks. The terms used are authentic to the sources and therefore reflect the diverse terminology in use.

From Florida's *Sunshine State Standards* in the area of reading, under the K–2 language arts curriculum (Florida Department of Education [FDOE], 1996):

- *Standard:* The student uses the reading process effectively

- *Benchmark:* Predicts what a passage is about based on its title and illustrations

From North Carolina's *Health Occupations Curriculum* for grades 9–12, in the Biomedical Technology course (NCDPI, 1995):

- *Competency:* Determine a career path based on personal qualifications

- *Objective:* Design a personal career path

From the *National Center for History in Schools History Standard Project* (Kendall & Marzano, 2000, p. 115) for grades 5–6:

- *Standard:* Understands the historical perspective

- *Benchmark:* Evaluates historical fiction according to the accuracy of its content and the author's interpretation

In these examples, it is clear that the first statement, whether called a *standard* or a *competency,* is a broad view of what students should know and be able to do. The standard, "The student uses the reading process effectively," could encompass many skills. The second statement, the *benchmark* or *objective,* describes skills or activities or products that will demonstrate whether students have achieved the standard. In the elementary example, making predictions is one of the activities needed to determine whether students can use the reading process effectively. In this manner the benchmark provides greater specificity than the standard about what students should know and be able to do. Therefore, benchmarks list a particular activity that students must engage in, or they recommend the creation of a particular product. These activities and products are then used to move students toward the achievement of the overall standard. Since the benchmark breaks the standard into smaller increments, several benchmarks may be written for each standard. By completing (or learning) all the incremental units of the benchmarks, the students achieve the whole, which is the standard.

Standards and particularly benchmarks should use action verbs. These verbs can help the teacher in determining the most appropriate method to use in assessing the standards and benchmarks. For example, in the second example of standards and benchmarks, the benchmark (objective) is to "*Design* a personal career path." This verb advises the teacher that the student must work out a career path for himself, not just answer questions about careers or list information about the path. Creating this career path is more complex than filling in blanks in statements about a career path, and calls for more critical thinking than would be needed to create a list. Such action verbs can mandate a certain cognitive level of performance by the student.

Unpacking Learning Targets

Learning targets in the form of standards and benchmarks are found in curricula and instructional strategies designed at the national, state, course, and lesson levels.

Standards, as we said earlier, are broad statements of what should be taught. Therefore, standards lay the foundation for the level of achievement, quality of performance, or degree of proficiency expected from students. Most states set content standards (like math standards) and often leave the performance standards or benchmarks to be set by the local educational agencies in their own curriculum.

At the national level, almost all disciplines have written standards. For example, Marzano and Kendall (1996, p. 20) list sources for standards pertaining to diverse disciplines (Table 2.3).

Standards devised at other levels, however, may be different. Here are some national and state comparisons. The National Science Education Standards (National Research Council [NRC], 1999, p. 104) list eight categories of standards, including

- Unifying concepts and processes in science
- Science as inquiry
- Physical science
- Life science
- Earth and space science
- Science and technology
- Science in personal and social perspectives
- History and nature of science

Seventy-two different standards are embedded within these eight categories (NRC, 1999). Conversely, at the state level for grades 9–12 science education, North Carolina lists only four "strands" of standards (NCDPI, 2000b):

- Nature of science
- Science as inquiry
- Science and technology
- Science in personal and social perspectives

Within these strands, seventeen standards are listed.

Moving to the course level, in the North Carolina Biology curriculum (NCDPI, 2000b) one finds the above listed four strands of standards present, with four additions:

- Science as human endeavor
- Historical perspectives
- Nature of scientific knowledge
- Science and technology in local, national, and global challenges

Within each of the eight listed strands, five competency goals are written. Under each competency goal, the biology course further explicates 5–6 objectives.

Teachers use all levels of standards and benchmarks when creating instructional lessons. It is in these lessons that the "rubber meets the road" because it is here that the teacher chooses those particular benchmarks (or objectives in North Carolina's terminology) that she will cover within a particular lesson. A biology teacher in North

TABLE 2.3. SOURCES FOR NATIONAL STANDARDS.

Discipline	*Source Document for Standards*
Science	*National Science Education Standards*
Foreign language	*Standards for Foreign Language Learning: Preparing for the 21st Century*
Language arts	*Standards for the English Language Arts*
History	*National Standards for History: Basic Edition*
Arts	*National Standards for Arts Education: What Every Young American Should Know and Be Able to Do in the Arts*
Health	*National Health Education Standards: Achieving Health Literacy*
Civics	*National Standards for Civics and Government*
Economics	*Content Statements for State Standards in Economics*
Geography	*Geography for Life: National Geography Standards*
Physical Education	*Moving into the Future: National Standards for Physical Education*
Mathematics	*Curriculum and Evaluation Standards for School Mathematics*
Social Studies	*Expectations of Excellence: Curriculum Standards for Social Studies*

Source: Marzano and Kendall, 1996, p. 20.

Carolina might create a lesson or section of a unit for the following objective: Compare and contrast the characteristics of asexual and sexual reproduction. This course objective falls within the Biology Competency Goal 2 (the learner will develop an understanding of the continuity of life and the changes of organisms over time) and closely reflects the "science as inquiry" strand. Table 2.4 illustrates this curricular hierarchy.

Table 2.4 also shows how a teacher might unpack the curriculum for a state standard for delivery within her classroom.

Another example of unpacking a learning target can continue with the effective-reader example from the beginning of this section. We have asked numerous reading teachers over the past few years, What do you want your students to know and be able to do in reading? Or, If a parent came to your school and asked what his child would know and be able to do by the end of the year, what would you say to him? Most of the teachers responded by saying something like this: I want my students to become effective readers who are on grade level proficiency in

1. Oral fluency

2. Comprehension

3. Use of reading strategies

4. Higher-order thinking skills

5. Motivation to read [McMunn, Williamson, and Reagan, p. 2004, p. xii]

TABLE 2.4. CURRICULAR HIERARCHY WITHIN NORTH CAROLINA BIOLOGY CURRICULUM.

Levels (From Most General to Most Specific)	Students Will Be Able to
Strand: science as inquiry	*State* problems, *hypothesize, collect* data, and *formulate* problem solutions.
Standard: competency goal 2	*Develop* an understanding of the continuity of life and the changes of organisms over time.
Benchmark: objective 2.01	*Compare and contrast* the characteristics of asexual and sexual reproduction
One lesson: Teacher-constructed specific objectives for that day's lesson	*View* slides of cell division in onion root, slides of yeast budding, and then *write* a paragraph (in the science journal) describing the similarities and differences observed in these two processes
One quick formative assessment for this	Students *create* a Venn Diagram showing the similarities and differences in cell division versus yeast budding

These five targets are what some reading teachers value and, ideally, the state, district, and school value them, too. Such targets are what drive instruction in the classroom. However, just stating these targets is not enough. The reading teacher must clearly articulate what each of the five targets means (Table 2.5) and know how best to measure them.

If the learning target is oral fluency and the teacher wishes to assess the student on this target, asking the student to read silently and then fill in a worksheet will not provide valid information. For oral fluency, the teacher must ask the student to read aloud. During this oral reading by the student, a teacher may note:

- Reads at an average pace

- Reads in a monotonous tone, little inflection

- Honors punctuation—for example, used emphasis with an exclamation point

- Does not pause at commas and reads past periods

- Reads in phrases

- Hesitates [McMunn, Williamson, & Reagan, 2004, Activity 7, Handout 4, p. 4]

This information provides accurate data on oral fluency. The teacher then determines from the criteria she has outlined for oral fluency (noted previously) where this

TABLE 2.5. TARGETS MATCHED TO INDICATORS OF AN EFFECTIVE READER.

Learning Target	*What Would Effective Readers Do?*
Oral fluency	Effective readers read aloud smoothly, easily, accurately, and with appropriate speed and inflection, pay attention to punctuation
Comprehension	Effective readers make meaning, build connections between prior background knowledge, and make decisions about what is relevant and important
Reading strategies	Effective readers apply multiple strategies flexibly, selectively, independently, and reflectively
Higher-order thinking	Effective readers don't just read the lines literally; they read between the lines and beyond the lines; they make inferences, analyze, and evaluate decisions about what is relevant and important
Motivation	Effective readers are motivated and enjoy reading; they read with perseverance and interest

Source: McMunn, Dunnivant, Williamson, and Reagan, 2004, p. xii.

student experiences difficulty with this learning target. One action this teacher may do to help with this student's oral fluency would be to provide the student multiple opportunities to read aloud using different texts at different reading levels to make sure that the particular text was not the problem. Once additional information is known about this student's oral fluency, then the teacher can determine whether his oral fluency is something that needs extra work or whether it is on grade level.

The assessment of the benchmarks can help determine what level of understanding a student has regarding a standard. Such assessment of benchmarks then leads to understanding of standards. Understanding of standards ensures student achievement of the prescribed curriculum.

As teachers unpack learning targets and begin to consider classroom assessments that will demonstrate achievement of those targets, they may find that when assessments are designed to push the cognitive complexity to higher levels, the target may inadvertently be changed in the process. For example, a group of educators reviewing constructed response examples chose to rewrite a question in which students were asked to find the perimeter of a fence. The original question was simple in design and asked students to observe a diagram, note the measurements on the diagram, and compute the perimeter of the figure (original question shown in Figure 2.2). The learning target driving the question focused on the concept of perimeter. After the group members discussed enhancing the cognitive complexity of the item, they added another sentence that asked the students to find the area of the fence as well.

FIGURE 2.2. PERIMETER QUESTION.

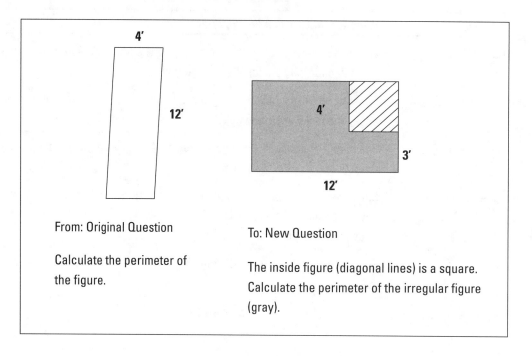

From: Original Question

Calculate the perimeter of
the figure.

To: New Question

The inside figure (diagonal lines) is a square.
Calculate the perimeter of the irregular figure
(gray).

What happened here? The educators expanded the cognitive level but also changed
the target being assessed. The original learning target (the concept of perimeter) no
longer aligned with the assessment (which now also incorporated the concept of area).
After some discussion, the educators realized that they had changed the target. A better way to address the perimeter issue at a higher cognitive complexity was to ask the
student to interpret a diagram and to justify his or her answers for finding the perimeter of a fence within a fence. Therefore, the question changed to address the learning
target at a higher cognitive level, as shown in Figure 2.2.

In this chapter we have presented a view of identifying learning targets that proceed
from the curriculum down to the classroom level. Understanding where curricula have
evolved may help us unlock our thinking for how they may develop in the future and,
most important, understand why and how curriculum affects the Classroom
Assessment Cycle. In Chapter Three, we look more closely at the classroom process
of unpacking these learning targets in order to define just what students are expected
to achieve.

Defining Student Expectations

3

As we stated in Chapter Two, teachers must gain a clear understanding of the learning targets before they can begin to plan actual instruction, student activities, and assessments. There is no hope of students achieving learning targets if everyone in the classroom (teachers and students) does not have a clear understanding of *what students should know and be able to do.*

This chapter explores one specific way that teachers might unpack learning targets or student expectations for learning (which, as we discussed in Chapter Two, can also be referred to as goals, objectives, standards, and so on, depending on the terminology used in the local educational domain). It looks at these questions:

- How can teachers use learning targets to set student expectations?
- How do student expectations differ for similar standards that traverse grade levels?
- Why has ensuring the teaching of all standards become a challenge for teachers?

Using Learning Targets to Set Student Expectations

One way to begin unpacking learning targets is to use a classification scheme such as that of Stiggins (2001a). Stiggins proposes five useful categories of learning targets, which he terms "achievement targets" (Stiggins, 2001a, p. 66):

1. Knowledge and understanding targets
2. Reasoning targets
3. Performance skill targets

4. Product development targets

5. Dispositional targets

This classification is not a cut-and-dried choice, where only one target may be embedded in a standard (since knowledge is probably a prerequisite of all standards). Even though these targets can overlap, we'll discuss them one at a time to enhance clarity.

Once a teacher has identified the learning targets needed for a lesson or portion of a unit of study, she might then categorize the targets. The category type can be a guide to unpacking the expectations for learning, the instruction needed, and the assessment method used.

We use examples of learning benchmarks (targets) pulled from the standard course of study for high school world geography (NCDPI, 1998) to illustrate how a teacher might define student performance in each category.

Knowledge and Understanding Targets

One "knowledge target" for world geography is found in the benchmark: "Identify major regions of the world." Knowledge targets, also called content or declarative knowledge by Marzano, Pickering, and McTighe (1993, p. 16), "can be thought of as information and can be ordered somewhat hierarchically according to their generality. At the bottom of the hierarchy are facts about specific persons, places, things, and events; at the top are concepts and generalizations."

The teacher might determine that students who could successfully list several world regions would be demonstrating a grasp of factual knowledge. Those who could state that regions can be categorized using cultural, physical, or political perspectives would be using the concept level of knowledge. Finally, students who could state, "elevation influences the physical geography of a region," would be evincing the generalization level of knowledge. Even at the higher levels of concept and generalization, knowledge targets are factually based. In other words, concepts and generalizations must be verifiable by facts.

To further explicate this hierarchy of knowledge we can use an example from foreign language. Asking students to memorize the Spanish words *problema, despacio, tengo, habla,* and *caballo* as facts may be necessary. Forming the words into sentences for effective dialogue requires more understanding of how the words are used within the sentence, such as *Habla despacio por favor* ("Please speak slowly"). If students are taught Spanish through memorization of vocabulary, they may never be able to generalize their learning to understand sentence structure or word endings or to actually communicate in the language.

Reasoning Targets

"Determine how to resolve a conflict that has arisen due to a proposed highway requiring the displacement of a historic cemetery" is one example of a reasoning target from the North Carolina high school world geography course. Reasoning targets require students to use knowledge and understanding in order to solve problems; such benchmarks may begin with verbs such as *compare, contrast, debate, analyze, deduce, develop, judge,* or *evaluate.*

This type of learning target requires students to think deeply and show *how* they know something, often through a product such as an open-ended question or through a performance such as a demonstration. Selected-response assessments such as multiple-choice items are usually inadequate to uncover the thinking process involved when the above verbs are used to assess a reasoning target.

Another example of a reasoning target is seen when students form opinions about what they have read. When they read articles from the news or read books these readings can often give rise to probing questions such as, Can we hide from our pain? or, Can we be anything we want to be? These questions can guide classroom dialogue to help students reason through their opinions and often re-shape what they are thinking. These targets become "real" for the students when they actually talk about why they hold the opinions they do.

Skill Targets

Skill targets are concerned with developing the capacity to perform or use strategies to sustain learning. Science students learning to correctly manipulate knobs on a microscope and elementary students taking their first measurements with rulers are focused on learning new skills. A world geography benchmark that exemplifies a skill target is, "Use maps to locate specific places and features."

However, before students are able to successfully perform skills, they must usually acquire knowledge. For example, students need to know the parts of a microscope and the function of each part prior to conducting an experiment that requires the skilled use of a microscope. Discerning the student's knowledge level before asking a student to prove her skill at operating the instrument could be done through a formative assessment process. In this process, the student must show and explain the parts of a microscope based on information in a checklist or rubric and using a self-, peer, or teacher assessment process. The teacher would then review the results and provide feedback prior to giving a student an extensive laboratory assignment to conduct using the microscope.

Students learning to work in groups is a good instructional strategy and is also a skill target; this type of learning target crosses grade levels and content areas. If teachers want students to work well in groups, then clearly articulating the group norms (behaviors), assigning roles, and creating procedures for the work all serve to unpack this skill target. If students know what is expected of them and have strategies to use, they can successfully perform the work.

Product Development Targets

Artwork, papers, projects, portfolios, models, and videos are all examples of student products. Product targets emphasize "the ability to use those skills to create certain kinds of quality, tangible products, such as samples of writing, reports, and art products, which exist independently of the performer but which provide concrete evidence of proficiency" (Stiggins, 1997, p. 54). The world geography benchmark that states, "Monitor the effects of pollution on a specific stream," is an excellent example of a product target. To complete this benchmark, students will certainly need to apply skills in measurement, to analyze results through reasoning, and to use knowledge of pollution; however, in order to monitor results, some record must be made of pollution levels at different times and places. Such a record (data log) is one example of a product.

Another example of a product that many students will learn to produce is an essay, whether narrative, expository, or informational. Science and math fair projects are also examples of products students may create. The work given to students as products must be aligned with the curricular targets, and the product must be designed not only to promote quality work but also to accurately measure these targets.

Dispositional Targets

To Stiggins (1997, p. 60), dispositional targets "go beyond academic achievement into the realms of affective and personal feeling states, such as attitude toward something, sense of academic self-confidence, or interest in something that motivationally predisposes a person to do or not do something." When teachers expect students to be self-motivated learners, possess positive self-concepts, or work well with others, these teachers are using dispositional targets. Like product development targets, dispositional targets can also be found in the North Carolina world geography curriculum. One example states, "Develop an appreciation of the racial, ethnic, cultural, and religious diversity of a region." To "develop an appreciation" connotes developing a positive view of such diversity. This benchmark, then, is clearly designed to have an impact on student attitudes.

When students are assigned homework, some do it, some do not, and others try. Giving homework assignments to enrich and motivate students instead of just to provide them additional practice can be a way to work on student motivation to complete homework assignments. Asking beginning readers to place labels on items around the house with the word it represents, such as a picture of a chair on a chair, may be a more motivating activity than just filling in a homework worksheet and circling the picture.

All five categories of learning targets add another layer to the curriculum cake. In Chapter Two we explored the development of standards and benchmarks and listed strands of standards at different levels of instruction (national, state, course, lesson). The strands can be further examined for the presence of particular themes, or targets, for student learning, as we have examined a world geography strand for knowledge, reasoning, skill, product, and dispositional targets. Figure 3.1 illustrates this relationship between strands, standards, and types of targets.

When designing courses of study, curriculum planners and writers consider all the levels we've mentioned, thereby relieving teachers of some of the burden when planning lessons. Teachers generally receive a course-of-study outline that includes all the standards and benchmarks, as well as other information, that help shape instruction and learning in the classroom.

Once teachers have a good grasp of the different learning targets, they may wish to try matching state or district objectives to learning targets. A ten-question matching exercise can be found in Exhibit 3.1 to encourage readers to try unpacking a piece of the curriculum. It should be noted, however, that targets do overlap, so many of the statements may encompass more than one learning target.

FIGURE 3.1. CURRICULAR HIERARCHY FOR WORLD GEOGRAPHY STRAND.

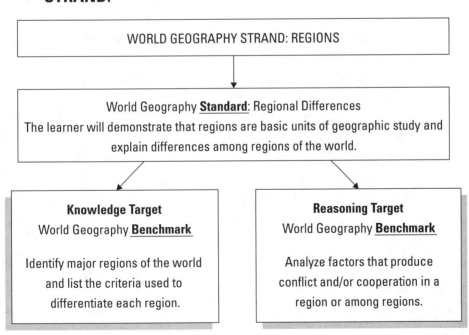

EXHIBIT 3.1. WHAT TYPES OF LEARNING TARGETS ARE THESE?

Instructions: Match the student learning targets on the right to the five types of learning on the left. Answers are open to interpretation; some responses are better than others. The important thing is to understand or explain *why* you have categorized the target as you have.

Type of Learning Outcomes	Student Learning Targets
a. Knowledge	1. Writes effectively for various audiences and purposes
b. Reasoning/Thinking	2. Develops knowledge and understanding of how language is used
c. Performance Skills/ Behavior	3. Contributes productively to both large and small groups
d. Product Development	4. Uses historical and contemporary information to demonstrate crosscultural understanding
e. Affect/Dispositions	5. Demonstrates knowledge of melody, rhythm, harmony, pitch, form, timbre, and tone quality
	6. Uses music vocabulary correctly
	7. Exhibits self-confidence, self-discipline, and self-motivation
	8. Develops a personal wellness plan that recognizes the impact of nutrition and fitness on personal well-being
	9. Chooses and devises appropriate strategies to solve mathematical problems
	10. Views self as capable of using mathematical skills and knowledge to make sense of new problem situations

Possible Answers: 1. C; 2. A; 3. E; 4. B; 5. A; 6. A; 7. E; 8. D; 9. B; 10. E.

Source: Adapted from Regional Laboratory Network, copyright © 1998. *Improving Classroom Assessment: A Toolkit for Professional Developers* (Toolkit 98), chapter 1, activity 1.2, handout A1.2, H3, p. 1. Reprinted with permission of NWREL.

Student Expectations Differ for Standards That Traverse Grade Levels

Often districts or schools use standards and benchmarks that are worded the same across grade levels. For instance, a mathematics standard that appears across K–5 grade levels might be, Understands and applies concepts of data analysis. Although the wording of the standard remains the same, the benchmarks may differ. One benchmark for this standard in K–2 states: The student understands that graphs are used to display objects or measures. For the 3–5 grades the benchmark changes: The student is able to understand the use of data, collect it, and express the data in multiple ways. Therefore, the standard is the same for all, but the benchmarks vary from kindergarten to fifth grade. The major difference for teachers is to figure out the level of sophistication that is expected of the students at each grade level.

Arthur Ellis (2004) explains that this across grade-level view of curricula theory goes back to Jerome Bruner's earlier notion of the spiral curriculum. In a spiral curriculum, "key concepts and methods from each discipline are identified, and visited and revisited at increasing levels of sophistication throughout the school years" (Ellis, 2004, p. 116). The cognitive challenge of the instructional activities and assessments therefore increases over time.

Look at the six assessment samples provided in Exhibits 3.2 through 3.7. Note the benchmark of each and how the assessment differs. For K–2 students the assessment is more about looking at data provided and pulling out or adding information, whereas in grades 3–5 the students move from reading and interpreting the graphs to creating their own.

EXHIBIT 3.2. KINDERGARTEN ASSESSMENT EXAMPLE.

Students use graphs to display data.

1. Count and circle the number that tells how many is in each column.

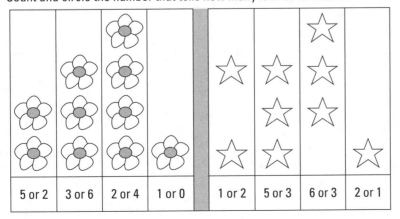

| 5 or 2 | 3 or 6 | 2 or 4 | 1 or 0 | 1 or 2 | 5 or 3 | 6 or 3 | 2 or 1 |

Source: Joyner and McMunn, 2003, K–5 Assessment Example for Math Graphing Skill Target. Reprinted with permission.

EXHIBIT 3.3. GRADE 1 ASSESSMENT EXAMPLE.

The student uses graphs to interpret and display data.

The children counted the buttons on their clothes. Look at the graph. Tell how many buttons each person has.

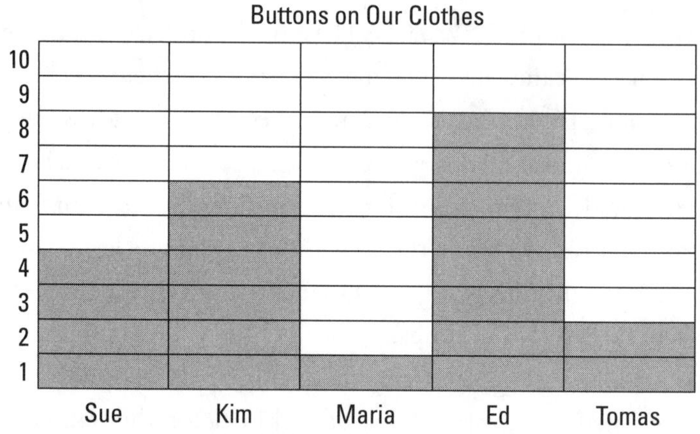

Buttons on Our Clothes

1. Sue has _____ buttons.

2. Kim has _____ buttons.

3. Maria has _____ buttons.

4. Ed has _____ buttons.

5. Tomas has _____ buttons.

6. Who has 2 fewer buttons than Kim? _____

7. Write a number sentence to show how many buttons Kim and Tomas have together.

    _____ + _____ = _____

8. Who has more buttons than Sue?

    _____ and _____

9. How many more buttons does Tomas need so that he will have the same number of buttons as Ed?

    _____

Source: Joyner and McMunn, 2003, K–5 Assessment Example for Math Graphing Skill Target. Reprinted with permission.

EXHIBIT 3.4. GRADE 2 ASSESSMENT EXAMPLE.

The student understands that graphs are used to display objects or measures.

Pat asked his friends about their favorite colors of paint. Here is what he found.

Favorite Paint Colors of Pat's Friends

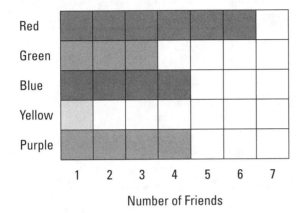

1. How many friends like blue best? _____

2. What was the least favorite color of Pat's friends? _____

3. What color did only 3 friends choose? _____

4. What colors did the same number of friends choose? _____ and _____

5. How many more friends voted for red than blue? _____

6. How many friends did Pat ask about their favorite color? _____

7. How many more need to vote for yellow to have the same votes as red? _____

Source: Joyner and McMunn, 2003, K–5 Assessment Example for Math Graphing Skill Target. Reprinted with permission.

EXHIBIT 3.5. GRADE 3 ASSESSMENT EXAMPLE.

The student understands uses of data, collects it, and uses it in multiple ways.

Third grade students voted on their favorite pattern blocks. Their votes are shown in the tally below. How many students voted? _____

Hexagon	Trapezoid	Blue rhombus	Square	Triangle	Tan rhombus
////	ЖЖ /	ЖЖ ЖЖ /	//	ЖЖ ////	//

Make a pictograph to show the information. Write a title in the first row below.

Hexagon	
Trapezoid	
Blue rhombus	
Square	
Triangle	
Tan rhombus	

⬭ Represents 2 blocks

Source: Joyner and McMunn, 2003, K–5 Assessment Example for Math Graphing Skill Target. Reprinted with permission.

EXHIBIT 3.6. GRADE 4 ASSESSMENT EXAMPLE.

The student is able to use data, collect it, and express the data in multiple ways.

1. Joy knows there are 24 hours in each day. She made a graph to show how she spends her time. How many hours does she have for things other than sleeping and school? _____

2. If Joy goes to bed at 9:30 P.M. each evening, what time does she get up? _____

3. School begins at 8:30 A.M. What time does school end? _____
   Is the time school ends "A.M." or "P.M."? _____

Source: Joyner and McMunn, 2003, K–5 Assessment Example for Math Graphing Skill Target. Reprinted with permission.

EXHIBIT 3.7. GRADE 5 ASSESSMENT EXAMPLE.

The student is able to understand the use data, collect it, and express the data in multiple ways.

1. The graphing grid below represents 100%. Twenty-seven percent of the calories in animal crackers come from fat. Shade the grid to show this percent.

Graphing Grid Title: _____

Graph Title: _____

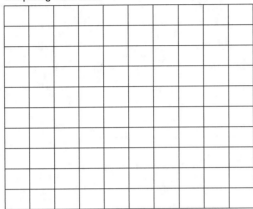
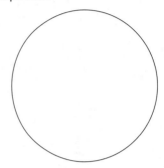

2. Use the circle to make a graph to show the percent of calories from fat and those not from fat in animal crackers. Label each part of the graph.

    <u>Use the fact sheet about Barnum's Animal Crackers to construct a graph.</u>

3. Using the space below, make a graph to show the sales of animal crackers for <u>all of the stores except</u> the Ballpark Snack store for the first quarter.
4. Label each side of the graph and write a title.
5. What scale did you use? Explain why you chose this scale.

Source: Joyner and McMunn, 2003, K–5 Assessment Example for Math Graphing Skill Target. Reprinted with permission.

Teaching Standards Has Become a Bigger Challenge for Teachers

It is clear from this brief overview of standards and benchmarks in Chapters Two and Three that particular themes recur at all levels, from the national level to the classroom level. However, we also offer a few cautionary notes for the reader to consider.

The modifications in education necessitated by global transitions have placed an additional planning burden on the teacher in the classroom. In the past, teachers simply relied on the textbook, not only for all conceptual information, but also for the sequencing and pacing of that information. The publishing of differing standards and benchmarks by states has made it impossible for textbook authors to write texts appropriate for all states. Therefore, selecting text information and planning the sequence of instruction to ensure the teaching of all standards has become a giant task for classroom teachers.

It is important for teachers to realize that the curriculum does *not* encompass every piece of information found in a textbook. The curricular standards and benchmarks must reflect reasonable course expectations, which are geared to the developmental age of the students. There are myriad activities that teachers can do in their classes. Activities, however, should not drive the instruction within the classroom. Teachers should choose the instructional strategies (activities) that actually advance the study of essential concepts. Such alignment has the most value because it helps the students achieve the curricular standards and benchmarks and therefore allows them to achieve the state's educational goals.

Once teachers read the curricular standards and benchmarks and then unpack them into their component learning targets, they must then begin to plan assessments for these targets. In this process teachers begin to gather evidence of achievement. Therefore, the next four chapters discuss gathering such evidence for learning. In reviewing the Classroom Assessment Cycle, remember that we are looking at the formative assessment process and using this as a lens to determine what evidence is good (that is, evidence that will help the learner). In this book, we cannot possibly cover *all* the evidence sources or the tremendous detail about these sources. However, the next four chapters discuss the strategies for gathering assessment evidence that we recommend to those attending our training sessions. These strategies represent the "meat," the essentials of evidence gathering that we want to share.

Gathering Assessment Evidence

Evidence is gathered in a variety of ways

The second quadrant of the Classroom Assessment Cycle involves collecting evidence of learning. To gain a better understanding of student learning a variety of assessment methods must be used, because decisions affecting instruction or achievement are not reliable if made from a single data source. Further, in order to collect valid data, quality assessment tools and methods are necessary. Finally, the criteria used for adequate versus excellent work must be determined before instruction takes place so the teacher can convey these criteria to students. In this manner, high expectations can be communicated, with a resulting positive effect on student achievement.

Chapter Four, "Understanding and Selecting Assessment Methods," provides details on using both product and performance assessments as tools for collecting evidence. Teachers need such ample evidence to accurately assess student performance. This chapter focuses on how evidence can be gathered and why it is important to collect the evidence of learning in a variety of ways.

Chapter Five, "Written Product, Portfolio, and Project Assessments," takes a closer look at product assessment by focusing on how to use written documents, portfolios, and projects as assessment tools.

Chapter Six, "Designing Quality Classroom Assessment Tasks," emphasizes the need to collect good evidence (evidence that can be used to help the learner identify strengths and weaknesses of performance and evidence the teacher can use to modify instruction to meet individual learner needs) of learning and describes characteristics of quality assessment tasks. Poor assessment decisions may be made if the tasks used are poorly designed and so fail to adequately measure the learning targets addressed.

Chapter Seven, "Creating Useful Scoring Guides," outlines the importance of using high-quality tools to score student work. If teachers give students assessment tasks of high-quality design, the rubrics used to score these must also exhibit this high quality. When high-quality rubrics are used they are powerful tools that can provide students and teachers with feedback on improving instruction and learning.

Understanding and Selecting Assessment Methods

4

Teachers need to gather evidence about student achievement or progress toward established learning targets in a variety of ways. This chapter answers the following questions:

- How do we choose when to use constructed response assessments?
- How do we gather assessment evidence in general ways?
- How do we gather assessment evidence in a variety of specific ways?

By using multiple and diverse sources, teachers can be sure they have ample evidence to accurately assess student achievement. The variety of assessments used by a reading teacher, for example, may include state testing results, individual reading conferences, written retells, and literature circle dialogues. If the teacher wants to know whether a student can comprehend what he reads, then conducting an individual reading conference (IRC), a performance method of assessment, may be the best tool to use. An IRC consists of a student reading orally (performance), retelling what was read (conversation), and giving responses to questions asked by the teacher (dialogue). These diverse assessment methods help the teacher accurately and completely determine the student's reading comprehension level.

Multiple assessment methods aid the teacher in triangulating the evidence for a complete picture of student comprehension. *Triangulation* is a technical term describing a method of, for example, pinpointing radio signal transmission sites, loci of earthquakes, and the locations of cell phone users by using three separate data sets. In education, teachers in effect triangulate when they use multiple assessment methods to collect diverse data about student achievement. By using more than one data source, the teacher can more accurately diagnose students' learning challenges. Of course there is no magic number of assessments that will accurately portray students' understanding of concepts. However, multiple and varied assessment methods give a more complete and accurate view of each student's level of achievement in relation to the learning targets.

When to Use a Constructed Response Assessment

In Chapter One, we distinguished between constructed response assessment and more traditional, selected-response assessments. *Constructed response assessment* is the direct, systematic observation of actual student work according to *preestablished* criteria. Such assessment may be manifested in products or performances, as both require that students *construct* their own answers rather than select answers from a given list.

Using performances as assessment tools is a good choice for assessing learning targets that require the student to demonstrate skills or processes. For example, assessing an oral presentation target of articulating ideas clearly, precisely, and accurately would require an actual performance. A selected-response assessment (like a multiple-choice question) would not be as logical a choice for this learning goal.

Although the approach to assessment may originate from either of these categories (selected or constructed responses), in this chapter we primarily focus on tools of constructed response assessment. Constructed response assessment methods involve real-world skills and are interdisciplinary in that they can be used for assessment purposes in all subjects. Further, they can be integrated with instruction, an essential part of the Classroom Assessment Cycle. These assessment methods also enable students to become more skillful in lifelong tasks and help students demonstrate their understanding of content-related concepts. Finally, they complement the growing emphasis on learning targets that require students to demonstrate proficiencies beyond the ability to simply absorb knowledge as well as those targets that ask students to actively work with knowledge and create new knowledge. When developing assessments, a teacher may begin by asking the following questions:

1. With which learning targets (standards, benchmarks, or objectives) is this assessment aligned?

2. Do the learning targets ensure that higher-order thinking skills are required?

3. Would a constructed response assessment be the best method by which to assess these learning targets?

4. If constructed response assessment should be used, what type of evidence should be selected (for example, products as essays, logs, or journals; or performances as oral reports, demonstrations of skill, or role-playing)? What will give the best information about the learning?

5. If constructed response assessment is used, what do students need to know (criteria) in order to perform at the expected level?

6. How will formative and summative feedback (as discussed in Chapter One) be provided throughout the learning process?

7. What instructional strategies will be necessary to aid the learning processes and prepare students for the assessment?

Gathering Evidence in General Ways

Many general methods can be employed in order to obtain student achievement data. For example, teachers may observe students during the oral performance, ask students questions before and after performances, and examine student work (McColskey and O'Sullivan, 1995). Teacher observations cross the categories of selected and constructed responses. Teachers watch students who are completing selected-response worksheets to see who is having difficulty, just as they observe student oral presentations. The first example is an informal observation and the second is a more formal one.

Teacher Observations

Observations of students may be formal or informal, with formal observations tending to be more structured than informal ones. The teacher using a formal method may collect data via an observation instrument, such as a rubric (discussed in Chapter Seven), for the performance. The teacher watches one particular student or one particular group and compares the behavior he sees to preestablished criteria. An informal observation may occur during instruction. In an informal observation, no one student or group may be singled out for an observation, and the teacher may not have predetermined criteria in mind. However, she may still collect data about students in the form of anecdotal teacher notes or narratives.

For example, informal observations are made every day in the classroom. It is through informal observations that teachers learn about their students. They may learn that Jackie tends to wander away from her group or that Matt never volunteers information. In contrast, formal observations are more likely to occur only on special occasions, when the stage has been set for them. A teacher conducting a literature circle (small groups of students engaged in critical thinking and reflection through discussions of what was read) as a formative assessment may use a form to jot down notes (see Table 4.1) concerning student understanding and student participation in the dialogue. At this point, the teacher is not part of the group but observing from the outside.

She may also ask her students to conduct a self-assessment of their learning (see Exhibit 4.1), so that she may conference with the students about their performances.

TABLE 4.1. DISCUSSION MATRIX: FORMATIVE USE.

Group: *Camels*	Students					
	Jack	Tim	Cora	Sue	Juan	Tia
Contributed to discussion	✓	✓		✓	✓	✓
Listened to others			✓		✓	✓
Referenced the text					✓	
Substantiated ideas with reasoning					✓	
Made inferences						
Notes or other observations:	*Discussion in Literature Circle today was limited. Text comprehension was not evident. Text may have been too difficult for this group or the students may not have read the text prior to their group discussion. Juan may need to be moved into a different Lit Circle group.*					

Source: Modified from Williamson, McMunn, and Reagan, 2004, p. 27.

In such conferences, the teacher and the student compare their assessments and jointly set learning goals for the student.

A formal observation such as this one, which leads to a goal-setting conference, is a good example of a formative assessment. Such formative assessments usually occur during the learning process, whereas summative assessments help define the proficiency level of a student after instruction. Formative assessments are more diagnostic in function, and their purpose is to provide students with needed feedback for improvement.

Questioning

Teacher observations, whether formal or informal, can serve as excellent data sources on student achievement, but they are only one of many assessment methods available to teachers. For example, questioning students is another general method teachers can use to probe student learning through both selected and constructed response assessments. The questions can be oral or written, with one right answer or many possible answers. The student may be asked to participate in an interview, write a paper, write an essay, complete a survey, give an oral report, perform a self-assessment, perform a peer assessment, or simply respond aloud to a short-answer question. In each of these cases, however, students are required to construct their own answers. Multiple choice, fill-in-the blanks, and matching questions are selected-response items that can also

EXHIBIT 4.1. SELF-ASSESSMENT: MY PROGRESS IN READING.

✓ Put a check in the appropriate box:

My Progress in Reading	Not yet	I'm getting there	I really improved
Comprehension: Do you understand what you read? Can you figure out problems? Can you retell what you read?			
Strategies: **Before you read** do you use strategies like: Looking over the text? Predicting?			
Strategies: **While you read** do you use strategies like: Rereading? Asking yourself questions?			
Strategies: **After you read** do you use strategies like: Checking predictions? Summarizing?			
Higher-Order Thinking Skills: Do you question as you read? Do you make connections? Do you make judgments?			
Motivation: Do you enjoy reading? Do you read often? Do you feel confident about reading? Do you like to talk about what you have read?			

After participating in Literature Circle, I learned

_____

_____

_____

_____

My goal in reading now is

_____

_____

Source: Williamson, McMunn, and Reagan, 2004, p. 33.

reveal student learning. Thus, through acute questioning techniques, a teacher can assess what students know and are able to do.

There are multiple ways to use questions to elicit information from students, but the questions should always be aligned to the assessment purpose. For example, if the learning target is reading for specific information, a language arts teacher may pose the following to the students as self-reflective questions:

- What information am I trying to find?

- What can I learn from the title, subtitle, or charts?

- What categories can I identify?

- Can I underline, or should I take notes? [Williamson, McMunn, & Reagan, 2004, p. 25]

A science teacher might ask her students to think about the following questions when reading a scientific report for the purpose of a critique or evaluation:

- What is the hypothesis underlying this study?

- What audience did the study target?

- What information was given to help the reader understand the study?

- How was the study designed?

- What data are given as evidence? Was there enough evidence?

- What are the results, and do they seem valid and reliable?

- What did the researchers conclude about the study?

- Were their findings supportive of the hypothesis?

- Was this study worth the money, time, and effort expended—does it have a significant impact?

- How could I use these results in my own life? [Williamson, et al., 2004, p. 25]

Using questions and conducting both formal and informal observations of students are two general methods of assessing student knowledge.

Student-Teacher Dialogues

One further general method of assessment is student-teacher dialogues. In the dialogues students reveal their thinking processes to the teacher. One such dialogue took place in Susan's chemistry class. Students were classifying chemical elements as liquids, solids, and gases. For the element mercury, Marsha answered, "solid." Susan reflected that Marsha might have seen mercury that had escaped from a broken thermometer. When this occurs, mercury rolls up into small spheres resembling BBs and these spheres do look solid. So Susan began a dialogue with Marsha to ascertain her reasoning. Without referencing thermometers, Marsha, now very exasperated, said: "Solid, of course it is a solid. Mercury is the planet closest to the sun!" Through this dialogue, Susan learned that Marsha knew the differences among solids, liquids, and gases and that Marsha's original answer was not wrong, given her perspective or reasoning.

Teachers can also conduct dialogues with students who are answering selected-response items. We have previously stated that teachers can certainly observe students while they complete worksheets or other selected-response assessments as multiple-choice tests. During the observation, if a teacher notes that a student is experiencing difficulty, what is more natural than beginning a dialogue with the student to find out the area of difficulty? So dialogues between students and teachers can have utility as assessments, as they reveal the depth of student knowledge.

Gathering Evidence in a Variety of Specific Ways

Table 4.2 classifies types of assessments under the two headings discussed in Chapter One, selected and constructed responses. Assessments that employ a selected-response method require students to choose answers from a given list. Constructed-response

TABLE 4.2. ASSESSMENT METHODS AND APPROACHES.

Selected Responses	Constructed Responses	
	Products	*Performances*
Multiple choice	Essays	Oral presentations
True/false	Logs	Demonstrations
Matching	Journals	Drama readings
Listing	Graphing	Debates
Fill in	Matrices	Panel discussions
	Paragraphs (short answers)	Oral reading (IRC)
	Webs	Artwork
	Portfolios	Projects
	Projects	Writing poems
	Notebooks	Musical recitals
	Flowcharts	Dance activity
	Concept maps	
	Research papers	

← Questioning →

← Formal and informal observations →

← Teacher/student dialogues →

assessments manifest as products or (literal) performances. Note, however, that the three general methods of collecting assessment evidence (teacher observations, questioning, and student-teacher dialogues) span the chart.

We realize that there are many ways to organize methods of assessments. Stiggins (2001a), for example, classifies assessments as selected-response, essay, performance assessment, and personal communication. From our work with educators, however, the organization of assessments into selected- or constructed-response categories has worked well and has led to enhanced teacher assessment literacy. Therefore, this book uses this two-tiered classification scheme. The constructed-response assessment category is further subdivided into products and performances.

In the remainder of this chapter, we describe a number of these specific constructed-response assessment methods introducing both simple products and literal performances. We devote the next chapter to discussing several more complex products, including logs and journals, projects, notebooks, and portfolios.

Simple Product Assessments

These assessment methods may include but are not limited to short answer sentences or paragraphs, diagrams and illustrations, graphic organizers, graphs and tables, and matrices.

Short-answer sentences or paragraphs may be used to answer specific questions. Such questions are currently more commonly used within school settings and can be found on high-stakes tests. These questions call for student-constructed responses but generally possess a "correct" answer. For example, the question, Who invented the electric light bulb? or word problems such as

> There are four wooden boards, each 16 feet long. If you used these boards to lay out a square on a playground for a proposed sandbox, how large an area would the square encompass?

are examples of questions that ask students to create an answer. Students do not choose their answers to these questions from a list but must construct the response. However, students who answer with other than *Thomas A. Edison* or *256 square feet* will find they have responded incorrectly.

Teachers frequently use this type of constructed response to check comprehension or to explore the recall of information by students. However, such questions have utility beyond this scope. Essay questions that encourage students to synthesize information or to evaluate solutions would be examples of the use of higher-order thinking skills in questions. For example, a high school business teacher could distribute information from various banking institutions and ask students to choose the best account for a specific business based on an analysis of the information provided. Students would review the information given and determine the needs of the business in order to choose the correct account. Such an evaluation of the needs of the business would constitute the use of higher-order thinking skills. This example demonstrates the use of a constructed response, in that students do not choose the correct answer from a given list; the example describes a question that requires the use of higher-order thinking by students. The question in this case is, Which account would be best to suit the needs of the business?

Other questions require students to create their own solutions but may have more than one right answer or more than one correct solution. Students are expected to justify their answers, based upon concepts learned in class or through their own study of concepts. For example, What physical characteristics of animals living in the arctic tundra would be most suitable for supporting and sustaining life? Similarly, The pie chart shown is not labeled: explain what this chart might represent, is a question requiring students to create a response, but there may be more than one right answer. With such questions there are many possible avenues for response. To answer the first question, students may focus on protection from cold (fur, feathers, fat), adaptive feeding mechanisms (claws, teeth, jaws, beaks), or locomotion devices (hooves, webbed appendages, wings). As long as students actually discuss physical characteristics (and not adaptive behaviors such as hibernation) and relate such characteristics to conditions within the arctic tundra, a variety of responses can be "correct." For the second question, an understanding of what pie charts tell a student is more important than the data expressed. For example, one student might indicate that the pie chart represents people who use certain brands of toothpaste. He would further explain that the largest pie section on the chart represents the most preferred type of toothpaste. Another might label the chart as test scores from the last unit test, showing the largest section as those students receiving grades corresponding to C on the test.

These types of questions encourage original, imaginative, and creative thought. The nature of the question usually demands critical thinking skills such as analysis, synthesis, or evaluation. In fact, the most common use of this type of question in assessment is to uncover the thinking processes involved in student decision making.

Like short-answer questions or student-constructed paragraphs, diagrams and illustrations are examples of student-constructed responses. These, however, use pictorial displays to uncover student knowledge. The uses of diagrams and illustrations for assessment purposes are varied. Students may diagram the set-up of equipment for a chemistry experiment or draw a blueprint for a house. Computer-assisted drawings may be created that show intricate details of engineering projects or visualizations of scientific concepts. Students may draw a picture of an animal to answer the question about the arctic tundra animal mentioned previously. A kindergarten teacher may use drawings as both diagnostic and summative assessments. She could first have her students draw a view of what an insect looks like prior to learning about insects and then at the end of a study on insects have these same students draw an insect again. The diagnostic drawing would probably be a circle with a face or dot in the middle; by

FIGURE 4.1. SAMPLE CONCEPT MAP.

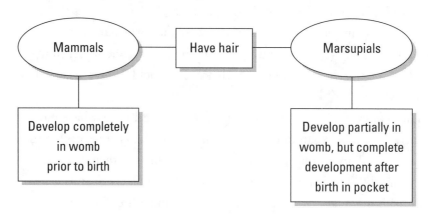

the time the study on insects is complete the summative assessment should include an actual drawing of the insect with a head, abdomen, thorax, and all six legs.

Graphic organizers, according to Burke (1994, p. 118), are "mental maps that represent key skills like sequencing, comparing and contrasting, and classifying and involving students in active thinking." The most common types of graphic organizers used in schools are webs and concept maps. Such tools help students to see the connections between and the differences among concepts. The simple *concept map* in Figure 4.1 may illustrate this use of graphic organizers.

Webs are simply more complex concept maps in which there are many cross-linkages between concepts. The simple concept map shown in Figure 4.1 could be converted to a web by adding more concepts. For example, other animal classifications such as reptiles, birds, and fishes could be added. There would be many cross-linkages between such groups, which would help students visualize the differences and similarities among animals in the animal kingdom and help the teacher assess what students do and do not understand.

Venn diagrams are also often categorized as graphic organizers. Like concept maps and webs, Venn diagrams show the relationship between ideas. However, Venn diagrams are uniquely adept at illustrating the overlap between concepts. An example of a Venn diagram appears in Figure 4.2, which shows the overlap between selected- and constructed-response assessments.

Flowcharts, another type of graphic organizer, may be used to encourage students to sequence events. Students may be asked to transform the written directions for a scientific experiment into a flowchart before beginning the procedure. Using this technique, the teacher determines that students read the procedure and understand the steps. Figure 4.3 illustrates part of the experimental procedure for a Geiger counter lab. The student-constructed flowchart in Figure 4.3 clearly shows the sequence of events to follow, and it helps the student determine data collection points.

FIGURE 4.2. VENN DIAGRAM: COMPARISON OF SELECTED- AND CONSTRUCTED-RESPONSE ASSESSMENTS.

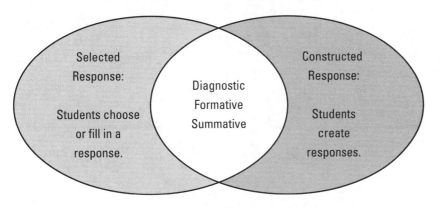

FIGURE 4.3. SAMPLE FLOWCHART: GEIGER COUNTER LAB.

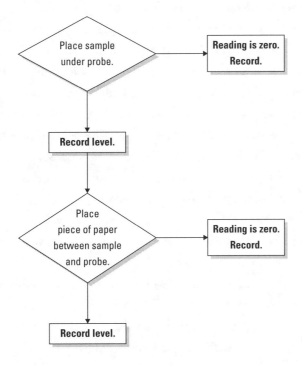

FIGURE 4.4. SAMPLE FLOWCHART: SQUARES AND RECTANGLES.

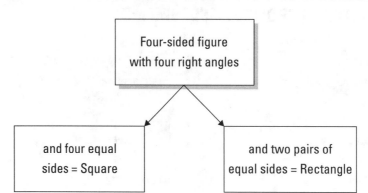

Flowcharts are also commonly used in order to classify objects into categories. For example, many field guides use flowcharts to help differentiate between species of animals (birds, insects, snakes, and so forth). The simple flowchart in Figure 4.4 shows the differentiation between a square and a rectangle.

Some flowcharts may use questions with yes or no answers to direct users toward classifications. Computer manuals often include these types of flowcharts in their "troubleshooting" sections to encourage users toward a step-by-step analysis of a problem.

No matter the form of the graphic organizer (map, web, Venn diagram, or flowchart) used for assessment, all such organizers explicate student understanding of concepts. Graphic organizers are particularly helpful in diagnosing student preconceptions or misconceptions of specific concepts. They also are logical choices for assessing whether students understand relationships among different components.

Graphs and *tables,* like the other forms of constructed responses, help make the thinking of the students evident to the teacher. Students in an elementary classroom might be asked to construct a *graph* to answer the question, What shoe type are most of the students in this classroom wearing today? The graph would then show the relative numbers of sneakers, dress shoes, boots, and other shoes worn that day. To aid younger elementary students in constructing the graph, stickers of shoes could be placed on a grid. Such a graph could be used to assess counting skills. Color recognition could also be tested in this manner, with a simple change in the original question.

Another use of graphing might be to display data collected in a science experiment. For example, one elementary teacher began a science activity by removing the lid from an electric popcorn popper. She placed the popper on a tablecloth spread on the floor of the classroom. Then she placed popcorn in the uncovered popper and turned it on. When the corn popped, some of it landed in the popper, some landed on the tablecloth, and some landed in the far corners of the room! She asked students to count the pieces of popcorn in each location and then graph this information. The graph helped students visualize the relative numbers of kernels landing in the various locations, and it helped the teacher assess how well the students understood how graphs display data. After students constructed their graphs, the teacher conducted a whole class discussion on the findings. By using the graphed data, the teacher was able to elicit descriptions that helped her teach and assess how well students understood how the movement of the popcorn was based upon energy. For example, the "high-energy" popcorn landed further away from the popper than the "low-energy" kernels. In this one assessment task involving the construction of a graph, the teacher was able to teach and assess graphing skills, reinforce and assess counting skills, and introduce and assess the science concept of energy.

Tables, like graphs, are often used to help students discern patterns. A science teacher may ask students to record masses and volumes of pure substances (carbon, tin, lead, zinc) in table columns next to the given column for density of the substance. From these data, the teacher may ask students to review and hypothesize the mathematical relationship between the three terms (mass, volume, and density). Similarly, a law enforcement class studying forensics may collect measurements of footprints, strides, and height. The class would then be asked to derive a relationship between foot size and height or stride length and height. In this manner, organizing the data into tables would help students see the patterns embedded in the data and help the teacher assess how well students discerned those patterns. A further example could be an elementary mathematics table-creation task that facilitates student understanding of estimation. A teacher could ask the students to estimate the time it would take them to run across a gym or baseball field. The students would create a data table to include a column for their estimated times and columns for actual times elapsed during their trial runs. The students would run the distance and record the results several times. The students would then either average the trials and compare the average to the estimated time or look at their best time for comparison. In either case, the students would have enough data to review to determine whether their estimate was on target or unrealistic. Once the table data were completed, the students could create a graphic picture of their results. Therefore, the assessment task of creating the data tables would help forward the teaching of a new concept (estimation).

Tables may also be used to organize data into easily reviewed units. This particular use of tables is often evident in math classes when students are solving word problems. For example, a teacher may require students to construct simple tables like Table 4.3, to solve a problem of rate × time = distance. Such tables help the student organize the data given in the problem, and help separate the relevant information from the irrelevant.

TABLE 4.3. SAMPLE TABLE.

Train	Distance	Time	Rate
Train A			
Train B			

Source: Butler, 1998.

A table like this one can be an assessment tool because it offers valuable feedback to the teacher on student understanding of the problem-solving process. Similarly, a table can clarify information that appears confusing when written in paragraph form. The sample paragraph below illustrates such a convoluted, bewildering mass of data:

> The Sesame Street students took three tests during the first nine weeks of school. Big Bird made a 52 on the first test, but improved to a 98 on the last test. Kermit scored an 87 on the second, Animal Kingdom, test, but only received a 72 on the last exam, Energy. On the Magnets test, Cookie Monster received a score of 78, but Kermit made a 48. Big Bird and Cookie Monster both received the same grade on the second test, which was 5 points higher than Kermit's score on this test. On the final test, Cookie Monster made an 88. Which student showed continuous improvement in test scores?

Before a table of the data is constructed, it is hard to see that Big Bird made the continuous improvement. However, this fact is easily perceived by studying Table 4.4. Student construction of this table would clarify for the teacher the students' ability to pull data out of text and organize it into a useful set of data for interpretation.

A teacher might ask students to construct a table like the one above in order to assess reading, organizational, or charting skills. When the data are even more complex, however, or when detailed comparisons of data sets are needed, a matrix takes the place of a simple table. When students are asked to think about characteristics or facts from the text they read, this can be a daunting task. Often textbooks may not cover all the facts about a particular topic. Sometimes the information is sparse or random. Asking students to complete a matrix of characteristics or facts is a good strategy to get students to prepare and organize their thinking about a topic, especially when facts are important. Table 4.5 shows how middle school science students used a matrix (only a section is shown) to compare and contrast the same characteristics of the planets and keep these facts organized for other uses during their study. Matrices, like this, can be used in all content areas.

Teachers could use a matrix as a teaching and assessment tool. We recommend that the teacher fill in a few of the boxes to model the process and ask students to fill in the remaining ones.

TABLE 4.4. *SESAME STREET* DATA TABLE.

Student	First Test: Magnets	Second Test: Animal Kingdom	Third Test: Energy
Big Bird	52	92	98
Kermit	48	87	72
Cookie Monster	78	92	88

Source: Butler, 1998.

TABLE 4.5. SAMPLE MATRIX.

Matrix of Planet Characteristics			
	Interesting Feature	*Temperature*	*Atmospheric Content*	*Distance to Sun*
Mercury	Smallest planet, dense, lots of craters	400°C by day −150°C by night	Mostly sodium	58×10^6
Venus	Receives lots of sunlight, but reflected, sulfuric acid gives yellow color	> 400°C	Mostly (97%) carbon dioxide, but trace amounts of nitrogen, argon, and oxygen	108×10^6
Earth	Life exists, 24-hour rotations	−21°C to a comfortable +14°C	Oxygen (77%), nitrogen (21%), and carbon dioxide	150×10^6
Mars	Dust storms common, polar caps	−133°C to 27°C	Carbon dioxide (95.3%) plus nitrogen (2.7%), argon (1.6%), and traces of oxygen (0.15%) and water (0.03%)	228×10^6
Jupiter	16 moons, light bands, 30,000°C core temperature	Above clouds −140°C to 21°C at deeper pressure	Mostly liquid and gaseous hydrogen . . .	180×10^6

Matrices, like tables, graphic organizers, illustrations, diagrams, and short-answer questions or paragraphs, may serve as assessment tools in the classroom. Using these constructed-response tools, the teacher integrates the instruction with assessment, thereby advancing the study of the content within the assessment task.

Performance Assessments

Performances differ from products because in performances an audience is normally present to watch the student. Like products, however, performances must conform to the definition of constructed response assessments in that they must be judged according to *preestablished performance criteria.* Of course, like all quality assessments, performances should also help forward the instruction of key curricular concepts.

Some examples of performances are oral presentations, demonstrations, enactments, debates, panel discussions, and videotapes or audiotapes. A further example of a performance is the writing and oral defense of a doctoral dissertation. Although including the latter example in a text designed for teachers of primary, middle school, and secondary school students may seem inappropriate, a performance not unlike that of the doctoral candidate's is rising in prominence among high school students in the form of the *senior project.*

The senior project program is a performance assessment and requirement (basics to honors) for twelfth graders with four components:

1. A research paper on a topic of the student's choice

2. A project related to the paper

3. A portfolio documenting the senior project process

4. A presentation to a panel comprising community members and school staff [SERVE Regional Laboratory, 2003]

The research paper serves to demonstrate the acquisition of new knowledge through researching, writing, interviewing, or other complex skills. The second phase, the project, is an extension of the research paper in which students work with a mentoring adult in a field related to the topic. In the third phase the students present their work to a panel of judges in a question-and-answer format. Through such activities, students "demonstrate complex knowledge and skills," including

- Gathering information through researching and reading
- Communicating information by writing, speaking, and using visual exhibits and verbal and nonverbal expression
- Using numbers, graphs, charts, drawings, and problem-solving techniques gained from math and science
- Using current systems of technology [NCDPI, 1999, p. 95]

This list of components and skills shows how the senior project program incorporates activities from both categories of constructed response assessments (products and performances). The senior project assessments benefit students, faculties, and communities. Students benefit in that they are given opportunities to present their best work, acquire new skills, gain self-confidence, and focus on career goals. Benefits to faculties include occasions to collaborate with colleagues in interdisciplinary studies, chances to raise expectations and standards for students, and opportunities to connect school curriculum to world-of-work applications. Community benefits from student work on senior projects include having more community members involved in school activities, gaining publicity for community problems or challenges, and acquiring new community members who are well prepared for the world of work as students matriculate.

Middle and elementary school students often like to debate topics in which they are interested. Debating is a structured argument in which teams or individuals defend or attack the informed opinions of other students on a topic or text. Real world examples draw students into the conversation. One such example from a *Newsweek* article (and now a movie) involves Coach Carter, who in 1999 padlocked the gym at Richmond High in the San Francisco area because fifteen out of forty-five students

TABLE 4.6. DEBATE SELF-ASSESSMENT FORM.

Criteria	*Often*	*Sometimes*	*Not Often*
1. I developed an informed opinion.			
2. I explained or justified my opinion.			
3. I considered new information.			
4. I was aware that I changed my opinion.			
5. I used textual evidence to support my opinion.			
6. I appropriately challenged others' opinions.			
7. I asked (raised) questions.			
8. Next time I need to work on the following target:			

failed to meet their signed contract agreements on keeping a 2.3 GPA (Lawson, 2005). Asking students to read this text and then decide whether they would or would not support what Coach Carter did is a great topic for a debate. Students can then debate the questions, Did Coach Carter do the right thing? Why do you think so? This process involves students' critical thinking. Making sure the students are given or determine the criteria being assessed prior to the debate is crucial. For example, Table 4.6 shares a student self-assessment form based on the criteria used to conduct the debate.

Like a debate, a panel discussion must also have pre-determined criteria. The following bulleted list displays the criteria for the background research performed by a group of elementary students prior to a panel discussion. After visiting a zoo and the library, the elementary students complete sets of cards with at least three facts, representing the following:

- Green card—General information about mammal. Lifespan?
- Blue card—Habitat where animal lives, giving the part of the world. Cave? Tree?
- Yellow card—What it looks like, weight and height.
- White card—Number of babies in litter, length of gestation.
- Pink card—What it eats, diet, baby's diet.
- Orange card—How it hunts *or* how it defends itself.

Each group completes the card sets and prepares a presentation on its animal. The group must include a description of the habitat seen at the zoo and evaluate the habitat based upon research about the animal. Students in the audience are encouraged to take the role of the zookeeper and to ask probing questions about how to enhance the life of an animal by improving its habitat. A checklist containing the criteria for the elementary presentation is displayed in Exhibit 4.2.

EXHIBIT 4.2. CHECKLIST FOR PANEL DISCUSSION.

Team:	Topic:	Date:
❏ Each team member presents information during discussion		
❏ Accurate facts about the animals are given		
❏ Presentation of information shows logical organization		
❏ Presenters show enthusiasm for subject matter		
❏ Courtesy is shown to other panel members and to audience		
❏ Presenters respond to audience questions with accurate, factual information		
❏ Group self-evaluates their discussion and sets goals for future presentations		
Notes:		

The senior project performance, the middle school debate, and the elementary panel discussion, however, like all constructed-response assessments, do not succeed unless carefully designed and planned. All such assessments must be based on curriculum standards, have clear expectations that are shared with students, and be judged by predetermined, quality criteria. The criteria are shared with the students before the performance and are derived from the learning outcomes or standards for the course. Before the constructed-response assessment, instructional strategies should be designed to aid students in developing the skills needed for the performance, and sufficient time for practicing these skills must be incorporated into the class schedule.

———————————

In Chapter Five we continue our discussion of specific constructed-response assessments with a look at portfolios and other complex products.

Written Product, Portfolio, and Project Assessments

5

Many types of assessment methods and approaches may require students to create products. In the last chapter we examined several such products as concept maps, Venn diagrams, and flowcharts. In this chapter we continue our exploration of products, specifically focusing on products that usually (but not always) have written components, as logs, journals, notebooks, portfolios, and projects. Although these products are familiar to teachers, the characteristics and uses of these assessments warrant a detailed discussion. This chapter answers the following questions:

- How are logs, journals, and notebooks used in assessment?

- How are portfolios used in assessment?

- How are projects used in assessment?

Logs, Journals, and Notebooks

First, let's examine three types of written documents that students may produce and that teachers and students may use as assessment evidence: logs, journals, and notebooks.

A *log* provides documentary evidence of events and concise summaries of information, and it may show the progression of events. Teachers may choose this assessment method when students need to track information and use it for later assignments. One example of a log is a patient's hospital chart. The ward clerk logs medications, laboratory test results, and therapy in this chart in order to establish a record of the patient's medical treatment. Police stations use logs to protect evidence from contamination, loss, or misuse. In schools, logs may be used in assessment to verify student actions. For example, students may be asked to keep scientific logs while running science experiments. The addition of growth factors to plants and the recorded heights of the plants at specified intervals are examples of data that might be included in such science logs. In order to reflect on reading habits, teachers may request that students keep a log of what and when they read. A detailed log can also help convince a teacher that the student actually performed certain actions. In addition, the log can reveal the exact nature of those actions. Because of their documentary properties, logs are frequently used to support assertions or conclusions students make about information they have gathered.

Exhibit 5.1 shows an example of a reading log. In it, the student provides a brief summary of the book and records questions she may still have about the text. If a teacher looks closely, she can see that Sara did not summarize deeply about what she read. Verdi is a yellow snake who did not want to turn green but, more deeply, he felt that this change would be a symbol of growing old and he did not want to grow old. Sara's questions may not reflect a deeper understanding of the story. In this manner, the assessment log reveals a glimpse of Sara's reading comprehension.

Journals are similar to logs in that they provide a record of the progression of events. In journals, students can record thoughts, observations, and questions and hold written dialogues with others. Generally, however, journals do not have the legalistic, evidentiary purpose of a log. Teachers may choose to use this assessment method when requiring students to record specific information based on the learning targets.

The *Diary of Anne Frank* is one example of a journal. Although this diary documents events, it flavors those events with the opinions, feelings, and perceptions of the author. This flavoring of data with the consciousness of the author is what makes journals so useful to teachers.

EXHIBIT 5.1. SAMPLE LOG.

Log: Questioning for understanding . . .		Student Name: Sara
Text read:	Summary of text:	Questions I'd like to discuss:
Verdi by Janell Cannon	Verdi is a yellow snake who did not want to turn green.	1. Was Verdi happy? 2. Why did Verdi want to challenge things? 3. Was Verdi just sad or was he angry?
Miss Rumphius by Barbara Cooney	When Miss Rumphius was a little girl she lived in a city by the sea. When she grew up, she wanted to travel and see faraway places, and then come home to live beside the	1. Was Miss Rumphius happy? 2. What are lupines? 3. How old is Miss Rumphius? 4. Why did Miss Rumphius want to live by the sea?

In the video *Good Morning, Miss Toliver* (Foundation for Advancements in Science & Education, 1993), Miss Toliver asks her math students to record in their journals "what they learned today." By reading the journals or asking students to read information from the journal out loud, Miss Toliver can ascertain not only which concepts were conveyed to students but also the level of understanding achieved by her students. She can also uncover any frustrations the students are experiencing. She uses formative assessment through conversations around journaling in her classroom.

Tobias (1993) encourages the use of math journals with students endeavoring to overcome math anxiety. When confronted with a difficult math problem, students are asked to write down their feelings and any information they think might be pertinent to the problem. The students' writings help Tobias diagnose misconceptions and knowledge gaps, and they direct the students' thoughts toward possible solutions.

The use of journals in the classroom deserves some words of caution, however, which support the importance of establishing guidelines for journals. When a teacher requests that students keep a journal, the students may share unexpected personal experiences or feelings. A teacher who reads about experiences involving abuse of the student by another student or adult or who finds evidence of threats made to others is compelled to act upon this knowledge. The fact that the teacher is legally responsible for reporting some information should be shared with the students before they begin their journals. Another concern may arise when students wish to write an entry in their journals that they feel uncomfortable sharing with the teacher. In this case, a teacher might ask that students flag private portions of a journal by folding down or stapling a page. Finally, the personal content of a student's journal should not be assessed for a grade—a teacher should not ask students to share their personal preferences and feelings and then judge the quality of those personal revelations. It is better for the teacher to use the journal only for informal assessment to better understand her students, uncover prior knowledge, or check the effectiveness of instruction.

A *notebook* is similar to a file folder in that it commonly holds a collection of all information pertinent to a particular topic. A cookbook is one example of a notebook. Recipes in the cookbook are divided into categories such as breads, vegetables, entrées, and desserts. Other sections may also be present, covering topics such as weights and measures, planning of meals, presentation of dishes, or table settings. However, all the information present in the book is related to preparing food. A good cookbook will contain all the information necessary to help the reader prepare and serve delicious, nutritious meals and thereby become a successful cook.

Students sometimes create their own "cookbooks" in the school setting by voluntarily compiling notebooks for their classes. A science notebook, for example, may contain lecture notes, copies of science exams, lab reports, and completed homework assignments. This science notebook is in effect a file folder for all the science information presented in the class. The student collects this information in hopes of using the notebook as a study guide for upcoming exams. The completeness of the information is of primary importance to such a student if he wishes to become a successful science student. A missing piece might result in a gap in knowledge, which could adversely affect the student's exam score.

Occasionally, teachers will require students to keep a notebook. The purposes of the notebook may vary but can include teaching organizational skills to students, verifying that students are completing ungraded assignments, providing parents with a collection of all of the students' work, and producing documentary evidence to justify a grade. In such teacher-required notebooks, the teacher usually sets the parameters for the collection of data. In fact, he may provide handouts to students that specify assignments to be collected and placed in the notebook.

Notebooks may be helpful for assessment purposes, as they contain the totality of work produced by a student. Such data can be analyzed to track student performance over time, determine particular content areas or concepts in which the student experiences difficulty, or serve as a basis for student self-assessment.

For example, elementary students often carry home folders (or notebooks) of work for their parents to review each week. A teacher can ask students to pull out of their folders one or two assignments that they feel they need to work on. The teacher then reviews what the students have pulled out and spends time in class re-teaching concepts the students identified as problems. In this manner, the notebook helps students keep up with their work and enables later reflection on learning.

Prior to a summative test, Nancy's ninth-grade physical science students were asked to pull out of their notebook the homework practice set that was the most difficult for them. Nancy would then decide whether she needed to re-teach the whole class or whether she simply needed to arrange for the students to work with a tutor or with her directly to review the concepts. Keeping the notebook in physical science was a way to help students reflect on what they did not learn well, and this information helped Nancy make appropriate instructional modifications.

Portfolios

Portfolios are often written collections of student work but, unlike notebooks, they do not usually include the totality of student work. A portfolio is defined as a *purposeful,* integrated collection of student work showing effort, progress, or a degree of proficiency. Portfolios are often defined by the purpose underlying the collection of artifacts, and the scope of such purposes is almost unlimited. A teacher may choose to use a portfolio when it is important to collect student work to reflect upon. We will discuss five portfolio types (there are many others) that are especially useful as assessment methods: 1) best-work; 2) memorabilia; 3) growth; 4) skills; and 5) assessment, proficiency, or promotion portfolios.

Long before the current boom in portfolio use in the classroom, artists and models assembled portfolios. Such portfolios could be classified as *best-work* portfolios, as the owner of the portfolio included only the paintings, drawings, or photographs that best displayed his or her talent.

Students who wish to showcase their creations, whether these are artistic or written products, can also assemble best-works portfolios. Generally, best-works portfolios in schools are used as evidence of mastery of learning goals. Best works prove that students have mastered techniques, gained skills, or exhibited talent. Although best-works portfolios are more often seen in art classrooms, language arts teachers may also use this portfolio type. In a language arts class this portfolio may be known as the creative writing portfolio.

Scrapbooks and photo albums constitute another common class of portfolios. Such portfolios are known as *memorabilia* portfolios because the artifacts in these portfolios are a collection of mementos. Almost everyone has assembled this type of portfolio at one time or another. To prove this claim, all one must do is empty a wallet or purse onto a tabletop and divide the contents into two categories, those used often and those that are strictly mementos. It is surprising to see the number of items people carry on a daily basis that have no practical use in everyday life.

Memorabilia portfolios are rare in schools, although many students may assemble scrapbooks to record their school experiences. However, for dispositional learning targets, a memorabilia portfolio would reveal much about student attitudes, interests, and self-esteem.

A *growth* portfolio is another type. Here the emphasis is on change. The excerpts from a portfolio shown in Figure 5.1 demonstrate how the writing of an elementary school student changed from second grade to third. Note in the second grade excerpt the student has self-assessed and corrected one capitalization error and one spelling error (but missed correcting the spelling of "pregnant"). In the third grade excerpt, the student has moved from writing about family events to addressing the president of the United States! The writing is now in cursive, and longer (albeit run-on) sentences are present.

Growth portfolios are common in classrooms. They are often used in student-involved conferences to help students focus on their own learning and to reveal to others the progress a student has made.

Yet another type of portfolio is the *skills* portfolio. Here, the owner of the portfolio assembles documentation to verify that she is proficient at a particular skill or set of skills. For example, many states require beginning teachers to assemble a skills portfolio, documenting evidence of effective teaching. Veteran teachers applying for National Board certification compile similar portfolios to demonstrate advanced competencies in teaching skills. In some high schools, students are encouraged to collect work samples that demonstrate employability skills. These student portfolios serve the same purpose as a résumé, in that the student can provide a potential employer with a copy of the skills portfolio so that the employer can ascertain what the applicant knows and is able to do.

FIGURE 5.1. SAMPLE GROWTH PORTFOLIO EXCERPT.

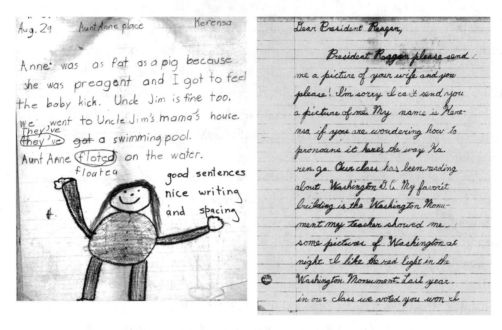

Source: Excerpts from the portfolio of Kerensa Butler, 1979. Reprinted with permission.

Another important type of portfolio is called an *assessment, proficiency,* or *promotion* portfolio. This type of portfolio can be used to show student growth toward or proficiency in standards of learning. These portfolios are often managed in an electronic format. For example, the promotion portfolio can house evidence that is used to judge whether a student is promoted out of or retained at a grade level. Since the stakes are high for this type of portfolio, the evidence used must be of high quality. For instance, a good promotion portfolio must contain an adequate sampling of good quality student work. It must record assessments of that work that are also reliable and valid, and the collected work must be aligned to the standards addressed within the grade level.

Another example of a proficiency portfolio is an electronic record kept for students, which organizes information about students and can serve transient families well by helping students and educators keep track of student information. Such a portfolio organization is shown in Figure 5.2 outlining three major parts: (1) proficiency areas containing organized student classroom work toward standards, (2) a student input section with an "All About Me" component where students store personal information such as logs of activities, and (3) communication information that is only available to parents or teachers and used to share student information among parents, teachers, or other educators. Any part of this portfolio record can be burned to a CD or made available online.

Each of these portfolios—best work, memorabilia, growth, skills, and assessment, proficiency, or promotion—has utility as an assessment tool. Asking students to

FIGURE 5.2. OUTLINE OF ELECTRONIC PORTFOLIO ORGANIZATION.

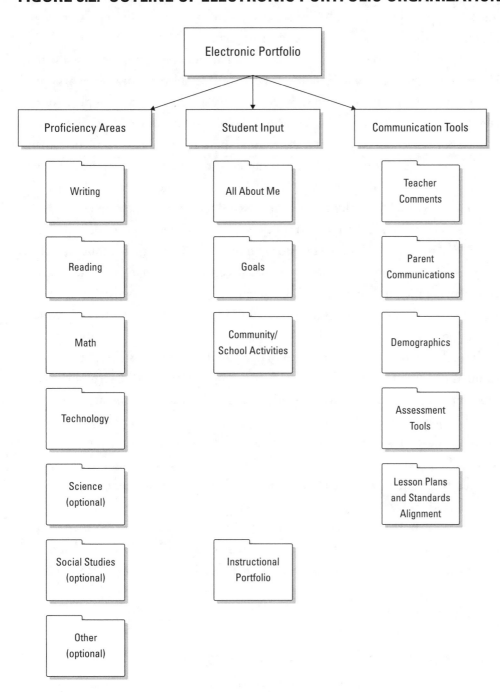

assemble best-work portfolios encourages self-assessment and builds self-esteem. The best-work portfolios can then be displayed at parent conferences, during Open House Night, or in the school's display case or media center.

Memorabilia portfolios may appear at first to have no function in the school setting. However, personal memorabilia portfolios may be assembled by students in art classes or used in language arts courses to stimulate writing, as students reflect on pieces or certain things in the portfolio and write a story about it. A teacher could also use a memorabilia portfolio to assess student self-esteem or motivation. Looking at these students' portfolios may tell a teacher the interests of her students, or what Jonathan's attitude about organizing a portfolio might be, or what might motivate Stacy to read more. This assessment method then helps teachers understand the needs of their students.

The elementary writing pieces from the elementary growth portfolio sampled in Figure 5.1 are a classic example of information within a growth portfolio in a classroom. At the end of second grade, the portfolios are passed to the third grade teacher. By reviewing the portfolios, the third grade teacher assesses the writing skills of the students, and then plans her writing curriculum for the year. Of course, this writing growth portfolio also makes a cherished keepsake for a parent.

In high school, a growth portfolio may be used in a business class. Students are required to research business careers and then explore a career through an internship experience. During the internship, students must create an instrument for assessing their own job performance and periodically perform self-assessments with this instrument. In addition, students collect required artifacts at specific time-intervals to document skills learned. By reviewing the portfolio at the end of the internship, the teacher, the student, and the actual employer have a clear picture of the student's progress and achievement over time.

The skills portfolio, of course, has a multitude of uses in the classroom. For instance, Long's (Long, 1997) math students designed their own report card and then documented their "grades" using a skills portfolio. The report card used the following Likert scale:

1 = Most of the time (seldom needs help)

2 = Sometimes (may need help to get started)

3 = Beginning to do (needs help to complete work)

4 = Does not complete work [Long, 1997, p. 37]

Long's students collected artifacts to demonstrate the "uses basic operations" skill (Long, 1997, p. 37). The students then assessed their own work and assigned one of the above descriptors to this skill.

Susan (Butler, 1997b) describes the design of the Skills portfolio used in her high school chemistry class: "The first portion of the portfolio was based on the Florida Department of Education Course Student Performance Standards. . . . I distributed these standards evenly into four Learning Activity sheets for students. Students were given one Learning Activity sheet for each of our four nine-week grading periods. The sheets were used as a basis for student proofs. Proofs constituted documentation that the knowledge described in the Learning Activity had actually been achieved by the student" (Butler, 1997b, pp. 71–72).

Therefore, Susan's students had to "prove," or collect evidence to document, the successful attainment of a particular skill. Skills for this chemistry-related portfolio included, "Explain the organization of the Periodic Table of Elements; determine atomic number and mass number when number of protons, neutrons, and electrons is specified; solve stoichiometric problems" (Florida Department of Education [FDOE], 1991). In reviewing these student-assembled artifacts, Susan realized how this type of assessment could bring out student strengths she had never previously witnessed, as some students were revealed as consummate artists or writers.

Before implementing any type of portfolio at the classroom, school, or district level, it is important to plan the purpose, design, and assessment of the portfolio. Here are some ways to learn more before plunging in:

- Talk with others who have used portfolios
- Look at sample portfolios
- Ask other districts or schools for samples of portfolios (they will share)
- Look at software options for electronic versions
- Ask yourself questions (Why do we want to do this?)
- Collect and read recent research
- Work with others

Then begin to address and make decisions about these general issues involved in implementing portfolios:

- What is the purpose of the portfolio?
- What type of portfolio is needed? (Is this portfolio a good match to the stated purposes?)
- How much time is needed for design, evaluation, and implementation?
- What will be the impact on teachers? on students?
- What guidelines or criteria should be considered?
- How will parents and students be educated about the portfolios?
- Can students be given choices about the material to include?
- Which parents will review the guidelines?
- What language is important for everyone to understand as it pertains to the portfolio as assessment?

- Will there be a self-reflection component?

- What portfolio format will be used, that is, electronic or written?

- How many students will be involved? Will different student groups be involved each year?

Getting down to a more detailed level, we also recommend that teachers answer each portfolio design question in the following list before implementing portfolios in their classrooms.

Portfolio Design Questions

1. Is the purpose of the portfolio to instruct, support learning, or assess? Answering this question will help determine the types of artifacts the students will collect. For instance, a portfolio assembled solely for summative assessment purposes may contain only best works rather than a continuum of student work.

2. What is the goal of using portfolios? Is the goal to promote self-assessment? Student reflection on their own learning? Problem solving? Particular skills? Higher-order thinking? The goal for the portfolio will determine the design of the portfolio. For example, to promote self-esteem, a best-works or memorabilia portfolio appears appropriate. However, if the goal is to improve students' proficiency at content-related skills, a skills portfolio would be best. A portfolio promoting student reflection would contain many subjective, journal-like artifacts, whereas a problem-solving portfolio would contain more objective work.

3. What types of artifacts will be collected in the portfolio? Will only written work be accepted, or will videotapes, posters, and computer disks also be acceptable? How many artifacts are necessary for documentation of a skill, goal, or purpose? The decisions made here will affect the size of the portfolio and its physical characteristics and may also be influenced by the storage capacity of the classroom. If a file folder or binder is used, then perhaps only written work can be accepted. If an electronic portfolio is planned, all data may be stored on a disk or CD. The use of a single *quality* entry to prove a skill is recommended over the use of multiple entries for that one skill. (Surely if the student was successful once, he can be so again!) The number of artifacts also defines the type of portfolio. If *all* student work is collected in the portfolio, the purpose is lost, and the assessment tool is just a notebook, not a portfolio.

4. How will artifacts be selected for the portfolio? Will the students or the teacher select them? How often will the portfolio be updated by adding artifacts? Must the students keep copies of all potential portfolio artifacts, or will the teacher

maintain a file for this purpose? What are the criteria for selecting artifacts (how will the teacher or the students decide whether a particular artifact documents a skill, purpose, or goal)? If the portfolio is intended to promote self-assessment, the students should choose the artifacts. Older students may keep their own working files, while younger ones may need help with this process, since they have not yet developed organizational skills sufficient to this task.

5. How will students be oriented to the use of the portfolio? The recommended method is to start slowly, giving students plenty of support and practice. A structured portfolio, in which expectations are explained to students, is recommended over a more open, unstructured design. Remember that change is difficult; be prepared for some student resistance to this new procedure. Perseverance and consistency are two key factors in the success of portfolio implementation.

6. How will the portfolio be assessed? A scoring guide, or rubric, is essential for this task, and this scoring guide should be shared with students before the assessment begins. However, if the work in the portfolio has already been assessed as individual pieces, should the overall portfolio also receive a grade?

7. How will the information in the portfolio be housed? Storage and handling of student information can be quite overwhelming, especially if the portfolio is one that travels with a student over an extended period. Many companies have developed software that helps manage the materials stored in a portfolio. Many of the student management systems used in districts also have a portfolio component housed within the management system for teacher and student use. It does not matter whether the information is stored in a file folder or by using a technical tool, as the purpose of the portfolio remains the most important aspect of the assessment tool. If an electronic storage system appears to be the best solution for a teacher, many Web sites are available to help with the selection.

8. What planning should be done before asking students to compile a portfolio? Constructing a portfolio-scoring guide before assigning the work will prevent student frustration, enhance the matching of the purpose to the artifacts, and ease the assessment task for the teacher. It is much simpler to assess an assignment if the plan for assessing it is written beforehand. Through careful planning, the teacher does not have to dread the moment he must confront a huge mound of papers, wondering what he will find in the contents of the portfolios his students have constructed.

Once these design questions are addressed, the portfolio can be planned and implemented. Although assisting students with portfolios may seem to be a monumental undertaking, portfolio assessment reaps huge benefits for the students and for the teacher. The following teacher comments demonstrate some of these rewards:

As I watch my students' portfolios fill up with entries each year, I become more knowledgeable about my students as individual learners (and people). This knowledge helps me effectively re-teach difficult math concepts and hone in on particular areas of weakness [Clarkson, 1997, p. 29].

As I reflect on my first year of portfolio activities, I am pleased with the increased commitment to learning I have begun to foster in my students. I have always felt that students need to feel safe, secure, and appreciated for their uniqueness before they take risks to try new ideas. Portfolios put this belief to the test [Long, 1997, p. 33].

Perhaps the thing I like best about portfolios is the time I gain for planning, instruction, and interacting with students. I am freed from collecting and grading papers all the time, because I don't look at every piece of work my students complete [Williams, 1997, p. 53].

From comments such as these, it is easy to see the advantages of well-planned portfolio implementation.

How Projects Are Used in Assessment

Like portfolios, projects are powerful assessment methods. Projects differ from portfolios in that students may not need to house a collection of work but rather demonstrate mastery of skills or completion of specific tasks. For this reason, projects appear under both the product and performance classifications in Chapter Four, Table 4.2, as to show such "mastery," students may need to both create written products and perform demonstrations (see the senior project example discussed in Chapter Four). Projects can offer students an opportunity to direct their own learning and integrate content across curriculums. A *project* may be defined as a compendium of complex assignments, each directed toward a common goal. Projects, like any assessment method, should be designed and selected to teach core curriculum content standards and should be scored by using a rubric, which is shared with students in advance. To support student autonomy and decision making, students should be given some choice as to the tasks they will perform or the roles they will assume for the project. In addition, students should be required to meet interim deadlines for the project (to aid the procrastinating student), to participate in planning the project (to aid the disorganized student), and to reflect on project activities (to aid the "surface" learner who seeks only to collect facts rather than understandings).

Of course, projects at different grade levels will vary in levels of difficulty. The following examples of appropriate projects may help to further clarify what is involved in projects at different grade levels.

In each case that follows both the process and product can be assessed. Students should understand the criteria used for both. For example, some processes might include use of class time, use of resources, engagement, and time management, whereas the actual product criteria could include content knowledge understood, method of presentation of the information, and accuracy of the information.

Elementary School Level

- Students study the origins of holidays and participate in meaningful activities, such as planting a tree for Arbor Day or visiting a veteran's hospital on Memorial Day.

- Students contribute articles to the "Daily News," a compilation of student essays about class activities that is distributed to parents each week.

- Students study the systems of the body and make life-size posters showing the location of major organs.

- Students plan and design an appropriate backyard play area for a pet.

Middle School Level

- Students design and build model racecars to test the effect of tire size, gear ratio, and body design on how fast their cars can go. They use appropriate mathematical formulas in their calculations.

- Students compete in science competitions in which they design and perform experiments to answer a research question.

- Students plan, write, and produce a video that addresses a historical event or presents a literature review.

- Students in history class produce a museum exhibit by collecting folksongs surrounding a particular period in history or historical event, such as the Civil War, pioneer life, or the Industrial Revolution.

High School Level

- Students in history classes plan and raise funds for a "Roman Tour of Great Britain."

- Students design, construct, build, and sell a house in the trade and industry program.

- Students in a science class reclaim an endangered estuary through cleanup efforts and then turn the estuary into a "living classroom" for elementary students.

- Students write a *Canterbury Tales*-like play during language arts class concerning modern American teenagers hanging out at the local fast-food restaurant and present the play to students at the school.

As evidenced by these lists, projects can be the result of both cooperative work and individual effort. No matter which type of project is implemented in the classroom, however, Lewin and Shoemaker (1998) warn of some common project pitfalls. The following are their descriptors of these negative phenomena:

The Razzle Dazzle: The performance has a lot of flash but no substance.

The Parasite: The parents pick the topic. The student may do the work but has no interest or ownership in the project. Moms or Dads, however, get to live out their dreams/interests/fantasies through their child's performance.

Scaffolding: The student picks a project of personal interest, but may not do any of the actual work. It is difficult to determine how much scaffolding (shoring up) by others (usually parents) occurred.

The Fizzle: Not enough guidance or direction is provided. The task is assigned, and students are expected to miraculously produce a fantastic project in six weeks. They rarely do.

The Celebration: This category results from an erroneous belief that performances should be showcases—festivals, parties, or other gala events—without evaluation. Everyone should be honored—no matter the quality of the work.

The Uneven Playing Field: Some students draw from many resources (e.g., parents, computers, libraries, and art supplies) in creating their projects, while other students draw from few or no resources.

Near Death: Teachers, near exhaustion, walk around school with glazed-over eyes mumbling, Why did I do this to myself? I will never do this again! [Lewin & Shoemaker, 1998, p. 104]

It is the responsibility of the teacher to minimize such project pitfalls and to maximize the learning experience for the students. Indeed, avoiding implementation problems and improving instruction is a responsibility whatever the assessment type chosen. This must be done in the assessment design phase.

———————

Our intent in Chapters Four and Five has been to review many types and examples of assessment methods and approaches and to aid the novice in differentiating one type of assessment from another. This differentiation can then aid the novice in choosing an assessment method appropriate to the stated purpose. For example, teachers choose to implement projects when related content, skills, and tasks are the targets of learning. Thus, projects are generally short-term in nature and tied to specific, clustered topics (such as Native Americans, the Federalist Era, and Dinosaurs). Conversely, portfolios are *usually* compiled over a more extended period and each included artifact is chosen to support the portfolio's purpose. Both portfolios and projects, however, require careful design, need to be closely aligned with the curriculum, and exemplify constructed-response assessment. In Chapter Six we introduce the concept of task criteria to ensure that whatever the assessment task chosen, it will be a well-designed, high-quality task.

Designing Quality Classroom Assessment Tasks

6

Chapter Two explored how curriculum changes in response to global transitions and how the curriculum outlines the standards and benchmarks to be met by students. This chapter delves more deeply into this subject from a slightly different perspective. The focus in this chapter is on conveying curricular expectations to students through quality tasks and assessment methods. This chapter answers the following questions:

- When is a task an assessment?

- How can teachers design quality assessment tasks?

- What are the characteristics of quality assessment tasks?

Before discussing these questions, let's visit a fourth grade classroom and observe the interactions between the teacher and the students. At the beginning of a lesson on creating a graph, the teacher is at the overhead projector modeling the creation of a graph on graphing paper. As she performs certain actions, she explains why they are necessary, for example:

> I will label this line with 10, the next with 20, and the third with 30.
> Notice that I have counted by tens to label these lines. It is necessary
> to count the same amount each time. It would not be correct to label
> this first line 10, the second 20, and the third 25. Why?

In this classroom, the students are first just listening to and watching the teacher. However, later in the lesson, graphing paper is distributed to students and the whole class (with the teacher) works together to create a graph of the number and kinds of pets the students own. The lesson ends with the students creating graphs on their own while the teacher circulates among them.

In this classroom, it is hard to discern where instruction ends and assessment begins. In Chapter One, we defined *assessment* as the act of collecting information about individuals or groups and explicated *classroom assessment* as an ongoing process through which teacher and students interact to promote greater learning. In Chapter Two, we reviewed the "big rocks" of the curriculum and noted that teachers should plan the assessment of these big rocks before planning the instruction. In this manner we defined instruction relative to both assessment and curriculum, in that the *instruction* should prepare students for the assessments and should be aligned with the standards and benchmarks of the curriculum.

Previously, we have looked at a variety of assessment methods the teacher may use in order to collect information about student learning, including selected-response items, constructed-response items, teacher questioning, teacher observations, and student-teacher dialogues. Whether we consider selected-response items or constructed-response items, however, we are giving students tasks to complete (as the teacher in the above scenario gave her students a graph to create). We then use the completed tasks to make decisions about student learning. So the question arises: Is the student task part of instruction or is the student task part of assessment?

A Task as an Assessment

Actually, to use the above scenario as an example, the graph created by the students is an instructional task as well as an assessment method. The task is instructional in that it is one of the instructional strategies the teacher is using to teach graphing skills. These instructional strategies include modeling (the teacher's work at the overhead), guided practice (the whole-class task of creating a graph), and individual practice (individual students creating the graph). So the act of creating a graph can be instructional in nature, if its purpose is to teach a process or procedure (how to create such a graph). Having the students construct graphs, however, is also an *assessment method,* since the teacher will assess student knowledge of graphing by examining their constructed products. Instructional tasks and assessment methods often overlap in this fashion. For our purposes, we will define an *instructional task* as any assignment teachers require of students. When teachers use such assignments to ascertain student levels of understanding or adeptness, the instructional task is also an *assessment method.* Therefore, in this chapter, when we use the word *task,* it often has a double meaning. A *task* can be an instructional strategy, as well as an assessment method.

How to Design Quality Assessment Tasks

The bulk of this chapter discusses specific questions, or criteria, that teachers can use to guide task design. Before introducing these questions, however, we examine the design process. For example, when designing assessment tasks, the teacher must first consider the purpose of the assessment. Assessment purposes were previously covered in Chapter One and include formative, summative, and diagnostic purposes. By first deciding on the purpose of an assessment, an appropriate task can be developed. For example, if the purpose is purely diagnostic, a high school language arts teacher could give a quiz on the summer reading selections to find out who read and who didn't. An elementary teacher might conduct individual reading conferences with all third graders to assess oral fluency in reading. A middle school math teacher might give a measurement unit conversion worksheet to students to find out what the students already know about the relationships among units of measurement. For formative purposes, all teachers may wish to use a constructed-response task incorporating scoring rubrics that provide the maximum amount of feedback for student improvement. For summative purposes, teachers may give a culminating multiple-choice exam or assign a culminating project. In all cases, the task chosen must align with the purpose of the assessment.

In addition to deciding on the purpose of the assessment, teachers must also unpack the curriculum for embedded learning targets that relate to the proposed task. *Unpacking* (analyzing and reflecting on) was previously described in Chapter Two, as well as aligning assessments to the learning targets. Assessments are *aligned* to learning targets when they support the successful achievement of the target. For example, if the curriculum specifies that students will "evaluate" the Constitution as a living document, this would be an example of a reasoning learning target. To achieve this target, students should be expected to offer arguments and evidence to support or refute this assertion. An assessment task (as an essay question or writing prompt) that requires such argumentation is aligned with the curriculum. A test question that simply asks students to list the ten amendments known as the Bill of Rights is misaligned with this learning target. Regurgitating a memorized list does not involve reasoning. "If assessment tasks are to tap higher-order cognitive processes, they must require that students cannot answer them correctly by relying on memory alone" (Anderson, et al., 2001, page 71).

Matching Tasks to Learning Targets

Therefore, after the curriculum is unpacked, the next step in the assessment task design process is to select a task that will align with the learning target. Table 6.1 provides a guide to aligning particular types of assessment tasks (and methods) to specific learning targets.

TABLE 6.1. MATCHING ASSESSMENTS TO TARGETS.

Learning Target	Selected Response	Constructed Response	Student/Teacher Dialogues	Teacher Observation	Questioning
Knowledge	Strong match–can be used efficiently to assess content knowledge	Products as essays or short answer questions can serve to assess student mastery of complex knowledge Performances as oral presentations can also be used to assess knowledge	Strong match for formative assessment of knowledge. There are accountability problems if this is used summatively, however, unless accurate records or audio-recording of the conversations exist	Can assess small domains of knowledge when short-term record-keeping is required. Usually requires an observation instrument to capture student actions/responses	Strong match for formative assessment of knowledge. Again, there are accountability problems if this is used summatively.
Reasoning	Can be an excellent way to assess some kinds of reasoning, but multiple choice questions must be carefully worded	Both products and performances are strong matches, as both can provide a window into reasoning	Adequate match–can ask student to "think out loud" to examine reasoning proficiency, but again, recordkeeping, is a problem	Weak match–it is hard to observe reasoning—some interaction, either verbal or written, must take place between the teacher and the student	Adequate match–can ask student to "think out loud" to examine reasoning proficiency, but again record-keeping is a problem
Skills	Can only test for mastery of simple prerequisite procedural knowledge; skills must usually be demonstrated	Products are a weak match, unless the skill is a writing one. Performances are strong matches, as skills can be demonstrated	Weak match, unless the skill is oral fluency (as in foreign language classes) or other oral communications	Strong match—when skill must be demonstrated, a teacher observation can be used to monitor the demonstration—some instrument should be used to capture student responses	Weak match—probing questions can be used to elicit student explanations of actions while demonstrating a skill
Products	Can only test for prerequisite knowledge of the attributes of quality products	Strong match–can assess (a) proficiency in carrying out the steps required to create a quality product, and (b) the product itself	Weak match, but student thought processes can be probed through such dialogues. This may reveal the planning steps they used to create the product	Not a good match, but can observe technique student used to create product	Weak match, but can ask students to explain process used to create the product
Affect/ Disposition	Strong match–surveys can convey student feelings, attitudes	Strong match–students can be asked to construct answers to questions that will reveal their feelings, attitudes	Strong match–student/teacher verbal exchanges can probe and reveal student feelings, attitudes	Somewhat strong match, as a behavior is the target (as how to cooperate in a group, how to conduct a debate)	Strong match–can ask students probing questions that will reveal student feelings, attitudes

Source: Adapted from Regional Laboratory Network, copyright © 1998. *Improving Classroom Assessment: A Toolkit for Professional Developers* (Toolkit 98), chapter 1, activity 1.7, "Target-Methods Match," handout A1.7, H2, p. 12. Reprinted with permission of NWREL.

Once all the above steps are taken and the actual task is selected, other considerations must be addressed. An outline of these considerations appears here in question form and will be further discussed in the closing section of this chapter:

- When will students complete the assessment task (homework, class work, other)?

- Will this be an individual, pair, or group task?

- What cognitive levels will be addressed in the task (higher-order thinking, basic skills, cognitive complexity)?

- Will the task promote student involvement in learning through student choice, self-assessment, and peer-assessment?

- Will the task "hook" the students by being motivating, engaging, feasible, integrated to other disciplines, relevant, and unbiased?

- How will the task provide differentiation (meet individual student needs)?

- How valid is the task and its scoring guide (does the task actually provide information about student achievement of the specified learning target)?

A Planning Template

Once these issues are addressed, the teacher can then begin to plan the instruction needed to prepare students for and support them during the completion of the assessment task. Exhibit 6.1 displays all of the steps discussed so far in a planning template. Such a template containing check boxes can greatly aid teachers in designing the assessment task.

As an example of how the planning template may be used, Exhibit 6.2 provides an overview for the design of an assessment task for interpreting graphs. This task might be used in a lesson taught prior to our scenario (in which students were already creating graphs). It would make sense to have students examine and interpret graphs before asking them to construct one.

Because of the diverse tasks assigned to students—for example, a skill practice worksheet, a test on learning targets, an instructional activity, or an essay to write for homework—we must continually monitor the quality of the tasks. We should be aware of why we are asking students to perform a particular task (purpose), ensure that it aligns with the curriculum, pinpoint the information we are seeking from the students, and determine what we will do with that information. One cautionary note before we move on to discussing other quality considerations: it may be necessary to design and

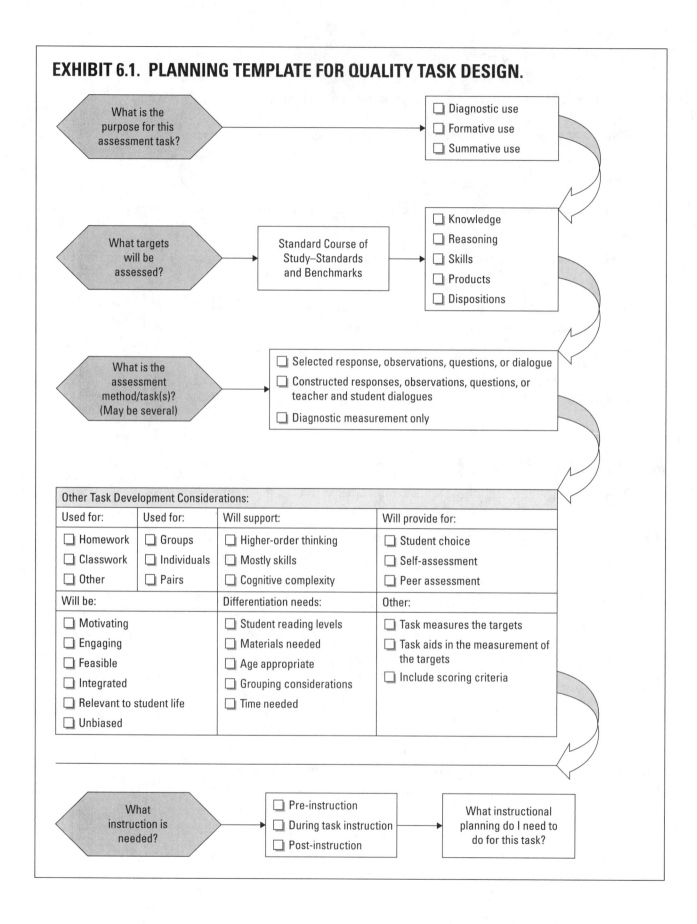

EXHIBIT 6.1. PLANNING TEMPLATE FOR QUALITY TASK DESIGN.

What is the purpose for this assessment task?

- ☐ Diagnostic use
- ☐ Formative use
- ☐ Summative use

What targets will be assessed?

Standard Course of Study–Standards and Benchmarks

- ☐ Knowledge
- ☐ Reasoning
- ☐ Skills
- ☐ Products
- ☐ Dispositions

What is the assessment method/task(s)? (May be several)

- ☐ Selected response, observations, questions, or dialogue
- ☐ Constructed responses, observations, questions, or teacher and student dialogues
- ☐ Diagnostic measurement only

Other Task Development Considerations:

Used for:	Used for:	Will support:	Will provide for:
☐ Homework	☐ Groups	☐ Higher-order thinking	☐ Student choice
☐ Classwork	☐ Individuals	☐ Mostly skills	☐ Self-assessment
☐ Other	☐ Pairs	☐ Cognitive complexity	☐ Peer assessment

Will be:	Differentiation needs:	Other:
☐ Motivating	☐ Student reading levels	☐ Task measures the targets
☐ Engaging	☐ Materials needed	☐ Task aids in the measurement of the targets
☐ Feasible	☐ Age appropriate	☐ Include scoring criteria
☐ Integrated	☐ Grouping considerations	
☐ Relevant to student life	☐ Time needed	
☐ Unbiased		

What instruction is needed?

- ☐ Pre-instruction
- ☐ During task instruction
- ☐ Post-instruction

What instructional planning do I need to do for this task?

EXHIBIT 6.2. PLANNING TEMPLATE FOR QUALITY TASK DESIGN: GRAPHING LESSON.

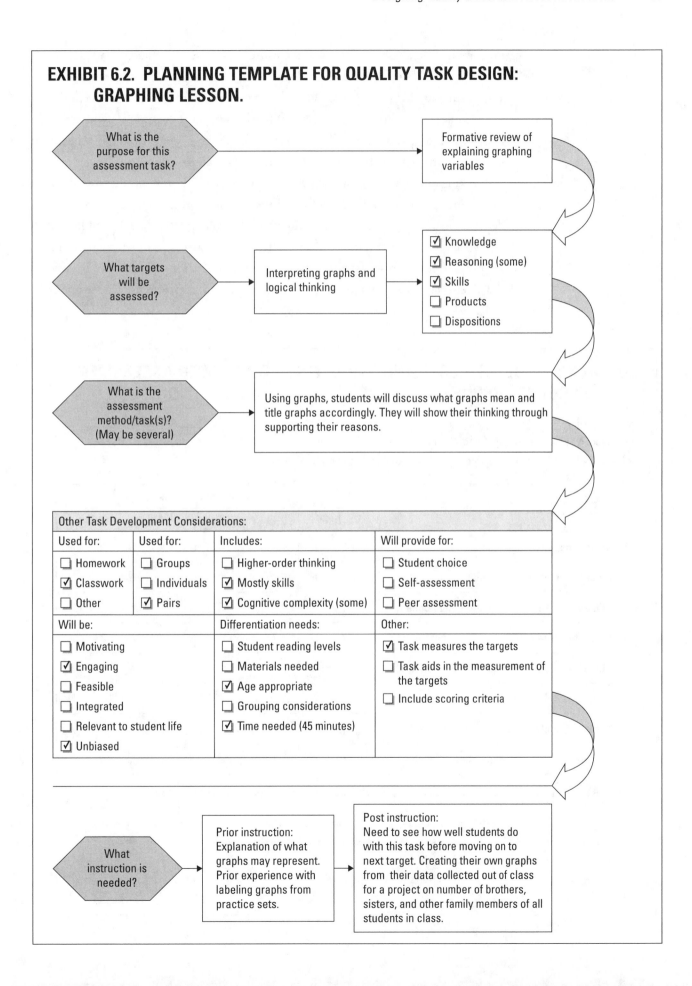

implement several assessment tasks to ensure that there is sufficient evidence of student learning. Shavelson and Ruize-Primo (1998) echo this caveat by stating that an ample number of tasks are needed to reliably estimate student performance.

For instance, a literacy coach has this learning target: Students will articulate informed opinions about a text. The literacy coach asks students to support their opinions with facts derived from the text. This coach may first demonstrate her opinion by thinking out loud, for example, "In my opinion, I think students do have too much stuff." She may review something from the text to support her opinion or provide students with an example from her background knowledge that has shaped her thinking. For example, she might say, "In this text the mother held down two jobs just to supply her children with name brand clothes, and I know many families where the parents also work two jobs." What task will she then give to her students? Should

---

EXHIBIT 6.3. TOOL FOR ASSESSING STUDENTS IN TEXT-BASED ASSESSMENT DISCOURSE GROUPS.

Group: __Blues_____   Date: _10/02_

Text used: _Newspaper article: Coach Carter_

Question Addressed: In your opinion, did Coach Carter do the right thing?

Learning Targets	Individual Students				
	Sally	**Ted**	**Timmy**	**Allison**	**Gary**
1. Student can give an opinion	**Y** – N	**Y** – N	**Y** – N	**Y** – N	Y – **N**
2. Student can explain or justify opinion (informed)	**Y** – N	**Y** – N	**Y** – N	Y – **N**	Y – **N**
3. Student takes new information into account	**Y** – N	**Y** – N	**Y** – N	Y – **N**	Y – **N**
4. Student is aware of changing his/her opinion	Y – **N**	**Y** – N	Y – **N**	Y – **N**	Y – **N**
5. Student is able to connect and use text info	Y – **N**	Y – **N**	**Y** – N	Y – **N**	Y – **N**
6. Student is able to use background experience	**Y** – N	**Y** – N	**Y** – N	Y – **N**	**Y** – N
7. Student can challenge the opinions of others	Y – **N**	**Y** – N	Y – **N**	**Y** – N	Y – **N**
8. Student is able to raise questions	Y – **N**	**Y** – N	**Y** – N	Y – **N**	Y – **N**

Overall oral teacher feedback (and teacher notes) for group members for this text-based discourse:

Allison and Gary–next week they need to work on being able to state their opinion and justify it, using facts and background knowledge. (Teacher note: I need to check on reading comprehension and assess next week to see if they can relate more to article)

Sally–can work on raising questions of others to challenge their opinion when the dialogue . . .

she move right to a quiz on whether the students' opinions agree with hers? No, of course not. First, she should let students practice through peer discussions (the instructional strategy) and she should observe them as they do so (the assessment method), providing feedback to the students about their achievement of the learning target (expressing an informed opinion). She might use an assessment sheet (similar to the one in Exhibit 6.3) to assess whether students were able to make an informed opinion and reference background knowledge, experience, or the text to support their opinions. The teacher would need to observe each discussion group to complete such an assessment sheet, and it might require several visits to each group before she could assess all group members. Finally, after the students have been given sufficient practice and time on the task, the teacher might ask students to self-assess their individual work on the learning target by comparing original opinions with ending ones. She could also provide feedback to individual students on noted strengths and weaknesses, drawing from the observations recorded on the assessment sheet.

In this case, at least two assessment tasks were used. The first involved the assessment of the group discussions through teacher observation. The second was the self-assessment done by the students. Asking the students to provide a written response could access this. For example, the literacy coach might ask students to write a paragraph and indicate whether any of them changed their opinions based on the group discussions and why their opinions changed. From these two assessment tasks, the coach can ascertain the level of student achievement and the data collected can inform the planning of subsequent lessons. This scenario, then, illustrates that multiple data sources may be needed to obtain reliable assessment information.

Characteristics of Quality Assessment Tasks

The planning template in Exhibit 6.1 provided an overview of the thinking involved in the task design process for creating assessments. However, the actual characteristics of quality tasks are only implied in this graphic. Therefore, we describe these specific characteristics in the next section.

From the template, we know that the purpose of the assessment task must be clearly defined and the task must align with the learning targets embedded in the curriculum. It is now time, however, to provide additional details on the "Other Task Development Considerations" section of the template. It is within this section that important characteristics of quality appear.

Beyond its specific goals (providing evidence of learning target achievement), every assessment task can function on a more general level to improve students' ability to learn, comprehend, and deal with more and more complex materials. The ability of a task to promote student metacognition is one quality characteristic. Here are three questions, discussed further below, that probe, from three angles, a task's capacity to improve cognitive abilities.

- Does the task encourage higher-order thinking and cognitive complexity?

- Does the task have more than one right answer?

- Does the task lead to deep understanding or does it simply promote surface learning?

• *Does the task encourage higher-order thinking and cognitive complexity?* If the task requires students to go beyond the simple recall of facts, it may encourage higher-order thinking skills such as application, analysis, synthesis, or evaluation. For example, when students categorize animals into reptile, mammal, and insect categories, they are demonstrating an understanding of these terms and showing that they can apply their knowledge to analyzing differences among the three groups in order to place animals into the proper category. This task could be even higher-order if students were asked to provide reasons for the placement of animals in particular categories and asked to provide other examples of animals that would belong in a category.

To encourage cognitive complexity, the task would need to aid students in making connections between discrete facts and in applying content knowledge in order to solve problems and examine issues. In the animal classification task, the teacher could enhance cognitive complexity by introducing some problematic animal examples—examples that could fit in more than one animal category. One such animal is the platypus, which hatches from eggs like reptiles but has hair like mammals.

EXHIBIT 6.4. QUESTIONING GUIDE.

Teacher Outline for Thinking   Book: *Verdi* by Janell Cannon

When Verdi's mother tells him to grow up big and green, Verdi cannot imagine why. All the big green snakes seem lazy, boring, and rude. Besides, he really loves his bright yellow skin and sporty stripes. So Verdi decides he simply *will not* turn green—which is why he finds himself in a heap of trouble.

Possible discussion questions:

1. What problems did Verdi face? Are they realistic problems?
2. What did he have and not have control over?
3. In our lives, what do we have and not have control over?
4. What kind of courage is expressed in this book?
5. How did the events in the book change the life of Verdi?
6. Which events in this story contributed to the change?
7. Can you think of a character in another story who had similar issues?
8. How and why does the author use comedy or whimsy in the book?
9. Can Verdi be anything he wants to be?

Source: McMunn, Williamson, and Reagan, 2004, resource section, p. 21. Graphic by Shelley Call. SERVE copyright © 2004. Reprinted with permission.

Another way to enhance cognitive complexity in the classroom is to increase the complexity of teacher questions. Complex questions require complex student answers. Consider the possible discussion questions found in Exhibit 6.4 on a questioning guide for the book *Verdi,* by Jannell Cannon. These questions require students to make connections (Can you think of a character in another story that had a similar theme?), examine issues (In our lives, what do we have and not have control over?), and solve problems (Can Verdi be anything he wants to be?).

• *Does the task have more than one right answer?* Such tasks seem to foster both higher-order thinking and inclusion, as they represent multiple avenues of approach and are therefore accessible to many students. The task might be to design an imaginary animal that could survive in a given environment (such as a desert). This type of task is in sharp contrast to a constructed-response task, where students are not given choices for a response, such as one that asks, Who was the first president of the United States? The president question is very low-order and factual in nature, as well as very closed (one and only one right answer). Conversely, the creation of an animal has multiple solutions, would call for higher-order thinking (at least analysis), and would be engaging to several types of students (such as those who have trouble memorizing facts, those who are artistically creative, those who like to problem-solve).

• *Does the task lead to deep understanding or does it simply promote surface learning?* Tasks that are more cognitively complex, connected to real life, and call for application, analysis, synthesis, or evaluation promote deeper levels of understanding than tasks that are simple, disconnected from student interests and experiences, and ask only for recall of information. An analogy here might be the use of a matching test to assess student knowledge of a vocabulary list as opposed to requiring students to write a story using the vocabulary words. Another example is asking students to discuss why a hydrangea bush blooms blue in one yard and pink in another yard, even though the plants were bought from the same nursery and both had blue blooms when originally planted. How could the students use their knowledge of acids and bases and the pH scale to answer this question?

These three questions focus on the capacity of a task to promote student metacognition. A second characteristic of quality assessment tasks is the ability of the task to encourage student success. Tasks must function on the motivational level or they will fail on all levels. They should be rewarding rather than frustrating, and they should seek to engage students in the processes of learning that the tasks are trying to teach or assess. Consider three additional task design questions:

• Is the task appropriate to the age level and preparedness of students?

• Can the task actually be done in the time allotted or with the materials available?

• Is the task motivating or engaging for students?

- *Is the task appropriate to the age level and preparedness of the students?* If young students are asked to perform tasks that call for the use of fine motor skills, frustration may often be the only outcome. Young readers get frustrated when asked to read text that is too hard for them. With older students, the tasks set should be predicated on past instruction. It is inappropriate to assign a research paper before time has been spent on writing a good paragraph or on note-taking procedures. Often students need to know how to use simple algebra equations before they do well in a physical science course. A science teacher may need to spend some necessary instruction on math prior to instruction on science concepts.

- *Can the task actually be done in the time allotted or with the materials available?* In other words, is the task a feasible one? In thinking about feasibility, the teacher should also draw upon his knowledge of his students. If students have home resources, a task might reasonably take the form of a homework assignment. If home resources are not available, the teacher must make time for students to complete the task during school hours. For example, asking students to type a report or find three Internet resources may work if the task is to be completed at school, but if the expectation is that the task be completed at home, considerations for students who do not have computers at home should be made. Students will be frustrated rather than motivated by tasks that are not realistic in their time and resource requirements.

- *Is the task motivating or engaging for students?* As we will discuss further in Chapter Ten, motivation is a complex issue. Students who are engaged in learning are motivated. Lack of engagement may reflect classroom management issues, a classroom environment that does not support student participation, or tasks that do not seem worth doing (low relevance to student's life). Moreover, assessment specialist Grant Wiggins (1998, p. 22) states, "authentic tasks supply greater incentives for students to perform." He defines an authentic task as one that is "realistic, requires judgment or innovation, and asks the students to 'do' the subject." Our experiences have shown that authentic tasks that appear relevant to students' lives will be more likely to engage students' interest and encourage them to persevere. Tying an activity to a particular career is one way to add realism and interest to a task. For example, an elementary math problem that gives students data on the length of a fireman's ladder and the height of a building and then asks students whether the fireman is able to rescue the people on the top floor is an example of a career-oriented task.

An inclusive task (one that provides a learning entry point for diverse students) can also be more motivating than a task that is not representative of all students. Inclusiveness can encompass a multitude of ideals, such as equity, fairness, multiculturalism, learning style, and multiple intelligences. Tasks that are culturally biased or that reinforce stereotypes are certainly less motivating to a diverse group of students than ones that emphasize positive attitudes. In teaching safety, for example, teachers may use pictures of safe and unsafe behaviors. Students depicted in such posters should be a mix of genders and races. One particular gender or race should be as well represented in the safe pictures as in the unsafe. Use of non-gender-specific names in written work can also enhance inclusion. For example, using "Jane is playing with matches" as the example given during a safety lesson may make girls feel unduly represented within the unsafe category of behaviors. Use of a non-gender-specific name such as Sam, Pat, or Chris can avoid this circumstance. Variety in use of gender, race, and ethnicity is important in assigning tasks, and it is a key ingredient in choosing types of tasks for students.

Tasks that enhance students' participation in their personal learning are more motivating and engaging. Tasks that are passive rather than active do not promote retention or understanding of concepts. A fill-in-the-blank worksheet on Robert's Rules of Order (Parliamentary Rules of Procedures) is one example of a passive task. However, having students conduct a classroom meeting using these rules is certainly a more active task, and one that engages students in applying learned concepts. Similarly, some teachers allow students to pick one book they want to read (based on their interest), but they also have to read the one the teacher picked out for them. Allowing students some choices in the task designed often leads to improving motivation to learn.

Compare the two assessment tasks found in Exhibits 6.5 and 6.6. Which is more cognitively challenging? Which is more engaging? Which exemplifies more of the quality characteristics this chapter has discussed?

The questions about task design and quality characteristics in this chapter can aid teachers in planning lessons that use quality assessment tasks to both promote knowledge acquisition and provide reliable evidence of student achievement and understanding. Such tasks may be geared to any of the learning targets or any of the "big rocks" of the curriculum. Teachers need to reflect on the work they are giving students and decide whether their assessment tasks are true to the purpose, aligned with the curricular learning targets, cognitively challenging, and engaging to students.

Once high-quality assessment tasks are designed, however, they must be scored in order to provide adequate feedback to students. Developing quality criteria for particular assessment tasks is addressed next, in Chapter Seven, our rubric chapter.

EXHIBIT 6.5. GRAPHS FOR STUDENT INTERPRETATION.

Graphs About Fourth Grade Students

```
                                X  X
                                X  X
                                X  X  X
                             X  X  X  X
                             X  X  X  X
               X          X  X  X  X  X  X        X  X
      ────────────────────────────────────────────────────
      3   3½   4   4½   5   5½   6   6½   7   7½   8   8½   9   9½
```
Graph 1

```
                        X
              X  X  X              X
        X     X  X  X  X           X
  X  X  X  X  X  X  X  X  X  X  X  X        X        X        X        X              X
  ───────────────────────────────────────────────────────────────────────────────────
  24 25 26 27 28 29 30 31 32 33 34 35 36 37 38 39 40 41 42 43 44 45 46 47 48
```
Graph 2

```
                        X  X
                        X  X
                        X  X
                        X  X  X  X
        X               X  X  X  X  X
        X               X  X  X  X  X  X           X  X              X
      ─────────────────────────────────────────────────────────────────
      0     ½    1    1½   2    2½   3    3½   4    4½   5    5½   6    6½
```
Graph 3

```
                    X        X
                 X  X  X  X
              X  X  X  X
           X  X  X  X  X  X  X
           X  X  X  X  X  X  X        X
      ───────────────────────────────────────
      50 51 52 53 54 55 56 57 58 59 60
```
Graph 4

```
                    X
                    X
                    X
                    X
                 X  X
                 X  X
              X  X  X
              X  X  X        X
              X  X  X        X
           X  X  X  X        X  X  X
      ──────────────────────────────────
      1     2     3     4     5     6     7     8     9
```
Graph 5

Talk about the following things with your partner. Be prepared to support your thinking.

1. Look at the range of numbers in Graph 2. Why is this graph not showing the ages of fourth grade students?

2. About how old is your teacher? (Be nice!) Why could Graph 1 not be the ages of the mothers of fourth grade students?

3. How many inches are in a foot? Why could Graph 3 not be the height of fourth grade students in units?

4. Match the graphs with the correct titles:
   a. Number of Letters in Students' First Names
   b. Ages of Fourth Grade Students' Mothers
   c. Height in Inches of Students in a Fourth Grade Class
   d. Weight at Birth of Fourth Grade Students
   e. Number of Hours per Day Fourth Grade Students Watch Television

Source: Reprinted with permission from *Measuring Up: Prototypes for Mathematics Assessment,* copyright © 1993 by the National Academy of Sciences, courtesy of the National Academies Press, Washington, D.C.

EXHIBIT 6.6. GRAPHING ACTIVITY WORKSHEET.

Look at the following questions and respond to them below:

1. What could this graph represent?

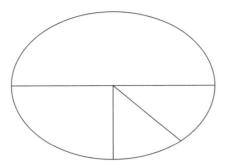

2. Create a graph using the following information in the data table.

Sports Teams	Number of Games Won
Bulls	15
Bills	20
Saints	10
Clubs	5
Sharks	12
Turtles	8
Hogs	6

Source: Joyner and McMunn, 2003, SERVE Regional Laboratory Performance Assessments in Math Project. Reprinted with permission.

Creating Useful Scoring Guides

7

As teachers design and select tasks in order to assess student work in a variety of ways and examine the evidence of learning from many angles, they should at the same time consider how they will score the assessments. Whether the assessment is for diagnostic, formative, or summative purposes, it is important to determine what "good work" means. The overall goal in selecting the task criteria that students should meet is to define and gather information that will improve instruction or enhance student performance. Although the actual scoring is done after an assessment is completed, setting up the criteria before the assessment and sharing these criteria with students ensures that the scoring will align with the instruction and that the criteria can be used to guide student learning as well as assess it. This makes scoring a critical link in the constant interplay between learning and assessment.

A word that is often used in discussing assessment scoring is *rubric*. Rubrics are scoring guides containing the criteria used to evaluate a student's performance for a particular task. By criteria, we mean the things that are important for students to know and do for their performance to meet the teacher's expectations. Designing a rubric can be a puzzling and challenging task for the novice. With practice, however, the rubric can simplify the teacher's job and answer the question, How am I going to score this complex assignment or task? Consider, for example, the world geography teacher who is faced with grading the project related to the benchmark: Monitor the effects of pollution on a specific stream. Some students have turned in written reports, some have prepared oral presentations, some have drawn graphs or charts, and others have a PowerPoint slide show prepared. Just deciding how to grade such diverse products can be overwhelming. The teacher sees quality in some of the student products and notes a complete lack of quality in others.

A rubric, then, defines what quality work looks like. It sets the criteria for scoring *before* the students begin work. The criteria used on the scoring guide, the rubric, help define quality for the students, and ultimately the rubric makes the job of assessing student work easier for the teacher and certainly more uniform and consistent.

In this chapter we answer the following questions about rubrics:

- What are the advantages and disadvantages of rubrics?
- What are the different formats for rubrics?
- How are rubrics designed?
- How can rubrics themselves be assessed?

The Advantages and Disadvantages of Rubrics

If student work is going to be scored and that score is going to be counted toward a grade, teachers should be able to justify how that score was determined. Constructing a rubric helps teachers instruct students appropriately before the assessment, provide feedback to students on their progress during learning, score the assessment objectively, and justify the scores that were given. However, rubrics are not the answer to everything in a classroom. Teachers do not need rubrics for every assignment they give students. Although using rubrics can be a positive experience for teachers and students, the use of rubrics does not substitute for one-on-one dialogues or conversations teachers have with students to explore understandings or misconceptions. Here are summaries of the positive and negative aspects of rubrics we have gathered from discussions with many teachers.

Some Positives About Using Rubric Scoring Guides

- Saves time during grading
- Defines quality work
- Justifies grades to parents
- Removes subjectivity
- Provides formative feedback
- Informs instruction
- Prepares students for summative evaluations
- Applies to multiple tasks
- Defines expectations up front to parents and students
- Involves students in creating the criteria for their tasks

Some Negatives About Using Rubric Scoring Guides

- Requires up-front planning time
- Needs revision frequently
- Requires parent education
- Requires a plan for transfer to report card grades (*Source:* McMunn & Schenck, 1996).

Formats for Rubrics

As you examine this section on the formats for rubrics, consider which rubrics would provide the teacher with better information to use in planning instruction. Which would provide the student with the best feedback about his or her work, and which would provide enough feedback for improvement? Which type of rubric would probably be more time-consuming to use or create? These questions will help focus your attention on the advantages and disadvantages of particular rubric formats.

Rubrics may be *generalized* or *task specific* in format. They may also be *holistic* or *analytical*. Each rubric format contains descriptions of performances, and these descriptions may be differentiated into performance quality levels (such as high, medium, and low). Rubric formats also usually assign points to particular levels of performance, thereby rendering the score earned on an assignment meaningful.

Generalized or Task Specific

Are the criteria we set for the task specific to this task, or can these same criteria be used for many tasks? If the criteria are task specific, they can be used only to score one specific task. For example, criteria used to assess a particular high school physical education skill for follow-through of a golf swing would be task specific in that other sports skills could not be assessed using a rubric designed to assess this particular skill. In other words, a list of criteria for judging the golf swing would be vastly different from a list used to judge other skills. Therefore, the task-specific rubric is unique in its purpose and design.

Another example of a task-specific rubric is one that many middle school teachers in physical science use, which is based on the specific task of arranging and understanding electrical circuits and the function of switches. The task might ask students to set up a circuit using a switch, battery, and miniature lights. Students would then explain the function of the switch (break in a circuit) and draw in their lab books a design of how the electricity flows. Students would also be challenged to make additional setups and explain whether the circuit works for each, explaining why or why not. A task-specific rubric used for scoring this assignment would include criteria such as

- Setup—Student shows setup of a complete circuit
- Product—In-lab notebooks

- Drawings—Shows all parts labeled correctly for all setups (circuit shows relationship of lights, battery, switches, and arrows showing energy flow)
- Paragraph—Students correctly explain how the electricity flows with each setup, explains the function of the switch, and explains the function of the battery

Task specific rubrics allow for particular facts or procedures essential to the task to be assessed. Once the criteria are set, scoring can be easy.

More generalized criteria, however, may be used repeatedly to score similar tasks. For example, teachers may use criteria for writing lab reports to score all such reports, even though the activities done for each lab may vary greatly. Arter and McTighe (2001) suggest that most teachers will find generalized rubrics more useful. Some reasons may be that these rubrics can be used repeatedly, thus eliminating the need for many rubrics, they can aid in teachers valuing the same criteria, and they do not give away answers. Therefore, they may save valuable time for teachers. In addition, generalized rubrics can help establish valued criteria and can enhance student performance, as students become familiar with requirements and teacher expectations.

To summarize, rubrics may be task specific if they can only be used to score one particular task. Rubrics are more generalized when they capture criteria that span several tasks. A teacher may create a generalized writing rubric, for example, that could be used to score all types of writing, such as narratives, expository paragraphs, or research papers. Headings for criteria for this type of writing rubric may include organization, mechanics, and content. This rubric would be generalized in that it could be used to score many writing tests. It could also be classified as somewhat task specific, however, in that it could only score writing tasks, not oral presentations or other performances. From this explanation, we can see that *task specific* and *generalized* are not true opposites. A rubric does not have to be all one or the other in format. Rather, task specificity or generalization exists on a continuum from less task specific (more generalized) to more task specific (less generalized).

Holistic or Analytical

All rubrics (whether generalized or task specific) fall into one of two further categories: they may be either holistic or analytical. These two terms are key for teachers in understanding rubrics. A holistic rubric is a scoring guide that responds to a student's work as a whole. It assigns a *single score* based on clearly defined criteria giving traits (descriptions) that define what the performance involves. Many state writing tests use holistic rubrics for scoring. For all the work done, the student receives one score (such as 2, 3, 4, or 5). Generally, holistic rubrics are used for summative purposes or for large-scale assessment. In contrast, an analytical rubric is a scoring guide that responds separately to each of the key criteria of the student's work. It assigns individual scores or quality descriptions for each criterion. An elementary writing rubric that assigns separate points for appropriate capitalization, word spacing, letters, shapes, sentence punctuation, and so forth is an example of an analytical rubric. From such a rubric, the student can determine the areas in which he or she did not receive the maximum points possible. This type of rubric helps students concentrate on improving one particular skill, rather than a set of skills. Analytical rubrics take more time to create but if constructed correctly can reduce grading time in the end, as teachers do not have to write the same comments repeatedly on students' papers. Analytical rubrics also provide students with more specific feedback than is possible through a holistic, single-digit score. An example of an analytical rubric is shown in Table 7.1. This rubric is analytical in that it awards points for each criterion (mechanics, narrative essay, and organization of writing).

Table 7.2 displays another analytical rubric, this time for math performance assessments in grades K–5. This rubric is labeled analytical because it provides scores for several different criteria.

TABLE 7.1. ANALYTICAL RUBRIC FOR PRACTICE ON NARRATIVE ESSAY.

CRITERIA: Main points/characteristics you valued from the student work. You should define each area and keep the information short, clear, and to the point.	*_4_pts*	*_3_pts*	*_2_pts* *REDO*
Mechanics of writing (circle problems) • Correct spelling • Subject/verbs agree • Writing is legible • Sentences are complete	No errors	1–3 errors or less	4–6 errors or less — correct these
Narrative essay - content (circle problems) • Essay gives a setting (time, place) • Essay gives a problem or defined plot • Events solve problem or elaborate plot • Writing follows the direction of the prompt • Ending has an appropriate conclusion	Essay meets all indicators given	Essay is weak in one or two areas (circled)—pay attention to these when teacher reviews	Essay does not include numerous indicators—student must rewrite essay
Organization of writing • Title given and it relates to the topic • Introduction given and relates to the topic • All supporting details relate to topic • Writing follows a sequence that makes sense from beginning to end	No errors.	One or two errors noted	Numerous errors noted—practice and redo
Range	12–10	9–6	6–4

SCORING: (Total points) _____out of 12

      10–12   (Performance meets expectations of grade-level work)

      7–9   (Performance suggests student needs extra practice)

      4–6   (Performance does not meet grade level work—student must redo this work and work with tutor)

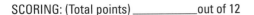
Source: McMunn, 1996, p. 38.

TABLE 7.2. ELEMENTARY PERFORMANCE ASSESSMENTS IN MATH: ANALYTICAL SCORING RUBRIC FOR GRADES K–5.

Level 4—(16–13 points)—Work beyond grade-level expectations
Level 3—(12–9 points)—Work is solid, on grade-level work
Level 2—(8–5 points)—Limited achievement on grade-level work
Level 1—(4–1 points)—Minimal acheivement on grade-level work

Criteria	Exemplary Level 4	Proficient Level 3	Progressing Level 2	Emerging Level 1	Not Scorable
Computational Fluency • **Accurate** • **Appropriate** • **Efficient**	• All answers/ computations are accurate • Work shows clear understanding and use of appropriate computation and gives an alternative computational approach • Solution is reached in manner more likely to be used at advanced levels	• Answer is correct but may have minor number fact error • Work shows understanding and use of appropriate computation • Solution strategy is efficient for grade level	• Has important errors in computation leading to incorrect answer • Work shows incomplete understanding of appropriate computation or solves only one step of multi-step task • Uses inefficient strategy for computing for grade level	• Answer is incorrect; may have multiple errors in computation • Has errors in choice of operation or in computation • Little evidence of use of strategy	• Work is non-existent or unrelated to the task
Understanding of Core Concepts	• Work demonstrates deep understanding of mathematics concept(s) in the task	• Work shows understanding of mathematics concept(s) in the task	• Work shows incomplete understanding of mathematics concept(s) in the task	• Work shows little or no evidence of understanding of mathematics concept(s)	
Problem-Solving and Reasoning Skills	• Work demonstrates thorough understanding and shows connections to other situations • Uses appropriate method of solving task and indicates alternative approaches • Work has evidence of clear reasoning, valid arguments, and generalizations	• Work demonstrates understanding of the task • Work is completed using a workable method/strategy • Work includes a clear argument and/or conjecture but may lack evidence for reasoning behind the conclusions	• Work demonstrates some understanding of the task • Work may begin with a strategy but student cannot reach a solution • May complete work but reasoning absent or flawed	• Work demonstrates little or no understanding of the task • Work shows difficulty setting up problem and choosing a solution • Answer is not reasonable	
Communication Representation	• Work communicates clearly the reasoning and solution is organized in a logical manner • Work includes accurate labels, vocabulary; includes multiple representations	• Work communicates ideas, reasoning, and solution • Work includes appropriate terms, notation, and representation	• Process/answer not clearly indicated and lacks full explanation • Representations not clearly labeled; vocabulary unclear	• Answer is incorrect and work is difficult to interpret • Lacks labels and/or other explanation	

Source: Adapted from Joyner and McMunn, 2003, K–5 Assessment Example for Math. Reprinted with permission.

Conversely, Table 7.3 shows a holistic rubric that can be used to score a writing assignment. This sample holistic writing rubric is holistic in that students receive *one* score (5, 3, or 1) rather than separate scores for separate criteria.

Whether rubrics are holistic or analytical (and generalized or task specific), they all contain descriptions that separate student performance into proficiency levels. When such levels are not needed, a checklist may be used instead of a rubric. For example, often teachers simply want students to check off components that are present or lacking in a performance or product. So a list of present or absent components is not a rubric but a checklist. Checklists contain basic lists of the criteria to be used in judging student work, and the teacher or student can check off criteria to show whether or not the student has met them. Checklists contain very few descriptive elements, unlike rubrics, and do not provide differentiation of levels of performance. Such checklists are simple and are used to show a student what they did or did not complete. A teacher using a checklist to teach students the proper way to submit papers might include some of these components:

- I placed my name in the right-hand corner

- I stapled my paper in the top left

- I looked over my paper for spelling mistakes

The checklist in Exhibit 7.1 contains some descriptions but fewer than a rubric would display. It basically allows a student or teacher to check off components of the

TABLE 7.3. SAMPLE HOLISTIC WRITING RUBRIC.

Points Awarded	Criteria
5	The sample has an effective opening and closing that ties the writing together. All the writing relates to the topic and has a single focus. Writing is organized and progresses logically. The writer takes compositional risks resulting in highly effective, vivid responses. Very few, if any, errors in usage, sentence construction, or mechanics are present. The variety of the sentences and/or rhetorical modes demonstrates syntactic and verbal sophistication.
3	The sample generally has an opening and a closing. The responses relate to the topic and usually have a single focus. However, some responses may drift from the focus. Development of the writing may be uneven with elaborated ideas interspersed with bare, unelaborated details. Some responses are organized with little, if any, difficulty moving from one idea to another; other responses may ramble somewhat with clusters of ideas that may be loosely connected. However, an overall progression is apparent in this piece. There may be some errors in usage, sentence construction, and/or mechanics. The writing avoids excessive monotony in syntax and/or rhetorical modes.
1	The writing may not have an opening and/or a closing. It may state a subject or a list of subjects and may have an underlying focus, but this focus may be inferred. Details are general and may appear random, inappropriate, or barely apparent. The paper may show little sense of planning or organization. There are severe problems with usage, sentence construction, and mechanics. The paper may appear incoherent or unintelligible.

Source: Adapted from Regional Laboratory Network, copyright © 1998. *Improving Classroom Assessment: A Toolkit for Professional Developers* (Toolkit 98), activity 3.3, overhead A3.3, 011, "Performance Criteria, Keys to Success," p. 24. Reprinted with permission of NWREL.

EXHIBIT 7.1. SAMPLE 2 CHECKLIST USED TO PROVIDE FEEDBACK: EXPERIMENT USING SCIENTIFIC METHOD.

Student: *Melissa*

☑ 1. Problem is stated in a clear statement.
☑ 2. Information was collected:
　　☒ 3 sources were used (1 reference book only) *2 given*
☑ 3. The written hypothesis is clear and meaningful. *Well-written*
☑ 4. The Experimental Design was complete with:
　　☒ A complete list of materials used
　　☑ The evidence showing the procedure was followed in a step-by-step order
　　☑ Observations noted during experiment
　　☑ A doable experimental design
☐ 5. Results are complete and
　　☒ Given in a checklist format and/or displayed in an organized data table
　　☑ Data is presented in a clear, graphic form
☐ 6. Conclusions are complete – evidence shows:
　　☒ Hypothesis was supported or not supported *Not stated.*
　　☒ Graphic results are clearly discussed in several well-written and organized paragraphs
　　☒ Applications for worthiness of this experiment were discussed *Not organized*
　　☒ Other variables that could have affected the experiment outcomes were
　　　noted and discussed

Revised project due on 10-10-98

Questions to think about for the summative assessment:
1. Why is it important for you to understand and know how to use the scientific method?
2. How would the world be different today if scientists had not organized data and used a systematic way to solve problems?

Source: McMunn, 1996, p. 38.

work as "present" or "absent." Like many checklists, this one would be easy to later convert to a scoring rubric.

What you may also notice about this checklist is that there is no scoring conversion or point scale attached to the criteria. As reviewers of teacher-constructed rubrics, we have frequently encountered samples such as those shown in Table 7.4. This construction is not a checklist, since it contains point scores and does not truly contain a checkable list of needed components. It is, in fact, a poorly designed analytical rubric. Students will have difficulty understanding the criteria, since no descriptions are given.

In the scoring tool (not a good rubric or a good checklist) in Table 7.4 it is clear that Sean earned twenty-five out of forty points on the report section. However, Sean will have no idea what he did wrong or, in fact, what he did right for the report section. The teacher might also have difficulty interpreting the score for Sean.

Melissa's checklist in Exhibit 7.1 shows she received more feedback via her checklist than Sean received on his flawed scoring guide. Melissa's checklist is useful for

TABLE 7.4. POORLY DESIGNED RUBRIC.

Explorer's Report		
Student: Sean	**Possible Points**	**Points Earned**
1. Cover	5	4
2. Title page	5	5
3. Map showing close-up of MS River	15	12
4. Drawing of explorer	15	13
5. Report	40	25
6. Bibliography	10	7
7. Presentation	10	9
*Extra credit for creativity, artwork, etc.	15	0
Total and Grade		75 (B)

Source: McMunn, 1996, p. 38.

providing feedback for improving on her written report about her experiment. She should be able to use the information shown on the checklist to improve the report before a grade is given. Sean received poor feedback and a poor final grade, and he received no extra credit.

Checklists have some utility in providing formative feedback, but to make such feedback meaningful to students, highly descriptive language must be used. But once a teacher starts adding such descriptive language, he or she is on the way to designing a rubric.

How to Design a Rubric

The following questions about rubric criteria focus on what is important to consider when constructing rubrics to be quality tools that will help teachers give richer and better feedback to students. Do the rubric criteria

- Reflect the skills and content taught?
- Emphasize significant knowledge and important concepts?
- Adequately differentiate between superior, adequate, and substandard work?
- Provide feedback to improving learning and understanding?
- Designate the most important qualities via the distribution of points?
- Clearly translate into grades?

Outlining the criteria by which students will be judged prior to the actual assessment and sharing these criteria with students help create quality rubrics that are an integral part of instruction.

• *Do the criteria in the rubric clearly reflect the skills and content taught?* Do the rubric criteria require student application of the skills and content taught by the teacher? It appears obvious that the assessment and scoring criteria should match the instructional content, but in our experiences it is not unknown for the opposite to occur. When teachers do not plan the method of assessment or the design of the rubric prior to instruction, or when teachers only assess because "it's been two weeks since I recorded a grade," the assessment and rubric often do not match the content taught. Assessments or rubrics, like cookies, are best when homemade—when the one who constructs them is also the one who instructs the students. In such situations the best fit is found between content and assessments.

One example where a "best fit" did not occur is in the following scenario: A teacher spent numerous instructional hours with students reading a text about peer pressure versus peer influence. The students then were given several questions to *prompt* their thinking and asked to discuss the text in groups and use their own background knowledge and experience to support how they felt about the questions asked. When the teacher was asked what summative assessment the students would do she replied, "I'll ask them to write several paragraphs about the text, and I'll grade the paragraphs based on mechanics, a topic sentence, two supporting details, and the concluding sentence" (Exhibit 7.2, part B, shows these criteria). What does this assessment method show? She was instructing the students to think and interpret, but the students were assessed in her rubric only on paragraph structure. This was clearly a mismatch between instruction and rubric criteria. Exhibit 7.2, part A, shows a prompt for an essay and *portion* of a rubric that would provide better criteria for assessing the students based on the text read and the thinking the teacher emphasized during instruction.

• *Do the criteria found in the rubric emphasize significant knowledge, enduring themes, and important concepts rather than irrelevant details or relatively unimportant skills?* In other words, do the criteria in the rubric focus student attention on the most important concepts, the "big rocks," rather than on minutiae? Is the emphasis on understanding or on coverage? Teachers who pride themselves on including test questions derived from text picture captions may be emphasizing minutiae to the exclusion of more important details. Teachers who have middle school students memorize all the bones in the body or require high school students to reconstruct the Periodic Table of the elements from memory may allot far more time and emphasis to such activities than they actually warrant when the overall curriculum is examined. How does the teacher decide which details are the most important? The curriculum is the guide to use for such decisions. It is clearly impossible to teach every concept covered in a text. The curriculum helps the teacher organize the instruction, so that the more important concepts are given top priority. In this same manner, the teacher

---

EXHIBIT 7.2. ESSAY PROMPT WITH PARTIAL RUBRIC SHOWING CRITERIA.

Write a well-organized (two pages or less) essay responding to the following prompt. Make sure you support your thinking through background knowledge, personal experience, and facts or quotes from the text read.

Prompt: In your opinion, does peer pressure or peer influence affect teens more today?

A - This criteria for the prompt

Criteria
Processing and Thinking • Opinion is stated clearly • Information is interpreted accurately and synthesized clearly • Insightful background examples are used
Organization • Evidence of explicit organization • Ideas, transitions, and relationships are clear

B - Or, this criteria only:

Criteria
Paragraph Structure • Topic sentence and concluding sentence given • Few grammatical errors • Two supporting details are given

---

plans the assessments and creates the rubrics to emphasize those same high-priority concepts.

If the history standards emphasize students making connections between the past and the present, the assessment should mirror this emphasis. For example, students might be required to trace the development of a current practice such as representative democracy to its roots in the democratic processes used in the city-states of ancient Greece. A rubric for such a question would focus on the connections made, not on the accuracy of specific dates or proper names.

Another history example may further explicate this need for emphasizing priority concepts. A middle school social studies teacher asked Susan to review a poster rubric.

The learning target for the activity was to learn biographical data on U.S. presidents. The poster rubric contained criteria on color, format, clarity, and illustrations. What it did *not* contain were any criteria concerned with content accuracy. Therefore, a student could make an attractive, visually pleasing, color poster and show Dolly Madison as George Washington's wife with no penalties for inaccuracy.

• *Do the criteria descriptors possess sufficient detail to enable students to understand the differences between superior, adequate, and substandard work?* Part of the detail, if at all possible, should include performance exemplars. An exemplar is an authentic example of student work. It may be annotated to exemplify significant features of quality, achievement, and learning in relation to the performance levels established.

In an oral report rubric, for example, one criterion might deal with body language. The descriptor for superior behavior in this category might read, "Purposeful movement, confident bearing." Adequate behavior could be noted by, "Twitches, nervous, somewhat confident," while substandard behavior would be described as, "Fidgets, shakes, lack of confidence shown." In this manner, the rubric clearly describes behaviors on three different levels of proficiency. Such descriptors model the expected behavior for students. In fact, by simply reading these rubric criteria, students understand the target performance required.

Often teachers do not like to show students exemplars of other students' work. The major reason appears to be a fear of students copying the work exactly. However, the authors' experience has shown that providing exemplars to students helps them comprehend the teacher's expectations. This enables the informed students to reach or exceed those expectations and produce quality work. This does not occur if students have no clear comprehension of quality. Exhibit 7.3 displays exemplar levels of a student assessment on number relationships. The teacher uses the rubric and the exemplars (high, medium, and low work) to help explain the differences in these levels to students.

Nancy required her students to participate in the science fair at the school. This project-based assessment was very involved, and Nancy learned that she needed to break the project into small increments for her students. The first increment was research on topics and writing a good hypothesis to test; the second was to submit the science fair project proposal outlining what the student would do. Once approved the students would conduct the project (research). They would then outline their results in two formats: one would be a mock project board set up on large construction paper and the other required a draft of their research paper. Nancy provided feedback to the students using preestablished rubrics and checklists and one-on-one discussions about the work. The students then prepared their final papers and project boards for the school science fair, and these were judged based on the same preestablished rubric used for the drafts. Each year Nancy kept the best work from students for each of

EXHIBIT 7.3. EXEMPLARS FOR MATH ASSESSMENT: HIGH, MEDIUM, AND LOW EXAMPLES.

High Level Response
1. Solve: $(6 \times 3) + 10 =$ _28_
2. Write a math story problem that this expression will solve: $(6 \times 3) + 10$. (Retyped for ease of reading.)

   Johnny has 6 sets of baseball cards. There are three in each set. He adds ten more and has 28.

Medium Level Response
1. Solve: $(6 \times 3) + 10 =$ _19_
2. Write a math story problem that this expression will solve: $(6 \times 3) + 10$. (Retyped for ease of reading.)

   They have 6 in each of the three baskets. Then he adds his eggs to Ben's pile of 10 and together they have 25.

Low Level Response
1. Solve: $(6 \times 3) + 10 =$ _73_
2. Write a math story problem that this expression will solve: $(6 \times 3) + 10$. (Retyped for ease of reading.)

   John adds all his apples together. He has 63 plus 10. A student can take 63 apples, add 10 apples, and get 73 apples.

Rubic for Scoring:

Criteria	High	Medium	Low
Answering the problem and writing the story	• Correct solution of problem • Appropriate mathematical purpose is evident in story	• Minor computational errors • Some parts of an appropriate strategy are given but may lack key math relationship	• Inappropriate computation • Evidence suggests student did not understand problem

Source: Adapted from Joyner and McMunn, 2003, K–5 Assessment Example for Math. Reprinted with permission.

these sets and used them for future reference as exemplars of excellent work. Nancy felt that having exemplars of quality work was one of the contributing factors for numerous state awards her students won. At first, she was hesitant to share these with her students because she thought they would just copy others' work, but she soon realized that having these exemplars provided an example of the teacher's expectations. Consequently, she spent less time going over and over her expectations to the students.

• *Do the criteria provide enough feedback to improve learning and understanding?* In other words, when the student receives the assessment, will the marks, point scale, and comments on the rubric be meaningful and useful to him or her? Do the criteria clearly identify the activities in which the student excelled and those in which further work are needed? Good rubrics always provide a target performance for students. Excellent rubrics provide students with the information necessary to ascertain how far away or how close their performance came to this target. Arter and McTighe (2001) suggest that there is no set rule for selecting rubrics that are best to use in the classroom. They do state (and we agree) that analytical type rubrics are best for formative measures, since the structure of these tend to provide feedback for improving both teaching and learning.

A scoring rubric for journal entries exemplifies the potential for meaningful feedback. The following descriptors occur under the heading "An Excellent Response":

• Is properly headed with name, date, book title underlined, and author

• Completely answers all parts of the journal prompts

• Is detailed and clear

• Shares the writer's own thoughts and feelings

From these descriptions of an excellent response, the students can evaluate their own entries and ascertain missing or incomplete portions.

• *Are the criteria prioritized in such a manner that the most important ones accumulate the greatest number of points?* For example, a student essay, whether written in science class or language arts class, will be assessed by a rubric containing criteria for spelling, punctuation, grammar, and capitalization. Depending on what is being targeted, such criteria may be awarded more points by the rubric used in the class on writing and fewer points by the rubric used in the science class. The science teacher wishes to reward and encourage the use of standard writing skills, but that is not his primary reason for assigning the essay. He may award more points for problem statements, hypotheses, descriptions of procedures, or inclusion of science content than for grammatical operations. The assessment instrument should emphasize the most important concepts from the instruction. These concepts should accumulate more points than other, more extraneous ones.

- *Is it clear how scores will be converted to grades?* If the assessment is to be converted to a numerical or letter grade, the point scale on the rubric for doing so should be clearly displayed and evident to students. For example, a first grade writing rubric might contain a total of thirty-two points for all criteria. The grading conversion at the bottom notes that

  - Exemplary (25–32 points)—Exceeds grade level expectations

  - Proficient (18–25 points)—Meets grade level expectations

  - Progressing (11–18 points)—Does not meet grade level expectations

  - Needs improvement (0–10 points)—Not working on grade level work

These four comments (exemplary, proficient, progressing, needs improvement) are the ones that actually appear on the first grade report card.

However, for higher grades, it is more usual to convert scores to letter or number grades. A middle grades rubric on the scientific method uses the following conversion scale:

> 9–11 points (11 points are the maximum)—Above grade level work (A or B)
>
> 6–8 points—On grade level work (C)
>
> 4–5 points—Redo (D or F)

A note of caution: When converting rubric scores to grades, using percentages *is not* the best route. In the scale above, if a teacher were to use percentages a student earning 8 out of 11 would earn a grade of 72 percent (a D for most schools) or a student earning 5 out of 11 would received a 45 percent, which is failing for most schools. However, on the scale above, a score of 5 would be a C. It is best to convert rubric scores into grades in ways that make sense and seem fair and reasonable for students rather than to figure scores as percentages.

Rubrics that convey the conversion method to be used can save time for the teacher and prevent student misconceptions about their final grades in a class. In fact, if the rubric is set up correctly, most middle school students can figure out his or her own grade from the rubric points.

The use of rubrics in a class can also help students keep track of their progress through a grading period. Exhibit 7.4 is one example of a grading system based on points earned by the students on classroom rubrics. A teacher using such a system would rarely have to answer, "What's my current grade in this class?" Students would have "surprise-free" report cards, as would parents. Explaining an overall grade for the class to parents would become much easier, as well.

EXHIBIT 7.4. ALTERNATIVE GRADING PROCESS.

(Based on Total Points)

Assignment	Number This Term	Possible Points Each	Total Points (Whole)	Point Earned (Part)
⇨ Assignment	5	12	60	54
⇨ Homework	10	5	50	45
⇨ Tests	3	25	75	60
⇨ Activities	4	6	24	20
⇨ Projects	1	20 (2)	40	35

Total			249	214

Part earned: 214 points
Whole possible: 249 points

Part/Whole × 100% = grade

214/249 = .859 × 100 = 86 grade

(We realize point systems for determining grades have some problems, as recently cited by Brookhart [2004] and Marzano [2000]. However, for some students and teachers this system is easy to work with. Before using this method, careful consideration should be given to what the grades measure, how zero grades are used, and if the point scale accurately reflects student attainment of targets.)

Source: McMunn, 1996, p. 42.

Assessing the Quality of Rubrics

Table 7.5 summarizes the design questions discussed in this chapter for the construction of a rubric. Teachers may use this summary chart to assess the quality of their own rubrics.

Once a teacher's self-created rubric is assessed using the quality rubric criteria found in Table 7.5, a score can be calculated. The actual score is not of crucial importance, of course. It is *the use the teacher makes of the score that is paramount.* An analysis of the score components can determine the strengths and weaknesses of the rubric. The teacher should ponder, What will make the rubric better? In order to improve the rubric, teachers can return to earlier sections of this chapter or work together in peer groups to discuss the points and questions outlined in Table 7.5 to gain more experience with rubrics.

TABLE 7.5. RUBRIC FOR ASSESSING THE QUALITY OF RUBRICS.

No.	Excellent (5)	Acceptable (3)	Unacceptable (1)
		Criteria	
1	Criteria identify all components necessary for high-quality work.	Sufficient criteria are present to define high-quality work, but some "fine-tuning" criteria may be missing.	Rubric fails to include critical criteria for excellence (Ex: content <u>accuracy</u>).
2	Criteria reflect alignment to all stated objectives.	Minor objectives are not sufficiently addressed by the criteria.	Major objectives are not sufficiently addressed by the criteria.
3	Criteria are feasible and measurable.	Criteria are measurable and reasonably feasible.	Criteria listed in the rubric may not be measurable, or they have low feasibility (e.g., they would require the teacher to individually observe each student, thereby using more time than warranted by the importance of the criterion).
		Descriptors	
4	Descriptors always use "kid-friendly" language, language easily understood by the target student population.	Descriptors usually use "kid-friendly language," but some "educationalese" is present.	Descriptors consistently use language inappropriate for the developmental/academic/grade level of the student population.
5	Descriptors use measurable quantities and avoid overuse of quantitative terms (e.g. several, numerous, some).	Descriptors rely more on quantitative terms than on measurable quantities.	The use of too many generalities (as sometimes, occasionally, some, etc.) detracts from the clarity and leads to confusion.
6	Descriptors accurately and specifically describe levels of performance within the criterion.	Descriptors accurately describe levels of performance, but specificity may be low (e.g., for a writing rubric, the descriptors might say the student "uses standard English." This does not specifically explain what "standard English" means).	Descriptors and criteria do not match OR there are no descriptors OR descriptors use one word (e.g., "always" for best performance, "sometimes" for acceptable performance, and "never" for unacceptable performance).
		Scoring Guide	
7	The most important criteria are allotted the greatest number of points, thereby allowing students to prioritize efforts.	All criteria earn the same amount of points, as all are equally important.	All criteria earn the same amount of points, but some are clearly more important or more aligned to the objectives than others.
8	The scoring guide clearly demonstrates how rubric scores will be converted to grades.	A conversion scale is present, but may not address all grading levels (e.g., "10 points is an A" is stated, but no distinctions are given for A+ grades or A- grades).	No conversion scale is present.

(continued)

TABLE 7.5. RUBRIC FOR ASSESSING THE QUALITY OF RUBRICS. (Cont'd.)

No.	Excellent (5)	Acceptable (3)	Unacceptable (1)
Format (Type) of Rubric			
9	Type of rubric used supports purpose of assessment (e.g., an analytical, task-specific rubric for a formative assessment; a holistic, generalized rubric for a summative assessment).	Type of rubric used is appropriate (e.g., analytical for formative assessments and holistic only for summative assessments), but generalized may be substituted for task-specific rubrics if students will perform several iterations of this type of work throughout the school year (e.g., an "oral presentation" rubric).	Type of rubric does not support purpose of assessment (e.g., a holistic rubric is used to judge performance on a newly taught skill).
Quality of the Feedback			
10	Rubric scores clearly pinpoint students' strengths and weaknesses; students obtain sufficient information to improve performance.	Rubric scores clearly pinpoint students' strengths and weaknesses.	Rubric gives insufficient information to allow students to improve.
11	Rubric is instructional in nature; students can read and understand what high-quality work will look like; students can use rubric to self-assess own performance without input from the teacher.	Rubric is instructional in nature; students can read and understand what high-quality work will look like.	Rubric does not contain sufficient information for students to understand teacher expectations and/or what quality work will look like.

We emphasize once again that the ultimate goal of assessment and instruction is to promote student achievement. Using quality tasks and quality criteria will help ensure that this goal is met. Chapters Six and Seven have emphasized ways to enhance the quality of these tasks and criteria.

The next part of the Classroom Assessment Cycle involves making sense of all the information gathered through classroom assessment. So in Chapter Eight we move toward analyzing the collected assessment data.

Making Sense of Assessment Data

Inferences, analysis of data, and interpretations are made

In the third quadrant of the Classroom Assessment Cycle (discussed in Chapter Eight) teachers look at the evidence they have gathered about student learning and formulate inferences and interpretations based upon this evidence. Any such analysis begins with a search for patterns. Once patterns are discerned, inferences are made. Next, it is necessary to reexamine the data to test the accuracy of the inferences. Often more data are collected to enhance the reliability of the inferences. Once reliability is established, inferences become assertions or conclusions. Such conclusions about student achievement are calls for action within the classroom.

Our research and experiences reveal that the Classroom Assessment Cycle often stops in this third quadrant. Teachers make inferences about students' learning, achievement levels, or abilities from the evidence collected, but then they often just formulate grades that may or may not reflect student learning of the targets, rather than continuing on to test inferences and draw high-quality conclusions. This practice does not support good assessment or differentiated instruction or provide good feedback for helping students improve.

In Chapter Eight, "Tracking and Analyzing Results," we discuss approaches to analyzing classroom data that will help teachers use the analyses to modify their instructional strategies in ways that make a difference to students.

Tracking and Analyzing Results

So far in this book we have focused on the classroom. This chapter on data analysis is no different. In the Classroom Assessment Cycle we are now in quadrant three. From the authors' work, this quadrant is often where things stop. Teachers may analyze the data but fail to move on to quadrant four, Making Instructional Modifications. Instead, they just label the student's learning with a score or a grade.

There are many programs to extract and use data throughout a department, school, or district, but we want *teachers* to think about how they can use data analysis in the classroom to help them better understand their students and better diagnose learning. The data analysis we are referring to in this chapter is about observing patterns and trends assessed more formatively to make inferences about student learning.

Used effectively, classroom assessment data can *diagnose* what teachers are teaching and what students are learning and *prescribe* how teaching and other factors that influence learning need to be improved. Clif St. Germain and Michael Guillot of the Center for Academic Excellence, quoted in *Parent Press* magazine, share a wonderful analogy of comparing the teacher's job to that of a doctor. They "note that doctors do not use one treatment for all patients. They see patients individually, evaluate temperature, blood pressure, and lab work, and then establish a personalized course of treatment." Like doctors, educators need to "resist the temptation to use only one" piece of data to determine whether a student is learning. "They must collect multiple forms of data, analyze the information, and then adjust teaching to meet the specific needs of the student" (*Parent Press*, 2001, p. 1). Analyzing the data involves looking for patterns, formulating inferences, testing or verifying inferences, and drawing conclusions, as shown in Figure 8.1. These conclusions may then spur changes in assessments or instruction.

FIGURE 8.1. DATA ANALYSIS PROCESS.

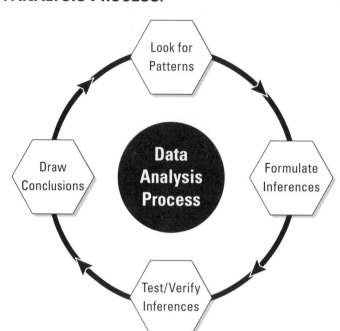

As we discussed in the Introduction, "There is a growing body of evidence that the use of high-quality, targeted assessment data, in the hands of school staff trained to use it effectively, can improve instruction" (Protheroe, 2001, p. 1). Indeed, data-based decision making has been a catchphrase in education for a long time. The question is not if data should be utilized in decision making, but *how* the data should be used. "In today's climate of accountability and assessment for public schools, 'data' is the watchword. When data shines a light on low performance in schools, stakeholders tend to wring their hands. Many times, educators are unaccustomed and sometimes afraid to mine the assessment data for information about underlying causes of achievement problems." These educators "often underestimate the value of the data. Data can give an accurate picture of the past and a clear indication of the present, based on reality rather than on perception" (*Parent Press,* 2001, p. 1).

The value of assessment data, in particular, lies in the fact that it can be used to

- Configure student groups
- Examine strengths and weaknesses of students and help them set goals for their own learning
- Determine which students may benefit most from differentiated instruction
- Determine whether recorded grades were derived from valid assessments
- Determine whether teacher-made tests are valid and reliable sources of student learning
- Set grade-level expectations for students in particular content areas

Moreover, people "need not be statisticians to look at classroom evidence and make good decisions" (Parent Press, 2001, p. 4). Data analysis simply means gathering appropriate data and analyzing it pertinent to its original purpose. The data (or evidence) needs to be collected and organized in a useful manner so that not only quantitative information (number results) but also qualitative (descriptive) information can be derived from it. In fact, qualitative information is generally more important to obtain during the learning process, as this formative, descriptive data may have the greatest impact on student performance when it is offered in a timely manner.

Chapters Four through Seven in Part Two discussed why teachers need to collect assessment evidence (qualitative and quantitative data) from multiple sources; what types of evidence need to be collected, analyzed, and interpreted; and the importance of designing assessments and rubrics so they yield high-quality data.

In this chapter, we now answer these questions relative to the data analysis process:

- How can assessment information be used to make valid inferences when analyzing student learning?

- How can classroom assessment evidence data be organized to create these valid inferences from multiple data sources?

How to Use Assessment Information to Make Valid Inferences

We will first look at examining individual assessments for clues to student performance on a particular assignment and then move to analyzing a series of assessments (cumulative assessments) to give a broader picture of overall student achievement.

Examining Individual Assessments

The following questions may aid a teacher in collecting and then analyzing the *most appropriate* assessment data for purposes of improving instruction and student learning. They may help uncover whether students learned and how well they learned. These questions emphasize the importance of looking at the assessment evidence to determine patterns or to see trends. This step must take place before inferences can be formulated. What did the students learn and how well did they learn it?

1. Does the student have any major misunderstandings about the task, the questions asked, or the instructions given? If so, were any misunderstandings due to a lack of information or a lack of understanding of the directions given?

2. Is this assessment evidence valid (Does it accurately measure what it was designed to measure?), and can it be added to other evidence about this student's learning?

3. Is this assessment evidence relevant? Does it address the learning target(s) either directly or indirectly (NCDPI, 1999)?

4. What clear and precise feedback can be given to the student because of this evidence?

5. How can the evidence be reviewed by the student and the teacher together, and when this occurs, is there sufficient evidence to make inferences about the student's learning?

The assessments and rubrics most likely to yield useful answers to these questions will have been designed as described earlier in Chapters Six and Seven. In particular, these assessment instruments

- Require the kind of thinking (cognitive challenge or intellectual work) that students are *regularly* exposed to in class during a grading period
- Align with important *learning targets*
- Require a *written, constructed response*
- Provide clear descriptions of expectations

Using a single example of assessment evidence is not recommended if the intent is to formulate inferences about overall levels of student achievement. Analyzing evidence from one source can help determine how well or how poorly a student performed on this particular assignment. In addition, any pattern noted in *one* assessment can be tracked through additional assessments for later verification on revision of inferences. Exhibit 8.1 illustrates an example of a teacher's examination of the results of a single assessment in order to draw some *initial* inferences about a student's learning. A fifth grade teacher was concerned about one of her student's reading comprehension so she pulled this student aside and asked her to retell what she just silently read. In doing so, the teacher discovered that the student, when prompted, could not explain what the story was about. Since the target of this assessment was to see whether the student comprehended what was read, the teacher persisted with the retell to probe the student for answers to some key questions about the text. In other words, the teacher sought more information before making inferences from her observational data. The teacher also asked herself a few questions about this assessment of reading prior to making any inferences or analyzing the evidence collected during the retell:

- Was the reading passage too difficult for this student? Could this be affecting the student's comprehension? That is, perhaps the teacher has made a faulty assumption about the student's reading level and is unable to assess comprehension on this text.

- Was the student intimidated with retelling the text out loud to an adult? If so, the emotional state of the student may have resulted in a poor performance even though the student's actual reading skills are high. Developing a risk-free learning environment for students is important for quality evidence to be collected.

- Was lack of fluency the problem? If the student's poor performance was due to a low pace of reading, the student needs to work especially on this skill. Assessing the student with a less complex, more easily comprehended reading passage may help diagnose whether fluency is the real problem.

- Was difficulty in focusing on meaning the problem, and if so, what other assessments and texts would help formulate a fuller picture of this student's reading level before making any inferences? In other words, creating a reading profile of the student's reading evidence may be needed.

These questions help demonstrate that reliable inferences about student learning cannot be made unless (1) there is an understanding of the purpose of the assessment, (2) the evidence collected is sound, and (3) there is sufficient evidence upon which to base good decisions. As in this case, further assessment is often found to be necessary. As stated previously, one assessment, or one type of assessment, does not give enough evidence to draw valid conclusions about the student's overall performance.

Cumulative Assessments

The data available for each student will be found in many forms. However, trying to use *every* piece of available data collected on a student can be overwhelming and unnecessary. What inferences can be made from the data is more important than the

---

EXHIBIT 8.1. STUDENT ASSESSMENT CONFERENCE FORM: FIFTH GRADE.

Student: Marge Evans — Individual Reading Conference 2/10. Marge is having difficulties in class and reading may be a problem. Will conduct an IRC for several weeks to see if I can isolate if and what her problems in reading are and get extra help for her.	
Text: Teen magazine article: Do Students Have Too Much Stuff?	
Teacher thinking questions	1. Did the student actually read the text? Was it interesting enough? 2. Was the text too hard to read? 3. Did the student have enough time to read the text? 4. Was the student off-task during read time?
Strengths	Marge, when asked, admitted she was more involved with looking at the pictures and did not read the article. I explained to Marge that I was assessing her reading comprehension and that she must read the text in order for me to do this.
Next steps for now . . .	Next week during read time, remind Marge to read the text. Send a note home to remind parents that Marge needs to read. Ask them to find some

actual number of sources to use. To get a useful cumulative picture of students' performance, teachers must learn how to select the most relevant, reliable, and valid information to use in making decisions about student progress.

As an example in selecting reliable (showing consistency of scores across evaluation over time or across different versions of the assessment) and valid (assessments that measure what they are intended to measure) evidence, consider Sam, a math student. To make reliable and valid inferences about Sam's performance level in math, which of the following pieces of evidence should a teacher select?

- Sam's IQ scores
- Sam's math scores on a state criterion referenced test of mathematical skills
- Sam's self-report of his math performance
- Sam's parent's assessment of his math performance
- Sam's portfolio of math work
- Sam's word problem solving ability from one assignment

Sam's IQ score, his self-report, his parent's assessment, and one example of his problem-solving ability would provide some evidence of his math performance, but basing inferences on such evidence is questionable. More valid and reliable inferences can be drawn by looking at criterion-referenced data or from a portfolio of Sam's work, since both assessments would show progress based upon clearly defined standards.

The following data analysis processes are useful in looking for patterns and trends (described both qualitatively and quantitatively) in student learning cumulative assessments:

- Change over time data
- Anecdotal data
- Grade distributions
- Assignments distributions

Change Over Time Data (Trends in Performance). An example of using change over time might be to peruse a student's portfolio of essays. A teacher could examine such a portfolio to note progress made. The portfolio could help diagnose particular areas or weaknesses that still need to be addressed. Perhaps the portfolio shows satisfactory performance, rather than highlighting weaknesses. In this case, the teacher could feel assured that the student is ready to progress to other forms of writing.

Growth portfolios (covered in Chapter Five) are excellent methods for documenting change over time. Such assessment instruments contain many data and therefore qualify as "bodies of evidence." *Bodies of evidence* can be defined as systematic, regular samplings of a student's performance relative to a range of learning targets. Bodies of evidence such as portfolios are used to make inferences about student learning and can aid the teacher in differentiating instruction for particular students.

Besides portfolios, other assessments that provide bodies of evidence include "running" records, student work samples, videos or audiotapes of performances, and anecdotal notes. Assessment bodies of evidence document changes occurring over time and elucidate patterns of student learning.

Portfolios and the other bodies of evidence easily portray a change (or conversely, a lack of progress) in student performance. However, other methods also exist for observing trends in student performance. One example is a learning analysis sheet Nancy used in her science classes. For the curricular standard, Students will acquire science investigation skills in measurement, Nancy unpacked seven learning targets:

1. Making comparisons
2. Unit understanding
3. Unit use
4. Unit conversions
5. Data organization
6. Graphing
7. Use of measurement tools

When students worked on classroom and lab assignments, she analyzed them for the successful achievement of these learning targets, plus other targets specific to the particular tasks they did (see Exhibit 8.2). The targets outlined on the portion of the observational tool shown in Exhibit 8.2 changed as new content or learning targets were introduced and assessed.

Over time, Nancy noticed that for the targets listed on the observational tool, Michael consistently had difficulty with his unit conversions and measurement tools. This was her cue to tightly focus her assessment efforts toward discerning the particular area of difficulty Michael was experiencing with these learning targets. Group tutoring sessions focusing on the particular problems were held either during class or after school and included Michael as well as other students identified with the same problem. In these sessions, Nancy modeled taking measurements using thermometers, cylinders, and scales to help Michael understand how to extrapolate between lines on a scale. Then Michael was given extra practice on this skill and was able to enhance the precision of his measurements. Nancy discovered that Michael did not know equivalent measures in different scales, so he was unable to convert between two different scales. Without the target analysis instrument for capturing science investigation performances over time Nancy would have remained unaware of Michael's (and many of her other science students') difficulties.

EXHIBIT 8.2. EXAMPLE: SCIENCE OBSERVATIONAL TOOL—PREASSESSING MEASUREMENT SKILLS.

Science Class: Period 4

TARGETS (GH = groupings for additional help on selected targets)

	GH-A				GH-B		GH-C			GH-D
	Making Comparisons	Unit Understanding	Unit Use	Unit Conversions	Data Organization	Graphing	Mass	Density	Weight	Measurement Tools
Michael	✓	✓	✓	No	✓	✓	?	?	?	No
Michael does not understand M, D, and W relationships and how to use science tools. Michael needs to work with Groups D, C, and A when I cover these relationships again.										
Sam	✓	✓	✓	✓	?	No	✓	✓	✓	✓
Sam has limited knowledge of taking data from a table and making a graph. Needs practice. Will give Sam some graphing activities for homework to work on. Attend Group B session.										
Terry	✓	✓	✓	✓	✓	✓	✓	✓	✓	✓
Terry can move on with mass, density, and weight lab.										
Donnie	Yes	No	No	No	—	—	—	—	—	—
Donnie will join Sandy, Bryan, Lakisha, and me in Group A on units. He also needs to join Group C and D sessions on mass, density, weight, and tools.										
Caroline	✓	✓	?	?	✓	✓	?	?	?	No

Similarly, another teacher who took the time to examine all the tests taken by one of her low-performing students found that the student simply marked the "C" choice for *all* multiple choice questions. By noting this trend, the teacher was alerted to perform further diagnostic testing and eventually design an intervention to address the student's reading deficiencies.

Anecdotal Data (Observational Data). Anecdotal notes are simply descriptions of student behaviors or performances written by the teacher either as they happen or shortly after they occur.

An example that may help elucidate this data analysis process (anecdotal data) is one drawn from the area of reading. The learning target emphasized in this example is oral fluency. The teacher must first decide what type of evidence (relative to the learning target) to collect that would be the most useful in determining the student's oral fluency. Many possible choices from which the teacher may select an appropriate evidence source include reading logs, audiotapes of readings, read aloud sessions with the student, written responses to prompts, and individual reading conference (IRC) notes (anecdotal in nature). These anecdotal notes are collected from the reading conference, which includes a student-teacher dialogue, a teacher observation, and student oral performance.

After the reading conference, the teacher records specific anecdotal notes about the reader's performance. Exhibit 8.3 displays conference notes from a sample IRC. Note particularly that the anecdotal record contains descriptions of the student performance, as well as suggestions of instructional modifications that may be attempted with this student. These suggested modifications are grounded in the inferences formulated from the data collected in the conference.

Grade Distributions (Range of Scores and Item Analysis). Sometimes it is only after an assessment is graded that weaknesses in the assessment design become apparent or patterns of performance in learning become clear. Grade distributions can be used to determine whether assignments or tasks used as assessments need to be readjusted or revised or whether concepts need to be retaught. Although it is more common to use test data to show individual student performance trends, trends embedded in test data can also illuminate the instructional needs of the whole class. For example, a graph like the one in Figure 8.2 might show that 66 percent of the students made above 71 percent on a particular assessment task. However, this also means that 34 percent of the students did not do well enough. Such data should cause the teacher to ask: What instructional strategies might help the low-performing students to understand this information before the class moves on to new material?

EXHIBIT 8.3. IRC CONFERENCE NOTES: ANECDOTAL DATA.

Conference Notes: Student B   Target: Oral Fluency

Reading: Sadako and the Thousand Paper Cranes

- Read word-for-word rather than in meaningful phrases
- Read a little more expressively at first; then used monotone
- Often pointed to each word
- Lost place several times
- Did not pause at commas and reads past periods

Teacher Modifications for Instruction: Conducted a mini-lesson. Modeled fluent reading by reading some passages to the student. Asked the student to take the videotape of his reading and listen to himself, then re-read and re-record the text. Also, gave student some easier text to practice reading at home.

Source: Reagan, 2003.

FIGURE 8.2. GRADE DISTRIBUTION DATA FOR AN ASSESSMENT TASK.

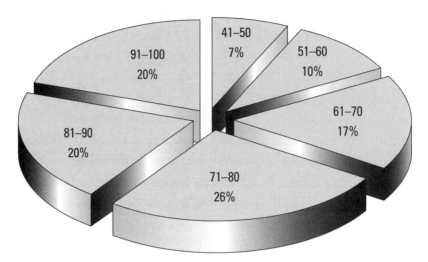

Or the teacher may need to ask: Is there a problem with the task that caused 34 percent of the students to perform poorly?

Another use of grade distribution data is portrayed in Figure 8.3. Here the teacher has graphed the class results for the past three chapter tests (all summative assessments). The graph clearly shows that students did not perform as well on the PS test as they did on the other two measures. Such data should lead the teacher to question the validity of this exam. He may wish to examine the test to see that the learning targets were aligned to the assessment method, and he may wish to reflect upon the instructional strategies used to prepare students for the exam. After such a process of analysis and reflection, the teacher may decide the scores are not valid and that they should not be recorded in the grade book. Susan and Nancy both used this type of test analysis for their science summative tests and found it useful to look at class test items also. If over 50 percent of students missed an item, the decision was made to throw out the item or reteach it based on what the students stated was the problem. Most high schools have Scantron machines (machines that score selected response items) that can quickly run a test item analysis so it is just a matter of looking at the items. More important, the key to this analysis is talking about the items most missed with students and making inferences as to whether the item was missed because students did not understand the item or whether there were other problems with the item.

Assignment Distributions (Assignment Trends). It is common for teachers to use several procedures for looking at trends and patterns when analyzing data and reaching a decision about instruction. For example, a teacher may look at trends over time and notice that Chris has not been completing homework assignments and is doing poorly on classroom quizzes. Anecdotal inferences of classroom assignments

FIGURE 8.3. GRADE DISTRIBUTIONS FOR THREE ASSESSMENTS.

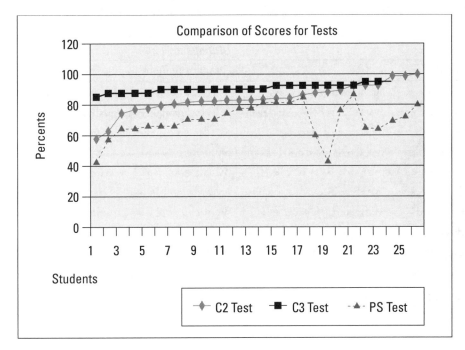

and grade results revealed that Chris does better when working in classroom groups or doing in-class work. In looking over grade distribution reports in Figure 8.4, the teacher finds that Chris may not work well independently or maybe has other problems. Table 8.1 describes inferences the teacher might make based upon these separate analyses and enumerates possible courses of action she may explore to aid Chris. This analysis may also force the teacher to rethink the purpose for and grading of homework if the whole class data showed the same trends.

FIGURE 8.4. CHRIS: PATTERNS OBSERVED IN QUARTER 4 WORK.

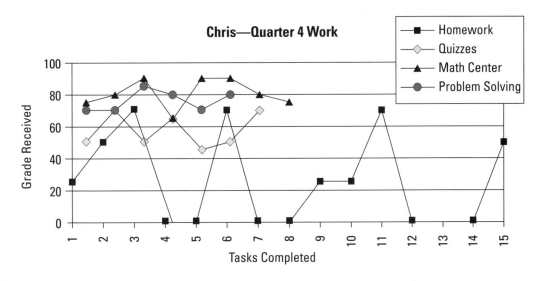

**TABLE 8.1. TEACHER INFERENCES AND ACTION PLAN:
POOR-PERFORMING STUDENT IN FIFTH GRADE MATH.**

Inferences	*Actions to Take*
Teacher thoughts:	Teacher thoughts:
Chris is not doing well on his homework assignments and does not complete most of them. This is affecting his total math grade. What is the problem with Chris on completing work on his own like homework and in-class quizzes? Chris is doing better in working with groups in the Math Center and on problem-solving activities. Do these grades represent that others are completing his work or does Chris have a reading problem that hinders his working independently?	I need to show Chris this assignment distribution graph and talk about any problems he has regarding completing his homework and see what we can do together. Maybe he needs a tutor after school to help him complete his math assignments. I also need to pay closer attention to his reading during scheduled reading times to note any problems he may have and begin making some formal observations during his group work time.

By observing behavior in various contexts, using diverse instruments, and implementing different analysis procedures, teachers will develop a more accurate picture of what their students know and are able to do.

Sometimes, however, the greatest challenge for teachers is not which data to collect or which analysis procedure to use. Rather, it is how to organize the data set in such a way that meaning can be derived from it. Organization, therefore, is the next topic of discussion in this chapter.

How to Create Valid Inferences from Multiple Data Sources

The challenge for the teacher is to lay out the data from daily assessments and tasks in such a way that shows which students need additional help in achieving the learning targets. None of the analyses of these assessments requires complex statistical knowledge. All are doable with simple mathematical computation, and all can be used to investigate gaps in student achievement and to learn more about underlying reasons for low performance (*Parent Press,* 2001).

Classroom assessment data may be organized in myriad ways. Some teachers use portfolios of student performance while others house evidence of student learning in electronic data warehouses. Some teachers create their own instruments to summarize the data (review Exhibit 8.2) and make it more accessible. Some teachers create charts or graphs to help them track student progress (review Figures 8.2–8.4). All of these methods are discussed in this section, and advantages as well as disadvantages of the various methods are enumerated. No matter which method is used, the purpose of data organization is to make the data accessible (easy to interpret). It is only by collecting quality data and then accurately interpreting such data that valid inferences can be formulated.

Portfolio Use

The use of portfolios is one type of organizational tool that allows both students and teachers to access assessment data. The purpose of the portfolio must, however, be aligned to the primary goal of data analysis. This goal is to first make valid inferences and then formulate conclusions that can be useful when forming decisions about the appropriate instructional modifications to make within the classroom.

Notebooks and student folders may not be good tools for organizing data for instructional purposes. Notebooks contain the sum total of all student work. Trying to use a notebook to inform instructional decisions may be overwhelming, as the quantity of data is simply too large. "Organizational folders" often found in elementary classrooms are examples of notebook-type artifacts that may also have little utility in classroom assessment data organization because of their bulk. Such folders often contain a plethora of formative information, including skill and strategy checklists, reading responses, logs, journal entries, teacher observations and anecdotal notes, student self-assessments, personal goal sheets, writing samples, reports, parent-student conference sheets, group and self-evaluation records, and perhaps even quizzes, reports, unit tests, and other products.

Portfolios, because they are purposeful collections of student work, are much less bulky than notebooks. *They do not* contain the entire spectrum of student work but a sampling of this work.

Teacher Centered Data: Worksheet Analysis

Observation is a powerful assessment process in a classroom, but organizing evidence collected on such observation is difficult. Nancy used the analysis sheet shown in Exhibit 8.2 in her physical science class to note when students grasped understanding of measurement. This method allowed her to organize multiple sources of information on measurement skills prior to allowing students to conduct a lab, where students needed to be skilled at each of the learning targets outlined. As noted in Exhibit 8.2 she made inferences about each student based upon her observations and then set up groups based on patterns of problems she noted. She was then able to work with each group and give far more in-depth instruction on noted problem areas.

Electronic Data Usage

Many schools have electronic data warehouses that allow teachers to keep track of classroom and school data and that can be used to analyze student learning results. However, entering the data can be a burden on already overworked teachers. If the data are already online, running information to show classroom sets or individual student profiles would help determine which students may need some additional help or which students should be grouped for extra instruction.

Three targeted learning goals illustrated in Figure 8.5 are the grade level results for student reading strategies, vocabulary, and comprehension. This graph could be created from a data warehouse based on the reported scores for each target in the last quarter. This graph (showing only nine students here) helps the teacher identify which student(s) may need additional help on a target. The teacher can then plan to conference with individual students or groups before instruction for the next quarter begins. Students 3 and 6 in Figure 8.5 are struggling with the learning-target reading strategies (both received scores of 3). The planning sheet in Exhibit 8.4 shows the inferences the teacher made from the data for student number 3. This reader is struggling with all three targets, strategies, comprehension, and vocabulary. Therefore, the teacher completed a planning sheet to note possible instructional modifications that may need to be made to help this student work on reading weaknesses. Often, working to enhance performance on one target (such as strategies) may pull up other targets (such as comprehension and vocabulary scores).

Thus, the planning chart in Exhibit 8.4 serves as a screening device that allows teachers to plan for students who need concentrated instructional modifications. The resulting plan in Exhibit 8.4 outlines some possible teacher actions. Of course, creating such a plan for *all students* and then following all the steps incorporated in Exhibit 8.4 would entail a lot of work from the teacher. The beauty of the plan is that not all students need this level of instructional modifications (see Chapter Nine).

FIGURE 8.5. STUDENT READING PROFILES.

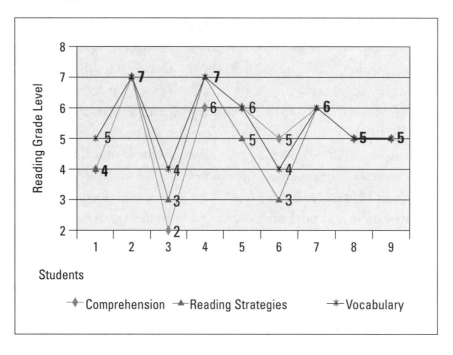

EXHIBIT 8.4. PLANS FOR STUDENT 3 FOR NEXT QUARTER.

Targets: Reading Strategies   **Student: 3**   **Group: C**

Analysis: Overall student is weak in strategies, comprehension, and vocabulary. Major need is to work on strategies so he can use them when no one else is sitting next to him reading.

Data Sources:
- IRC
- Cloze activity
- Short readings
- Strategy checks

Tools to Use:
- Strategy checklist
- Easier text
- Group help
- Tutor

Review

Modifications:
- Post and model appropriate strategies usage
- Ask student to self-assess use of strategies by using self-checks
- Practice before, during, and after reading strategies
- Will begin vocabulary strategies and reassess comprehension with IRC

Date: October 25th
Reassess for strategy use December 15th

Alert: Check with former reading teacher and student's record to see prior use of strategies. Check with reading specialist for instructional strategies other teachers can use with this student.

Source: McMunn and Reagan, 2004.

In Part Two we emphasized the need to collect quality assessment data. In Part Three we built upon this need for quality data and attempted to describe multiple ways to analyze collected data and make inferences from the data. In this chapter we have also endeavored to present sample analyses that teachers may find useful as guides when they begin their own data analysis processes. As teachers begin to analyze, make inferences, and formulate interpretations, they also need to focus on the primary goal of all these activities. This goal is to use data to advance student learning. Educators should beware of using data just for the purposes of calculating grades or for labeling students. Data analysis that does not lead to instructional modifications designed to improve student performance is data wasted. Chapter Nine is designed to address the challenge of linking assessment information to such instructional decision-making processes.

Linking Assessment to Instruction

Instructional plans and modifications are carried out

As we discussed in Chapter Eight, "Tracking and Analyzing Results," the teacher diagnoses student deficiencies and then plans strategies to help the student. When assessments reflect high-quality practices, these give the teacher good information about the students' learning needs. Then, any decisions related to instructional modifications can take into account and accommodate these student needs and ultimately lead to improved learning. Moreover, classroom assessments should blur the border that separates assessment from instruction. When assessments define learning targets for students and describe quality performances, they are, in fact, instructional for the students. Students can use the assessment instruments to measure their own academic progress. Such instructional assessment methods can increase student motivation for learning, as well as enhance students' abilities to self-assess.

Assessments should provide students with strategies to use to enhance performance. Students who experience excellent classroom assessment become more self-reliant learners. Through classroom assessment, they internalize learning strategies taught by the teacher and can later access these strategies when confronted with similar assessment challenges. For example, a student who learns about context clues during an individual reading conference can easily use this strategy on a large-scale, high-stakes assessment test. Thus, determining whether students have and use the right learning strategies is key to quality assessment.

Once assessment data describe a level of proficiency for the student, the teacher's next step should be to design instructional modifications to help the student improve. The instructional modification step, however, is one that is rarely completed. It is far more usual to see teachers perform an assessment, assign a grade, and move on, regardless of individual student understanding. One author of this book piloted the development of a reading program with third through eighth grade teachers over several years. The data collected consistently showed that most teachers stopped at the "making inferences" quadrant of the Classroom Assessment Cycle without either formulating interpretations of the data or planning instructional interventions. Mostly, the teachers simply moved on to the next content-block or topic.

For the Classroom Assessment Cycle to be complete, it is imperative that teachers diagnose problems by looking at the evidence (data) and then plan appropriate instructional modifications or interventions as next steps for each student.

We address these issues in Part Four (Chapters Nine and Ten). Once assessment data are collected and conclusions about student achievement are drawn, an instructional plan or strategy for helping the student should be formulated and implemented. As we describe in Chapter Nine, "Revising Feedback and Instructional Plans," for maximum effect, the modified instruction must address the individual differences in achievement. For example, students may earn the same low score on a standardized test, but the reasons behind their poor performances may differ. Some students may be lacking content knowledge, whereas others have reading difficulties that hamper their understanding of the question. "One size fits all" instruction will not address the different needs of all students.

Differentiating instruction requires a repertoire of instructional approaches to align with different learning targets. It requires giving students effective feedback about performance. Ultimately, it requires that teachers examine their beliefs about assessment and make a conscious effort to modify teaching practices so they focus on what students need to know.

In Chapter Ten, "Using Assessment to Motivate Students," we approach the question of modifying instruction from the viewpoint of instruction that supports student motivation to learn.

Revising Feedback and Instructional Plans

9

This chapter focuses on rounding out the Classroom Assessment Cycle by following through with feedback to students and instructional modifications. Once assessment data are collected and inferences about student achievement are drawn, an instructional modification or strategy for helping the student is planned. This planning can address any achievement gaps uncovered in the process of data collection and analysis.

This last and fourth quadrant of the Classroom Assessment Cycle addresses carrying out instructional modifications for one learner, a group of learners, or a classroom of learners. Often teachers have the evidence to identify weaknesses in student learning, but fail to follow through by providing the instructional support the student needs to improve his performance. Here we focus on methods of making that follow-through occur.

This quadrant of the cycle emphasizes differentiating instruction for one or more students based on the analysis of assessment data. It is not helpful to ascertain that several students earned the same low score on a summative test and then decide to use the same instructional intervention with all of the low-performing students when the reasons underlying each student's poor performance may differ. Differentiating instruction to match the needs of students is critical if learning is to improve.

In addition to identifying differentiation needs, this quadrant of the cycle also emphasizes modifying instruction to improve the overall quality of that instruction. Dimensions of quality instruction include assignments that are cognitively challenging, aligned to standards, validly assessed, have value beyond school, are motivating to students, and are appropriate for diverse learners. Properly understood, "Instruction involves directing students to appropriate learning activities; guiding students to appropriate knowledge; helping students rehearse, encode, and process information; monitoring student performance; and providing feedback as to the appropriateness of the student's learning activities and practice performance" (Merrill, Drake, Lacy, Pratt, and the ID$_2$ Research Group, 1996, p. 6).

As we presented in the Introduction, there are four "outside" factors that continually affect the Classroom Assessment Cycle, and two of these factors are deeply interwoven with modifying instruction: (1) a classroom environment promoting learning and (2) teacher beliefs and practices. We will also discuss teacher beliefs and practices in this chapter because modifying instruction to meet student needs does not occur without corresponding modifications in teachers' views of teaching. This chapter answers these questions:

- Why is it important to uncover teacher beliefs and examine current practices?

- Which instructional strategies best fit particular learning targets?

- What is good feedback and how does it improve instruction?

- What is differentiated instruction?

- What are research-based best practices of teaching and how are they translated into classroom instruction?

Teacher Beliefs and Current Practices

The authors have found that teachers' beliefs greatly influence their teaching practices. For example, if a teacher believes that some students are simply unable to learn, he will not invest a great deal of time in teaching these students. Similarly, if a teacher feels that the only way to motivate students to learn is through grading, very little formative assessment will be found in that teacher's classroom. Such beliefs and practices bear directly on the ability of teachers to implement new assessment and instructional strategies.

If teachers wish to improve their assessment and instructional practices, they often must first examine the underlying beliefs that inspire these practices. To this end, we frequently begin our professional development sessions with a reflection activity in which teachers are prompted to respond to survey questions that help uncover their deep-seated assessment beliefs. One such survey can be found in Table 9.1. Before continuing, the reader may wish to pause and respond to this survey.

Typically, in professional development sessions, several mismatches between "desirability" and "implementation" are found. The statements showing the widest disparity are often statements 1, 2, 4, 8, and 9, which deal with assessment of learning

TABLE 9.1. ASSESSMENT BELIEFS AND PRACTICES.

First, react to each statement by placing an "X" within the "Desirability" column to indicate whether you feel the statement is of high or low desirability. Then read each statement again and place an "X" within the "Implementation" column to indicate whether you, personally, implement the stated actions rarely (low) or regularly (high).

Statements About Assessment	Desirability					Implementation				
	Low				High	Low				High
	1	2	3	4	5	1	2	3	4	5
1. Conscious efforts are made to assess student progress relative to instructional goals that go beyond recall of information.				X				X		
2. Students' instructional needs are often assessed, and instructional decisions are often made based on student needs.			X			X				
3. Students can articulately discuss their progress on key instructional goals.				X		X				
4. Students are involved in self-evaluating their progress by gathering evidence (using a portfolio or other means) to show that they have mastered key competencies.	X								X	
5. The number of assignments for which letter grades or percentage scores are given is limited so that students focus more on learning than worrying about "the grade."				X					X	
6. Students often receive individualized feedback on assignments (oral and/or written comments) that will help them improve.					X		X			
7. The number of high grades given in a class is never limited. ?			X							X
8. Students have many opportunities to make choices and take charge of the way they will learn a particular topic.			X					X		
9. Talking with students about strengths and goals for improvement is key.		X					X			

Source: McMunn and Schenck, 1996.

targets, student involvement in assessment, and student learning autonomy (choice). Although most teachers agree that the actions described in these statements are desirable, most also admit that they are rarely implemented.

Another beginning survey is the self-checklist found in Exhibit 9.1. Like the previous survey, this instrument also asks teachers to examine their own assessment beliefs and practices. You may wish to complete this survey also. In the survey, the statements that get question (?) marks ("I need help on this") most often are numbers 2, 4, 5, 7, 8, and 9. These statements encompass assessment of learning targets, student involvement in assessment and learning, and instructional modification based upon assessment data.

EXHIBIT 9.1. SELF-CHECKLIST: PROMOTING ASSESSMENT FOR LEARNING.

Please react to the statements below, using the following codes:
✓ : I understand and do
○ : I understand but do not do this
? : I need help on this

1. I understand and can articulate in advance of teaching the achievement targets my students are to hit.
2. I inform my students regularly about the achievement targets in terms they can understand.
3. I can transform these achievement targets into dependable assessments that yield accurate information about learning.
4. I understand the relationship between assessment and student motivation, and I use assessment to build student confidence.
5. I consistently use classroom assessment information to revise instruction.
6. I give frequent and descriptive (often specific) feedback to students that inform their learning.
7. My students are actively involved in their own assessment.
8. My students actively communicate with others about their achievement status and improvement.
9. My students can describe what achievement targets they are to hit and what comes next in their learning.

Source: Adapted from Stiggins, R. J., Arter, J. A., Chappius, J., and Chappius, S. (2004). *Classroom Assessment for Student Learning: Doing It Right—Using It Well* (Figure 2.3, p. 51). Assessment Training Institute, 317 S. W. Alder, Suite 12000, Portland, Oregon 97204. Reprinted with permission.

From the results we have reviewed in numerous training sessions using the two surveys, it is clear that the majority of respondents do not routinely

- Inform students about assessment results or instructional goals
- Involve students in assessment
- Assess student performance relative to instructional goals
- Differentiate instruction based on assessment information.
- Encourage student autonomy

All of these bulleted activities are important in carrying out the Classroom Assessment Cycle. For example, the first three activities in the bulleted list are critical both to clarifying learning targets and to collecting evidence of student learning, the first two quadrants of the cycle. Encouraging student autonomy whereby students are given some choice in assessment or learning is significant to these quadrants also, as well as to modifying instruction. Last, differentiating instruction based on assessment information clearly involves the quadrants of analyzing data and modifying instruction.

Once the survey results are tabulated for the participants in our professional development session, we often discuss the results with the whole group, particularly highlighting the mismatches found between the desirability and implementation sections of the first survey and also highlighting the numbers with question marks on the second survey. It was in one of these whole group discussions that Marcie, a math teacher, articulated a response representative of the feelings of many other teacher participants:

> When you lay it out like that, it makes me realize that I'm still assessing students the way I was assessed. My teachers never told us what we were supposed to learn and we were never involved in the assessment process (unless we graded each others' papers when the teacher called out the answers). The only results I really got were graded papers and report cards and those always came *after* a task. I don't remember ever having an assessment that helped me understand what I needed to study in order to improve. It's depressing, but I see myself doing these same things, now that I'm a teacher. Assessment is something I do at the end of teaching [Butler, personal communication, 1999].

Marcie's statement reiterates sentiments we have heard again and again: (1) teachers assess as they were assessed and (2) assessment is viewed as an ending activity, rather than as an ongoing activity.

If such beliefs and practices perpetuate, there is little chance that improvement in assessment will take place. How can teachers climb out of this unrelenting cycle of "assess as you were assessed?" What might help teachers see assessment as a continuous process, constantly interwoven with instruction? The kind of information we have presented so far may be helpful. In addition, in the remainder of this chapter we will examine instructional concepts that may help teachers see practical ways to begin the process of changing their own instructional strategies and practices.

Instructional Strategies to Fit Particular Learning Targets

To improve instruction, teachers need to choose instructional strategies that meet the student needs they have identified. Instructional strategies are approaches to instruction that enhance student learning. For example, Marzano, Pickering, and Pollock (2001) list nine instructional strategies that they find to have the greatest impact on student achievement. These nine are "identifying similarities and differences, summarizing and note taking, reinforcing effort and providing recognition, homework and practice, nonlinguistic representations, cooperative learning, setting objectives and providing feedback, generating and testing hypotheses and questions, cues and advance organizers" (2001, p. 146). Most qualified teachers would read this list and immediately recognize and identify with it, as most are using these types of learning strategies already.

Instructional strategies in general, then, are all the classroom activities that support student learning. Experienced teachers have found, however, that some work better than others. Which ones are the "good" instructional strategies? They are the ones that enable active learning to occur in the classroom; ones that involve students in their own learning. Is there one "magic" strategy? No. The teacher must differentiate strategies; she must use a variety of strategies in order to activate the diverse learning styles of the student population. Consistent use of the same strategy (note taking, for example) can quickly turn students off. Thus, using a variety of instructional strategies is a key to unlocking student motivation, an accomplishment that can then lead to enhanced learning.

One way to categorize instructional strategies is to organize them according to the instructional model they tend to support. For example, the *direct instructional model* often features teacher-centered instructional strategies (lecturing, modeling, and demonstrating). However, such strategies may also be categorized according to the purpose (or target) of instruction. Table 9.2 presents a modified table used by Prince William County Schools in Virginia (2004) that associates learning targets (behavior, cognitive, application-process, and other) with general instructional strategies. Such an organizing scheme can be useful to teachers who are seeking to choose appropriate instructional strategies to match particular learning targets.

If the learning target (refer to Table 9.2) is a skill target, strategies listed under Behavior will be the best match, as these include demonstrating and modeling the skill for the students.

The modified chart displayed in Table 9.2 is a useful tool, then, for helping select appropriate instructional strategies. As we saw in Chapter Two when unpacking

TABLE 9.2. INSTRUCTIONAL STRATEGIES.

Behavior	*Cognitive*	*Application/Process*	*Other*
More skill mastery, learning facts symbols, recalling content, or just rote learning. Learning is more teacher directed.	Creative, critical, and reflective thinking are key. Concept attainment and development are important. Learning is collaborative between the teacher and student.	Process is key. Learning focus is problem-based or activity-based. Creative, critical, and synthesizing thinking are important. Teacher is a facilitator of learning.	Some strategies are common to all areas of learning. They are appropriate for all content areas also.
Strategies include:	Strategies include:	Strategies include:	Strategies include:
• Demonstrations • Modeling • Lecture • Puzzles/games • Mnemonic strategies • Discussion • Cooperative learning • Jigsaws • Choral readings • Creating lists • Vocabulary building	• Brainstorming • Reciprocal teaching • Concept mapping • Simulations • Role playing • KWL • Direct reading • Thinking activities • Kagan structures (Think/Pair Share, Round table, etc.) • Summarizing and note taking • Conversations • Creating metaphors • Using analogies	• Conflict resolution • Information management • Advance organizers • Debates • Inquiry based (like scientific method) • Interviews • Projects • Socratic seminars • Thematic units • Seeking out answers to questions • Testing hypothesis • Problem solving	• Homework • Practice • Providing feedback • Identifying similarities and differences • Questioning • Reinforcing effort • Providing recognition • Setting learning goals • Cooperative learning • Conducting learning styles questionnaires • Guided practice • Self-assessment

Source: Prince William County Schools, Virginia (http://www.pwcs.edu/curriculum/sol/flowchart1.html).

standards for embedded learning targets, there is a great deal of overlap among these categories. Just as the knowledge learning target overlaps all others (including reasoning, skills, products, and dispositional targets), the Cognitive category overlaps all the others in Table 9.2. This means that some strategies listed under Behavior or Application/Process would also apply to Cognitive and vice versa. When using this chart as a tool, teachers should simply view strategies listed under categories as strong matches, but should feel free to "borrow" strategies from other categories, if appropriate.

In the following sections, we describe one or more specific instructional strategies that a teacher might choose for each of the learning target categories (what students should know and be able to do).

Behavior

Since behavior-learning targets (see Table 9.2) are concerned with skill mastery or recall of information, the instructional strategies employed must aid students in learning basic facts. Although recall of information is not a higher-order thinking skill, it is still a very important one. For example, many vocations have specific vocabulary words associated with them. *Mnemonic strategies* use a systematic procedure to aid memory. Teachers can model such strategies for students, like the science teacher who teaches the phrase "<u>K</u>ing <u>P</u>hillip <u>C</u>ried <u>O</u>ut <u>F</u>or <u>G</u>oodness' <u>S</u>ake" to help students remember the classification hierarchy of organisms (<u>K</u>ingdom, <u>P</u>hylum, <u>C</u>lass, <u>O</u>rder, <u>F</u>amily, <u>G</u>enus, <u>S</u>pecies). Most people use aids like this often in everyday life, and mnemonic devices such as this have shown high effectiveness as memory aids (Mastropieri, Scruggs, Bakken, & Brigham, 1992). The brain works to make meaning of concepts "by establishing and reworking patterns, relationships, and connections" (Ewell, 1997, p. 6). Mnemonic strategies help students associate data into large chunks, which are more easily accessed and retrieved from storage "compartments" in the brain. Therefore, helping students use mnemonic devices could be useful, especially when it is important for them to remember many data.

Other instructional strategies that enable students to achieve behavior-learning targets include choral-reading and vocabulary-building exercises. Both of these exercises can improve student comprehension of concepts, particularly when students are expected to glean information from text materials. If students cannot read well or use the information they read, comprehending content becomes very difficult. Instructional strategies that enhance a student's reading abilities are appropriate to use in all content areas. (The best reading teacher for content is the content area teacher, as he knows the specialized vocabulary needed to understand course concepts.)

One of us (Nancy) was given a wake-up call about reading levels among her high school students during a tenth grade biology class. In a lesson on photosynthesis she spent a lot of time unpacking vocabulary terms new to students, through analogies, prefix-suffix, and Latin routes to break words down for meaning. Nancy asked the class to look at *photo* (which means "light") and *synthesis* (which means "to make") which together mean "to make with light." This sounds too simple for high school students, but Nancy felt that it was an excellent instructional strategy.

After class was over one of Nancy's students approached her (a student who had already failed biology three times) and said, "Today you helped me understand that what you were writing on the board was what you were saying to us. I never realized that the words in books were the same as what you write and say, thanks."

After the student left, Nancy stood there thinking, "I've got students who cannot read, in fact, who have a very difficult time understanding text. How did he ever make it to the tenth grade? And how am I going to help him understand biology?" He passed that year, and that day's experience prompted Nancy to take more steps to understand her students before instruction took place.

Teachers, like Nancy, who wish to aid students in vocabulary building need to provide a variety of texts to students and help them draw on context clues as well as interact with words in order to continue to build their vocabulary for specific content.

Cognitive

When the target is cognitive learning (see Table 9.2), students are asked to go beyond simple recall and instead perform critical or reflective thinking to delve deeply into content. One instructional strategy that can aid students in achieving this learning target is the use of a Question Quilt.

The Question Quilt, illustrated in Exhibit 9.2, is simply a graphic organizer in which students create and then record various kinds of questions about a unit of study, text they are reading, or other specific content currently being studied. Before students can complete a Question Quilt, however, they must understand that questions can be classified by categories. The typical hierarchy can be that of Bloom's taxonomy (Bloom, 1956) (recall, application, analysis, synthesis, and evaluation) or the Bloom's revision (Anderson, et al., 2001), which lists six categories, rather than five (remember, understand, apply, analyze, evaluate, and create). During each week of instruction, student groups work together to create questions designed to conform to these levels. The process of question generation focuses student attention on concepts that they have difficulty comprehending. This process also enhances the cognitive challenge of classroom activities, as students are asked to create (and be prepared to answer) questions that require higher-order thinking skills.

Teachers need to create classrooms that enhance cognition, ones that incorporate open-ended activities, higher-order questioning, and problem solving. In such classrooms, students are held to high expectations and the instructional strategies used by the teacher help the students meet these expectations.

Application/Process

Instructional strategies used for application/process learning targets (see Table 9.2) tend to be activity-based and higher level. Here, students may grapple with problems,

EXHIBIT 9.2. QUESTION QUILT: CLASSROOM EXAMPLE.

Questions created and posted by students for a particular unit of study and displayed in the classroom for review can be outlined in this format.

Bloom's Level	Questions Week 1	Questions Week 2	Questions Week 3	Questions Week 4	Questions Week 5
Recall (Often broken down into Knowledge and Comprehension)	Label the parts of the human cell.	Define in writing the word *mitochondria.*	Name three functions of the nucleus of an animal cell.	Who coined the term cell?	Match the structure with the function of the listed parts.
Application	Categorize the cell structures as plant, animal, or both.	?	?	?	?
Analysis	Compare and contrast plant and animal cells	?	?	?	?
Synthesis	Using the graph, predict the influence of salt water on the celery (plant) cells.	?	?	?	?
Evaluation	Argue that cell size is limited and that number of cells determines size of animals.	?	?	?	?

Source: McMunn and Schenck, 1996.

EXHIBIT 9.3. SEMINAR PLAN.

Topic: Dolley Madison's Role in American History
Key Skills: Reading Comprehension, Analysis, Research

Goal: To explore a female citizen's role in history.

Pre-Activities	Seminar Questions	Post-Activities
Students: Read the letter from Dolley Madison to her sister Read the letter from Dolley Madison to Mrs. Benjamin Latrobe **Teacher:** Pose probing questions	**Opening (Exploring):** In the first letter, to whom is Mrs. Madison writing? Where is she located? In the second letter, to whom is Mrs. Madison writing? What has changed in the time between the two letters? **Core-Examining Stage:** Why is James Madison not present at the White House? What has the president asked Mrs. Madison to do while she is there? What has she been doing while she waits? Who else is with her in the White House at the time? At what point does Dolley Madison decide she needs to leave the White House? **Expanding and Relating Stage:** What additional information do you learn about Dolley Madison in the second letter? About the White House? Which letter is more "emotional?" "personal?" Explain.	**Language Arts and History:** Create a theatrical scenario using the events that Dolley Madison described as the basis for your script and then use your imagination to complete the scene. Include the following: major characters, setting, and dialogue. **Art:** What major historical artifacts were saved by Dolley Madison? Make a list and then research to find where these pieces are located today. **Social Studies:** Modern first ladies have called Mrs. Madison a role model. Choose at least one other first lady and examine how she viewed her role as first lady. Then, based on her views and on Dolley Madison's views, write a job description for the post of "first lady." Go further and describe the desirable attributes for a first lady.

Evaluation Plan
Language Arts and History: Assess with Dramatic Enactment Rubric
Art: Assess with Research Rubic
Social Studies: Assess with Essay Rubic

Source: Butler, 2004.

pursue inquiries, or create projects. One instructional strategy that many teachers use to help students achieve application/process targets is the presentation of a seminar.

Exhibit 9.3 displays a planning sheet for a high school history class seminar on the role of a particular female citizen in history, Dolly Madison. This planning sheet contains both pre- and postactivities and lists probing questions the teacher will ask students during the seminar. The probing questions help students recall important information and then enhance the cognitive challenge of the activity, as students are pushed to think creatively and critically. The postseminar activities continue this push toward cognitive complexity, as students are required to create products, perform research, and produce a theatrical scenario.

This type of required student activity changes the role of the teacher from disseminator of knowledge to facilitator of knowledge and actively engages the students in their own learning processes.

Other

Within the Other category of learning targets (see Table 9.2), instructional strategies that cross disciplines are collected. These strategies (like the Question Quilt strategy discussed in the Cognitive section) are appropriate for use in all content areas as they provide basic learning support to students and can be used to strengthen behavior, cognitive, and application strategies. Examples of instructional strategies falling within this category include guided practice, homework, self-assessment, and teacher questioning as described in Chapter Four.

As the chart of instructional strategies (Table 9.2) demonstrates, there are multiple and diverse instructional strategies available to teachers. The bottom line, however, is finding the right strategy that helps students learn.

Good Feedback and How It Improves Instruction

In a synthesis of research on assessment, Black and Wiliam (1998) found five key assessment factors that lead to enhanced student learning. Among these factors was effective feedback. (The remaining four were student involvement in learning, modifying instruction based on assessment data, recognition of assessment influences on student motivation and self-esteem, and student self-assessment practices.) The relationship between feedback and modifying or improving instruction is illustrated in Figure 9.1. For learning to take place, three cyclical actions must occur:

FIGURE 9.1. LEARNING TAKES PLACE.

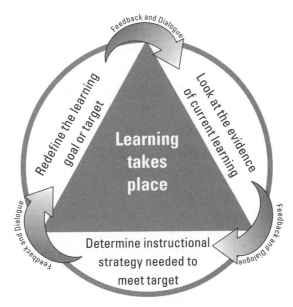

1. Teachers and students must examine the current evidence of learning relative to a learning target and decide whether additional instruction is needed.

2. They must determine an instructional strategy to meet the learning target, if one is warranted. After the strategy is applied, teachers and students reexamine evidence to see whether the learning target has been achieved ("learning takes place"). If it has, students may move on to address other targets. If it has not been achieved . . .

3. Teachers and students must refine or redefine the target based on the evidence. Throughout all these steps, feedback to the student and dialogue between the student and the teacher is essential.

Similarly, Black and Wiliam (1998, p. 143) state, "When anyone is trying to learn, feedback about the effort has three elements: redefinition of the desired goal, evidence about present position, and some understanding of the way to close the gap between the two. All three must be understood to some degree by anyone before he or she can take action to improve learning."

The following example and the illustration in Figure 9.1 set parameters for effective feedback. This example drawn from a middle school Spanish class may help clarify these parameters. Marcie, a Spanish student, is learning to speak fluent Spanish. The Spanish teacher, Mrs. Garcia, observes Marcie and comments, "Your *g* sounds need some work; your *g* sounds are the same for words like *amigo* and *guerra*." With these comments, Mrs. Gracia has provided feedback to Marcie on her performance by giving specific and clear information. Is this feedback effective? Perhaps Marcie understands the feedback and can improve, but an instructional strategy would certainly clarify the feedback for her. Mrs. Garcia might model for Marcie the difference in the *g* sounds once or several times. She may stand by as Marcie practices the sounds in several words, stepping in when needed to correct the sounds. Mrs. Garcia may also review the rules for the sounds with Marcie, stating that the *g* sound at the beginning of a word or after *n* is pronounced like the English word *guy* as in *guerra* or *ángulo* and that the *g* in other words, except before *e* or *i,* is pronounced like the English *g* in *sugar* as in *pago* or *amigo.* Mrs. Garcia may also ask Marcie to practice her pronunciations with other, more fluent Spanish speakers. Such modeling behavior (an instructional strategy) on the part of the teacher and students would greatly facilitate learning and be much more effective as feedback than simply oral statements.

Why was modeling the action and suggesting the student work with groups more effective than simple oral feedback? The answer to this question lies within the definitions of feedback and guidance. Mrs. Garcia gave *feedback* with her oral comments. However, she gave *guidance* to Marcie by modeling the correct behavior for her. *Effective feedback* includes both of these parameters, as defined below:

- Feedback is information that can be oral or written and should focus on helping pinpoint areas of strengths and weaknesses. Feedback should provide a person with information on how to improve, and if the feedback is "good" enough, guidance may not be needed. Feedback answers the "what do I need to know?" questions about the work. (Feedback needs to be addressed in the positive as much as possible.)

- Guidance is giving someone specific directions on what to do to improve performance. It usually follows feedback. Guidance answers the "how do I improve my work?" questions that students often may not ask [Wiggins, 1998].

The most effective feedback is

- Clear—Easily understood and legible, if written

- Accurate—In both the student's behavior and the teacher's conclusions

- Precise—Based on specific behavior, not just on generalizations

- Selective—Including important observations, especially patterns of behavior noted

- Timely—Given as soon as possible

Modifying or improving instructional strategies and giving effective feedback in response to assessment enhance student learning.

Exhibit 6.3 showed a feedback form a teacher completed as her students performed a text-based assessment discourse session. Once this teacher is finished giving individual students and groups their feedback on what their strengths are and what they need to work on, she may then look over all the completed assessment forms for the whole class and determine whether all her students need an instructional lesson on how to summarize facts and quotes or whether they need help in documenting specific information to support their thinking before discussing the text they read. She may also note that for the student groups to continue to improve in their thinking about texts they read, a survey of interests may need to be done. This would involve them more in the selection of the next text to read and discuss. Thus, this teacher is using the feedback from her observations and completed assessment forms to inform future instruction. In the process, this teacher is able to focus on some of the factors Black and Wiliam (1998) found as key assessment factors that lead to enhanced student learning (such as effective feedback, involvement of students, and modifying instruction).

Similarly, "The assessment environment of a classroom can vary from feedback that is very standardized and structured (test scores) to feedback that is very informal and unstructured (classroom dialogue). If the only feedback students receive is test scores, then they will likely assume that judgment, not improvement, is the teacher's goal. . . . Observations of the more- and less-motivating teachers subsequently showed that the more-motivating teachers used more informal, unstructured feedback mechanisms. The less-motivating teachers relied more exclusively on test scores as feed back for students" Meece and McColskey (1997, p. 43).

Differentiated Instruction

When teachers modify instructional plans to meet the needs of specific students, they differentiate instruction. *Differentiated instruction* simply means "teachers reacting responsively to a learner's needs" (Tomlinson & Allan, 2000, p. 5). Tomlinson (1999, pp. 7–8) states: "Differentiated classrooms feel right to students who learn in different ways and at different rates and who bring to school different talents and interests. More significantly, such classrooms work better for a full range of students than do one-size-fits-all settings. Teachers in differentiated classrooms are more in touch with their students and approach teaching more as an art than as a mechanical exercise."

This description is one that all teachers can strive to achieve. In striving, however, it is *not* necessary to differentiate instruction for every student, every day. Tomlinson (1999, p. 14) notes that such behavior is "impossible, and it would destroy a sense of wholeness in the class. Instead, the teacher selects moments in the instructional sequence to differentiate, based on formal or informal assessment. . . . Differentiation is an organized yet flexible way of proactively adjusting teaching and learning to meet kids where they are and help them to achieve maximum growth as learners."

The following scenario involving Hope Reagan, a reading teacher, and Christopher, a student in Ms. Reagan's class (identified here by a pseudonym), illustrates how a teacher uses all the elements of the classroom assessment cycle—including identification of learning targets, conducting quality assessments, and applying knowledge of instructional strategies—in order to differentiate instruction.

Ms. Reagan conducted an individual reading conference with each of her students at least every six weeks to pinpoint problems. Christopher was a sixth grade student. To unveil his patterns of performance, Ms. Reagan used the following five learning targets for reading: (1) oral fluency, (2) comprehension of what was read, (3) use of reading strategies, (4) higher-order thinking, and (5) motivation. Ms. Reagan's notes on Christopher during one conference relative to these learning targets are displayed in Table 9.3.

From this assessment, Ms. Reagan made the following inferences about this reader's comprehension:

- He is not reading *this text* for meaning.
- He is possibly letting his background knowledge overshadow the author's intent.
- Maybe he does not understand a fable.
- Maybe he needs help with key comprehension skills.
- Maybe he is unmotivated to read this text.

TABLE 9.3. IRC-TEACHER NOTES: MODIFYING INSTRUCTION.

Student: Christopher	Assessment: Individual Reading Conference Reading: Fable by Arnold Lobel, Crocodile in the Bedroom
Targets	Teacher notes after the conference
Oral Fluency	Read at a brisk pace Somewhat monotone reading No distinct voices for dialogue
Comprehension	Did not retell sequential events from the story Unsuccessfully attempted to summarize the passage Attempted summarization but did not follow the story line the author intended
Use of Strategies	Re-read for a second start, many times Inserted and substituted words that did not maintain the author's meaning Syntax now happy and secure (no self-correction). He must put on a pair (no self-correction) to protect . . .
Higher-Order Thinking	Interpreted "order" in his own way Avoided using textual evidences that explain moral choices
Motivation	Gave short answers with very little discussion Had head in hand most of the conference Gave very little eye contact—looked around the room when talking Sighed several times

Source: McMunn, Williamson, and Reagan (2004). SERVE copyright © 2004. Reprinted with permission.

Ms. Reagan had many thoughts as she unpacked Christopher's comprehension evidence from the fable he read. However, Ms. Reagan did not stop there. She knew Christopher and she had a lot of information collected on him, but from this one formative assessment she determined instructional strategies she would try with Christopher prior to assessing him again. She chose to do three things: (1) she found some text for him to read that would be more interesting to him, (2) she worked with Christopher on using visualization techniques to help him with his comprehension, as it was evident he had not visualized what the garden looked like and thus had missed an important fact in the original story, and (3) she also decided to dialogue with him more often during silent reading to ask specific questions that would help her see whether his comprehension was improving. By applying these differentiated instructional strategies after making her inferences, Ms. Reagan modified Christopher's instructional plan and greatly enhanced his success as a reader.

Another example from high school may provide further insight into the instructional modification process. A teacher inferred that several students were having difficulties in their unit on force and motion in physical science. The teacher plotted test data, homework grades, and practice sheet scores completed for the unit so far for her four lab groups to see what particular part of their work on force and motion needed some attention. From the score analysis, half the class showed they were passing this unit of study. However, the other half was not. The teacher pulled the students into a group and talked with all the students in the two lab groups. Together they came up with two major targets with which they needed help: (1) mathematical computations needed to figure out problems presented in the unit, and (2) understanding of the units of measurement for force and motion used in the unit study. Computations and units are skill-learning targets and were covered initially in the class. However, the teacher failed to realize that these students were "weak" in math. They were unable to make connections between concepts taught in math class and concepts in science. It had also been several months since the particular computational skills used in this unit were taught. In order for the students to do the science work they needed math skills. Based on this information elicited from the students, the teacher conducted two lessons for half the class (while the other half conducted a lab) on the algebraic skills they needed. She showed the students how to work the math problems by using units and *no* numbers. They were then asked to go back over previous assignments and to practice computations and unit conversions. The teacher also talked with several math teachers about helping these students on these required skills. After allowing time for practice, the teacher re-assessed the students in these groups for their math skills to see whether the modification was working and whether there were other problems that came up that might call for additional modifications.

Many teachers, like the elementary teacher and the high school teacher described earlier, take the time to differentiate instructional practices. When they do, they are blending instruction and assessment strategies that help students improve in their academic performances.

Research-Based Best Practices of Teaching

Recent educational literature may hold a key to helping teachers use assessment and instructional modification routinely in their classrooms. Researchers are constantly striving to define best practices in teaching. Some of these best practices have implications for assessing students and as an aid in making instructional modifications. After reviewing educational literature on factors relating to best practices, Guild (1997) identified six areas that were common to the multiple intelligence theory, learning styles theories, and theories of brain-based education. All these theories advocated education that

- Was learner-centered
- Required the teacher to be a reflective practitioner and decision maker
- Encouraged a reflective practitioner student role
- Mandated that the curriculum embody substance, depth, and quality
- Supported education of the whole person
- Promoted diversity

These areas of commonality found by Guild are closely tied to some of the areas that the professional development participants who took our surveys, as described earlier in this chapter, found difficult to implement. These commonalities are also emphasized by many of Marzano, Pickering, and Pollock's (2001) nine instructional strategies. These nine, presented earlier in this chapter, are "identifying similarities and differences, summarizing and note taking, reinforcing effort and providing recognition, homework and practice, nonlinguistic representations, cooperative learning, setting objectives and providing feedback, generating and testing hypotheses, and questions, cues, and advance organizers" (2001, p. 146). For example, teachers need to consider a learning-centered environment where students can actively learn how to identify similarities and differences, summarize and take notes, complete homework and practice, and generate and test hypotheses. All of these activities support a reflective practitioner student role and support the teaching of the whole child. By presenting nine different strategies, Marzano, Pickering, and Pollock (2001) also advocate diversity of instructional strategies. In support of a teacher reflective practitioner role they write, "no instructional strategy works equally well in all situations. We strongly recommend that you keep this in mind as you review the strategies presented . . . and apply them in classrooms. Instructional strategies are tools only" (Marzano, Pickering, and Pollock, 2001, p. 8). The authors imply that teachers must perform action research in their classroom to determine which tools work best in particular situations and for particular students.

Since teachers' beliefs and practices will, in large part, determine what they want their students to understand and be able to do, as well as how they instruct and assess students, it is important that teachers understand each of the above commonalities before planning instruction and implementing assessments. Once teachers begin adopting these best practices they will find that changing assessment practices and modifying instruction is often a logical next step. We have already discussed the demands of the curriculum and the importance of differentiating instruction to respond to student diversity. Therefore we concentrate here on the remaining four areas. We define each of the areas, describe appropriate instructional strategies, and make clear the connections to classroom assessment.

The Environment Is Learner Centered

Learner-centered schools, according to Guild (1997, p. 30), "focus their energies on helping all students to be successful learners. They weigh decisions about structure, rituals, routines, class composition, curriculum content and materials, and assessments and evaluation for their effect on learners." In learning-centered classrooms, learners are actively involved in all stages of learning, from planning through evaluation. Thus the learner-centered classroom is in contrast to the teacher-centered classroom, where the teacher is the primary planner, source of information, and assessor. The concept of learner-centeredness arises from the educational philosophy of constructivism.

Unlike an approach in which the role of the teacher is to transmit existing knowledge from teacher to student in as efficient a method as possible ("knowledge is piped from the full container of the teacher's head to the empty vessels of the student' heads" [Tobin, Briscoe, & Holman, 1990, p. 410]), the constructivist approach sees that the role of the teacher is to guide the student in gaining knowledge through personal experience. Each new experience is evaluated in light of knowledge gained from past experiences. This leads to rejecting and revising some ideas. The individual changes his perceptions and experiences intellectual growth. Since the individual must *construct* knowledge, this is an active process.

Constructivists, then, believe that they must provide experiences to students that will allow them to construct knowledge. They believe that students must take an active role in this process, and they reject the idea that knowledge can be passively transmitted from one individual to another.

Teachers with learner-centered classrooms tend to value learning that demonstrates constructing and applying information, rather than memorizing what the teacher or text has stated. Their assessments are more likely to ask students to demonstrate their understandings or to apply information. They plan classroom activities and use teaching strategies based upon these beliefs. They encourage student involvement in all aspects of learning and assessing.

One learner-centered, or constructivist, teaching strategy is the cognitive apprenticeship approach. In this model, the role of the teacher is to stimulate student thinking. The three behaviors most often used to do so are modeling, supporting, and fading. "Teachers first model their strategies in the context and/or make their tacit knowledge explicit. Then, the teacher supports the students' attempts at implementing the strategies . . . and finally, they leave more and more room for the student to work independently" (Roth, 1993, p. 147).

Susan used this model after a unit in her classroom culminated with oral reports given by the students. The students had been given the assessment criteria one week in advance of the report and were given time in class to prepare the report. However, when the reports began, Susan was disappointed in the quality of the students' work. The students did not exhibit the behaviors outlined in the criteria (attention-getting introduction, clear speaking style, organization of thoughts, and so forth). It became obvious to Susan that the students did not know what an excellent oral report looked like.

To help students understand the art of oral reporting, Susan asked the class to evaluate another group's oral report, using the pre-arranged criteria. Then she asked for student feedback about the report during a whole class discussion session. During this session, students shared the strengths and weaknesses in the delivery of the oral report. By reiterating and emphasizing particular student comments, Susan reinforced the knowledge she hoped to teach. She also used questioning techniques to elicit comments about some behaviors that were not immediately apparent to students. For example, she asked, "Did José seem comfortable when he was speaking to the class?"

to draw student attention to distracting behaviors such as twitching or shifting from foot to foot. Through these comments and questions, as well as using the assessment criteria, Susan *modeled* an example of excellent oral reporting. She also encouraged student self-assessment, an important aspect of a student-centered environment.

The next stage in the cognitive apprenticeship mode of teaching is to *support* student efforts. After the class discussion concerning the oral reports, Susan asked the student groups to revisit and redesign their own reports. During this activity, she circulated around the room, again using questions and comments to probe student understanding and to encourage student reflection on what they had learned. These revised oral reports showed great improvement over the first attempt. Later in the semester, students were once again called upon to make oral presentations. Susan repeated her supporting strategies but found she needed to interject fewer and fewer of her own comments when speaking with student groups. In fact, she was able to *fade* into the background at this point. She was still available to assist students but found less need to do so. In her "fading" role, she often simply circulated among groups, listened to their discussions, and waited for students to elicit assistance, if necessary.

As this example clearly indicates, Susan did most of her teaching during the modeling phase. In her support role, she was not actually teaching new behaviors, just reminding students of concepts or skills previously learned. Then, during the fading phase of teaching, Susan was primarily responding to student questions, unobtrusively monitoring their learning, or using what is often referred to as the formative assessment process to provide feedback to improve student learning.

In all three phases, however, Susan used questioning (discussed in Chapter Four) to assess student understanding, stimulate student thinking, and help students become more perceptive self-assessors.

By applying the cognitive apprenticeship model and questioning, she fostered a learner-centered environment, encouraging student involvement and facilitating communication between teachers and students.

The Teacher Is a Reflective Practitioner and Decision Maker

Teachers who are reflective practitioners stay abreast of educational reforms, innovations, and research. Their goal is to create and maintain a developmentally appropriate, safe classroom environment by examining available information, selecting appropriate management models, and reflecting on the effectiveness of those models. They monitor the application of new teaching ideas in order to evaluate benefits or detriments of each. Then they integrate practical, sensible teaching skills garnered from examination of research into instruction. In the process, they apply new theoretical knowledge, reflect on the efficacy of the application, and refine their teaching techniques over time.

In other words, reflective practitioners perform action research in their classrooms. Grundy (1987), suggests that action research encourages reflecting on practice in order to comprehend the practice and thereby create more meaningful opportunities for students to learn. In this way, action research "fosters interpretation and understanding, and promotes rational decision-making as the basis for classroom practice" (Grundy, 1987, p. 191).

This teacher-as-action-researcher role can encourage teachers to undertake all the Classroom Assessment Cycle steps we have presented. Teacher researchers collect data via classroom assessments of many types in order to (1) judge effectiveness of instruction and (2) evaluate student achievement. They reflect on the assessment results (analyze the data) to find patterns and formulate inferences about student learning and instruction strategies to explain the patterns. To examine these inferences, more data collection may be necessary. The teacher may need to review lesson plans to ascertain whether important concepts were actually explored by the students. She may look at the format used for student assignments, the number of assignments, and the grades on the assignments before finding evidence to support one or more of the inferences. Viewing all these findings, the teacher may decide to revise teaching strategies or assessment methods. This implementation-reflection-revision process is an ongoing, iterative cycle of teacher activity.

Reflective practitioners, then, view their teaching as a continuous research project, where scrutiny of current practice is used to refine the art of teaching. They regard information from student assessments as feedback for the effectiveness of their instructional strategies and assessments, as well as feedback for student achievement. In order to implement such self-examination, they know they must schedule time for reflection.

One strategy that fosters the reflective practitioner role for the teacher is switching metaphors. In order to enact new teaching behaviors, the teacher may need to reconceptualize his teaching role. This is no easy task. Identifying a metaphor for the new teaching style often facilitates this change process (Tobin, 1990). For example, when Susan was using the lecture-example-practice model, her teaching metaphor was "teacher as initiate of the temple of sacred knowledge" (Butler, 1997a). She says, "I viewed my pupils, then, as novices, or suppliants who could capture the pearls of wisdom if properly initiated. However, to advance from the novice to the initiate stages, the students had to perform certain rites. They had to listen in class, do their homework, read the textbook, and perform laboratory experiments. Through these activities, however, the mysteries of the sacred knowledge would unfold for the students" (Butler, 1997a, pp. 235–236).

In order to change her mode of teaching Susan first had to identify a new metaphor for herself. She was at first hesitant to share this new metaphor, fearing ridicule. However, she eventually confessed, "I began to see my role in the classroom to be not unlike the role of the holodeck computer on the Starship Enterprise in the TV program, *Star Trek: The Next Generation.* On the show, this computer is responsible for the settings: Paris in springtime, London in the time of Sherlock Holmes, a Spanish galleon sailing the seas, etc. The holodeck computer also introduces holographic characters that interact with the protagonists and it maintains safeguards to ensure that no one gets hurt (gunshots or phaser blasts don't injure the real people). However, the behaviors of the protagonists direct the action—the computer simply reacts to these behaviors by introducing new characters or changing the scene. In times of emergency or when the action goes awry, the protagonist can stop the program and call for help from the computer. So, like the holodeck computer, which everyone understands is running in the background, I, too, was present [in my classroom], but unobtrusive" (Butler, 1997a, pp. 256–257).

This change in teaching metaphor enabled Susan to incorporate new teaching behaviors into her classroom repertoire. However, metaphors can be used for more than just making behavioral adaptations. By identifying a teaching metaphor, instructors can "become aware of their belief systems and how their perceptual frameworks affect their teaching roles and the roles their students play in response" (Marshall, 1990, p. 128). In other words, the metaphors teachers use can structure the way they perceive situations, opening their eyes to some possibilities while shutting out others.

There is of course no one right metaphor for teaching. However, since everyone's actions are often governed by unconsciously held metaphors, teachers must bring these underlying perceptions to the surface in order to understand their own behavior. By identifying their own current metaphor for teaching, they can evaluate its power in determining their actions. And they can use a change in teaching metaphors to help them change their teaching behaviors. Therefore, reflective practitioners seek to uncover the metaphors that govern their teaching. The examples in Exhibit 9.4 are commonly held teacher metaphors. You may wish to review these metaphors and identify the one that guides your own teaching. An examination of personal teaching metaphors can be the focus for reflection and change.

The Students Are Reflective Practitioners

Student reflective practitioners, according to Guild (1997, p. 31), "are engaged in exploring, experimenting, creating, applying, and evaluating their ways of learning, as well as interacting actively with the content and concepts they are studying." Such a definition again evokes the constructivist epistemology. To learn, students must be active participants rather than passive receivers of teacher-disseminated information. They must become self-assessors rather than relying on the teacher as the sole judge of the quality of their work. When teachers are the source of knowledge, practices will include lecturing, requiring students to raise their hands in order to be selected to speak, and using classroom assignments that have only one right answer or that include no room for student choice in the method of completion or assessment.

To foster student autonomy, teachers may need to rethink these traditional student and teacher roles. Only by abdicating some control in the classroom can teachers empower students to monitor and make decisions about their own learning. Students must have the freedom to move around the room or even be absent from the classroom in order to pursue alternative pathways for learning. To facilitate learning,

---

EXHIBIT 9.4. METAPHORS FOR TEACHING.

- *Teacher as Boss:* Student-workers are supervised by teacher-managers, who cajole students to "get back to work" or "do your homework" or "finish your seatwork."

- *Teacher as Nurturer:* The teacher cares for the students, protecting them and fostering their learning. The images of caretaking, affection, love, and warmth are stimulated by this metaphor.

- *Teacher as Captain of the Ship:* No mutinies allowed here. The teacher barks out orders and the students jump to comply.

- *Teacher as Expert:* The purpose of the teacher is to be an information source. Teaching, in this context, is telling others. The "others" (students) are passive receivers of the knowledge.

- *Teacher as Doctor:* The teacher diagnoses the learning needs of the students and prescribes appropriate interventions for them.

- *Teacher as Coach:* Students are novices who must practice skills in order to develop expertise. The teacher models the desired skills, structures practice times and events, and encourages student achievement.

- *Teacher as Performer:* The teacher must capture the interests of the students by acting in an entertaining way.

- *Teacher as Traffic Cop:* Many avenues of learning are open to students, but the teacher as traffic cop helps prevent collisions, introduce order, and ensure safety.

- *Teacher as Judge:* The teacher sets the standards for learning and assesses students against this standard.

- *Teacher as Co-Learner:* The teacher is no longer the expert, but a seeker of knowledge who works with the students. The "right" answer to questions is not known but must be researched or created through reasoning and problem-solving activities.

Source: Adapted with permission from Lakoff, G., and Johnson, M. (1980), *Metaphors We Live By,* Figure 9.8, pp. 25–26, University of Chicago Press, Chicago, Illinois.

---

self-assessment, and the exchange of ideas, they must be free to engage in conversations with peers and to participate in peer tutoring. Students must be given opportunities to assess their own work, as well as the work of others. Through such activities, students develop decision-making skills and enhance their judging capabilities. They learn to budget time and resources in order to accomplish goals. In short, when students are given responsibilities and the freedom to make choices, they are more likely to become autonomous, self-directed learners and confident self-assessors.

One instructional strategy that fosters the reflective practitioner role for the student is pursuing *emancipatory interests.* Grundy writes of human "interests" (people are interested in that which gives them pleasure) (Grundy, 1987, p. 8) and contrasts three classroom interests: practical, technical, and emancipatory. *Emancipatory interests* have as their aim justice, equality, autonomy, and responsibility. Grundy states that the *technical interests* cannot fulfill these aims, since this interest is an interest in control, viewing others and the environment as "objects." Teachers pursuing technical interests will make all the decisions for the students, for example, mandating how students will demonstrate mastery of knowledge. Generally, these teachers assess all students in exactly the same way (for instance, all students take the same written exam). Therefore, students as reflective practitioners are rarely found in classrooms governed by teachers operating in the sphere of technical interest.

Practical interests view the universe as subject, rather than object, yet they are still insufficient to promote autonomy. They do not promote the equality of participants in the classroom. For example, a teacher pursuing a practical interest might invite students to aid in the design of scoring rubrics. A class meeting is held, and student suggestions are aired. However, the comments of the teacher "lead" students to incorporate only the ideas that the teacher endorses into the rubric design. Although the assessment in this classroom appears more emancipatory than that in the technical interest classroom, true autonomy has not been achieved.

Grundy (1987, p. 19) identifies the emancipatory interest as "a fundamental interest in emancipation and empowerment to engage in autonomous action arising out of authentic, critical insights into the social construction of human society." She further states that, "at the level of practice, the emancipatory curriculum will involve the participants in the educational encounter, both teacher and pupil, in actions which attempt to change the structures within which learning occurs and which constrain freedom in often unrecognized ways." In the classroom utilizing emancipatory interests, teachers and students share the assessment workload, with students having major responsibility for formative assessments (ongoing assessments that monitor growth) and teachers assuming the responsibility for summative assessments (final assessments that evaluate achievement). In their roles as formative assessors, students are expected to perform peer reviews and give feedback to other students about performance. For example, students in a biology class learning to use microscopes might be given "check-off" skill sheets. The students would first practice the skills listed on the sheets individually, performing self-assessment. Next, when they felt confident in their ability to correctly manipulate the microscope, these students would demonstrate their proficiency to other students (formative or learning assessment). Finally, after successfully demonstrating their microscope skills to themselves and to others, the students would ask the teacher to perform an evaluation of their performance (summative or final assessment). In this fashion, students are empowered to critically review their own and others' work and yet the legalities of grading are respected, in that the teacher serves as the official grader.

In short, if students are to become reflective practitioners and autonomous learners, they must be given opportunities to develop these skills. Teachers can foster these roles for students by giving them choices in how they will be assessed, eliciting their input on assessment practices, and encouraging them to practice self- and peer evaluation.

The Whole Person Is Educated

Teaching that emphasizes the education of the whole person connects classroom learning to the student's life outside the classroom. To Guild (1997, p. 31) this means paying attention "to the cultural, physical, social, and emotional life of the learner as well as to his or her academic life." Teachers interested in this holistic approach to education take the time to know their students, not just as students but also as people. While taking into account the developmental stage of the student and planning for experiences designed to best meet the student's learning needs, the teacher also adapts instruction to capitalize on the interests of the student and on the student's future plans.

Enhancing the reality of learning may mean branching out from the specific discipline taught by the teacher in order to help the student make connections to other academic content. For example, few "real" people operate in only one academic discipline. A scientist may be primarily concerned with science, but she will also certainly use communication, language arts, and mathematical skills. Therefore, when teachers educate the "whole person" they emphasize the necessity of incorporating content from several different academic disciplines into their work. In this context, assessments should reflect an incorporation of content across disciplines, and possibly from the world of the arts as well, and provide opportunities for students to demonstrate how well they understand and can apply connections.

Educating the whole child promotes personalization of education, emphasizes the relevance of the instruction and assessment, aids understanding of the connections between and across academic disciplines, and encourages the development of cultural literacy.

One instructional strategy that fosters education of the whole person is problem-based learning. Bridges and Hallinger (1991) define problem-based learning as learning that begins with a problem. The problem should be one that students are apt to face in the future or at least similar in context to possible future problems. The subject matter in the course or class should be organized around the problem rather than into separate disciplines. In working through the problem, learning occurs mostly within the context of the problem in small groups, rather than in large, lecture-oriented assemblies. Within the small groups, individuals assume the major responsibility for their own learning and, indeed, for their own instruction and self-assessment.

This learning progresses through group and individual efforts, as follows. Students are first presented with the problem and then work in small groups to separate known facts from learning issues. Once the "know" and "need to know" categories are designated, students perform research activities to change the unknown into the known. Groups analyze the results of this research, formulate solutions, and present these solutions to a public. An evaluative activity then follows the solution presentation. This entire process is illustrated in Figure 9.2.

FIGURE 9.2. FLOWCHART FOR PROBLEM-BASED LEARNING.

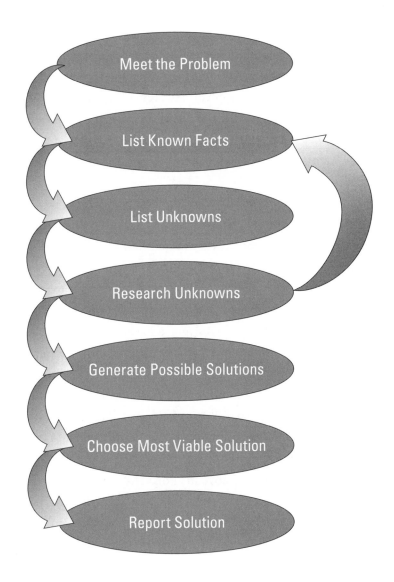

Middleton (1994, p. 151) uses the term "ill-defined" to describe the complex problems typically used in the problem-based learning (PBL) classroom. Gallagher, Stepien, Sher, and Workman (1995) call them "ill-structured." Cordeiro and Campbell (1996, p. 8) concur with this view, dividing PBL problems into "high ground" or "swampy" problems. High-ground problems are of a technical nature, where a well-rehearsed procedure for solving is available. A mathematical word problem or a science laboratory experiment in which students re-perform work previously discovered by others is a high-ground problem. Cordeiro and Campbell (1996, p. 8) discard the idea of using high-ground problems in problem-based learning, urging the use of swampy problems instead. Swampy problems, they state, are more complex, and occur "when one only vaguely understand the situation, has no clear way of knowing what would be better and lacks procedures for addressing obstacles or constraints of the situation." Gallagher, Stepien, and Rosenthal (1992) further describe such problems as having no one single best way to be tackled and no single right answer. In fact, they state that students may never be 100 percent sure of making the correct solution selection, since some information is always missing.

Such ill-structured problems best resemble the nature of problems as they occur in the real world, and this "real world" essence of PBL problems is what makes them so valuable. Boud (1985) points out that these "real" problems are also inherently interdisciplinary, as real-world problems do not usually limit themselves to one particular discipline.

How does assessment fit into the PBL picture and how does this assessment aid in the holistic education of students? PBL problems are reality-based and interdisciplinary, leading students to a connected view of academic disciplines. The assessments used for PBL experiences can enhance this connectivity. For example, rather than using a multiple-choice test at the end of a PBL unit, the teacher can choose a more realistic form of assessment. The assessment or capstone performance for the PBL unit should match the problem presented and should engage students in real-life roles. For instance, students working as forensic scientists to determine the cause of death in a potential poisoning case could serve as "expert witnesses" at the trial of the accused. A problem concerning mosquito infestations might culminate in a town meeting in which the Mosquito Board has to field questions from concerned citizens. Students examining the implementation of school uniforms could present their finding to the parent-teacher association. Engineering students could submit competing bids to a homeowner wishing to move his house from point A to point B. In each of these examples, students remain in the role created by the PBL problem even through the evaluation process. Each would also require students to use skills from several academic disciplines. These capstone performances could also incorporate the arts (visuals and graphics for presentations, role playing, perhaps even an enacted skit for the parents that shows advantages and disadvantages of school uniforms, and so forth). The imagination of the teacher and the creativity of the students are the only limits to the possibilities for assessment of PBL.

Creating a learner-centered environment, becoming a teacher researcher, encouraging student autonomy, and providing holistic education are all endeavors endorsed by current educational research. They may also be mechanisms for change, if change is desired. Before a teacher can know whether she wishes to implement changes in her classroom, however, she must first examine her own beliefs and teaching practices. In light of the information presented here, the teacher may wish to take the surveys at the beginning of the chapter (if she has not done so already), identify a personal teaching metaphor, and reflect on possible changes to be made.

Such changes will not, however, be easy to make or be instantaneous. Work within school districts facing assessment change indicates that such change is slow and it must be supported and revisited as people construct new plans. These plans for creating changes in current assessment practices and for learning to modify instructional plans must also fabricate a "feedback spiral" for continuous growth (Brewer & Kallick, 1996, p. 186). People must plan, experiment, gather evidence, reflect, modify, and revisit. While they are moving along this route, they must realize they will never finalize their work, or reach the endpoint, since the destination will change based upon input and reflection. Therefore change should be viewed as a continuous process of growth, a journey not a destination.

Implementing best practices of teaching, modifying instructional plans in the light of assessment data, and improving instructional strategies will make it more likely that students will meet their many learning targets. One more factor vital to this goal, student motivation, is discussed in Chapter Ten.

Using Assessment to Motivate Students

In this chapter our focus continues to be on both the Classroom Assessment Cycle itself and some learning factors that are *external* to the cycle but that *strongly influence* its functions. The external factor that we examine here is the importance of a classroom environment that promotes learning. At the same time, we look inside to recall the many activities of the Classroom Assessment Cycle we have already discussed that motivate students to learn.

Factors that may help motivate students to learn are (1) involving students in their own assessment, (2) matching assessment strategies to student learning, and (3) considering thinking styles and using assessments to adjust the classroom environment in order to enhance student motivation to learn. Conversely, poorly thought out assessments may dampen student motivation to learn.

Another way of expressing the major concept behind this chapter is *shaping learning with assessment*. However, shaping learning is an elusive goal because learning itself is such an abstract concept. Learning takes place inside the minds of students. It is possible to seek and even find evidence of such learning, but it is hard to pinpoint the actual mental processes that determine whether learning is occurring. In essence, teachers never "learn" students (pardon the grammar); students learn themselves! However, if *the will to engage the material* is not present, student learning cannot occur. Therefore one teacher responsibility is to encourage this will to engage by creating motivating learning opportunities for students.

Teachers generally react violently to the statement above. "I'm not an entertainer; I'm a teacher!" is the comment that best exemplifies the attitude of some. Teachers do not see the motivation of students as one of their responsibilities. They feel that motivation must come from within the student. This is true; teachers cannot "motivate" their students, any more than they can "learn" them. Kohn (1993) makes this point when he describes two "myths" of motivation:

1. You can motivate other people.

2. There is a single entity called "motivation" that students have more or less of.

People who believe myth 1, Kohn suggests, are likely to be those who demonstrate a control-oriented approach to teaching. They "motivate" others in the sense that they have the power to direct others' actions. This power usually takes the form of offering or withholding rewards and punishments. Persons who subscribe to myth 2 offer it as an excuse or rationalization when students remain unmotivated—these students are thought to simply lack the motivation "chip." Kohn recommends that teachers stop asking how motivated students are and instead concentrate on asking how students are motivated. Or, as we would put it, teachers may not be able to motivate their students, but they can create motivating learning opportunities.

In this chapter we endeavor to explain the reasoning behind this assertion, exploring the link between classroom assessment and motivation of students. We discuss these three questions:

- What is motivation?

- How do the concepts embodied within the Classroom Assessment Cycle enhance student motivation?

- What process can teachers follow to address motivation needs?

What Is Motivation?

In workshops dealing with student motivation, we ask teachers to describe a typical motivated student. Before they begin this task, however, they invariably describe a nonmotivated student first. Here is a compendium of typical elements teachers use to describe these nonmotivated students:

- Never does homework

- Sleeps in class

- Has frequent absences

- Is often off-task

- Has failing grades

- Is easily distracted; may bring toys to class or play with writing implements

- Is often out of seat

- Does "shoddy" work

- In counseling sessions, states that he or she does not care about grades or school

Almost every teacher can identify a current or former student who fits this unmotivated student profile.

Teachers often find it harder, however, to write characteristics of motivated students. Often, we must allow more time and ask coaching questions before teachers can generate characteristics of a motivated student. This reluctance to list characteristics of motivated students may arise from teachers' attitudes about motivation. As stated previously, some teachers are reluctant to take responsibility for creating motivating learning environments. It may seem easier to blame students for their own motivational problems. In any case, we often find it easier to elicit descriptions of nonmotivated students than motivated ones. However, with some probing and coaching, the following characteristics of motivated students usually are mentioned:

- Attends class, pays attention, does not disrupt
- Begins work with little prompting, follows directions, participates in activities, completes tasks on time
- Persists and tries different approaches before seeking help on difficult tasks
- Invests time and effort in doing a "quality" job
- Is reluctant to stop working on a task, volunteers materials to share in class, asks questions often
- Shows enthusiasm and obvious pride in work
- Selects challenging rather than easy tasks
- Sometimes engages in learning activities that go beyond course requirements

Everyone would like to teach a classroom filled with students matching these descriptions. It is possible to do so because motivation is a learned construct. Therefore, teachers can help students become motivated. Brophy's (1987, p. 40) definition of motivation best expresses this view: "Student motivation to learn is an acquired competence *developed through general experience,* but stimulated most directly through modeling, communication of expectations, and direct instruction or socialization by significant others (especially parents and *teachers*)"(emphasis added). If motivation is a learned competence, then instruction and assessments can be structured to foster this competence.

It is of course also possible to give students a motivation to learn by offering rewards that are extrinsic to the learning activity or the result of learning. External factors that drive the effort to learn may take the form of grades, parent approval, or food (pizza parties), for example. Students driven by *extrinsic motivation* ask questions such as

What do I get if I do this?

What will I get to do if I make a good grade?

Kohn (1993) argues that an overuse of external motivators undermines students' abilities to take responsibility for their own learning: "The famous 'Wad-ja-get' preoccupation of students—compulsively comparing their own grades to others—is not a function of human nature but of the performance (ability) orientation that suffuses most American classrooms and stifles children's interest in what they are learning" (Kohn, 1993, p. 158). (External rewards and grading are discussed further in Chapter Eleven.)

Therefore, if teachers would like a classroom of motivated students, Kohn (1993, p. 187) recommends changes in classroom management styles, routines, and strategies in order to incorporate more of what he calls the three Cs:

Content: What is taught should be flexible and acknowledge student and teacher needs.

Collaboration: True collaboration is about creating a climate for learning in which all participants (teacher and students) are involved.

Choice: There should be flexibility in the instruction and assessment in order to meet the individual needs of the students.

These are all issues that we have addressed in discussing the design of assessment tasks for improved instruction and differentiating instruction. They are among the classroom qualities that contribute to the type of motivation all educators should hope to foster in students: intrinsic motivation. *Intrinsic motivation* is the internal drive to master or accomplish tasks. Students with this drive ask questions such as

What did I learn?

What can I do to improve?

Did I try hard enough?

Too often, teachers rely on external factors to motivate students. If such rewards in fact increased motivation, there would not be such an outcry in the literature about students' lack of motivation as is currently found. However, study after study documents the lack of student motivation in American schools (Brophy, 1987; Butler, R., 1988; Ames, 1990; Tomlinson, 1993; Ginsberg & Bronstein, 1993; Anderman & Maehr, 1994). The practical distinction between extrinsic and intrinsic motivation is also addressed in the current literature on motivational theory as it relates to student learning, where it may be expressed in terms of learning that emphasizes student ability (how "smart" the student is) versus learning that emphasizes learning itself.

The self-worth theory of achievement motivation as expressed by Covington, for example, "assumes that a central part of all classroom achievement is the need for students to protect their sense of worth or personal value" (Covington, 1984, p. 5). A student's sense of worth depends heavily on that student's accomplishments or performance. The quality of performance results from both ability and effort. Research done using this model has led to several conclusions. First, students perceive ability as the dominant causal factor in achievement. Second, effort seems to supplant ability as a main source of reward and satisfaction only in environments where learning for its own sake is the goal. This suggests that the most important task for the teacher is to instruct students in ways that prevent a preoccupation with existing ability from interfering with students' willingness to expend effort to learn. In order to accomplish this task, teachers can use noncompetitive learning structures that increase the number of intrinsic rewards available to students so more students experience achievement and a sense of self-worth. A noncompetitive learning environment will promote a pursuit of success rather than an avoidance of failure.

This emphasis is also found in Ames's discussion of cooperative, competitive, and individualistic goal structures in relation to motivation: "A competitive structure promotes an egoistic or social comparative orientation, a cooperative structure elicits a moral orientation, and an individualistic structure evokes an achievement-mastery orientation" (Ames, 1984, p. 189).

Competitive systems of motivation (the best work gets posted, those who finish first line up first, ability grouping, grades) focus children on their ability. Winning can become associated with public pride, competence, and confidence, while losing can evoke public shame, embarrassment, and humiliation. Cooperative systems encourage members of a group to work toward a common goal and to receive common rewards for attainment or common punishment for nonattainment of goals. Helping each other or sharing effort promotes positive interdependence among the group. Consequently, group work becomes a moral situation in which the focus of evaluation is on intent or how willing one is to put forth effort to meet the group goals. In contrast, individualistic approaches link individual effort directly to individual achievement, and the focus of behavior is on achieving task mastery. In competitive settings, the student's response to task difficulty involves a self-assessment of his or her ability relative to the ability of others. However, in individualized settings, the response to task difficulty evokes an assessment of the amount of effort necessary to accomplish the task.

Ames suggests that varying the classroom environment in terms of these three goal structures will affect the character of student motivation. Again, ability-focused students are concerned with being judged as "able" by outperforming others or by achieving success even when the task is easy. Students focused on the task are concerned with understanding, insight, or skill and accomplishing something that is challenging. Classrooms that incorporate Kohn's three Cs also move closer to the learning-oriented end of the educational continuum and further from the ability-oriented end.

Classroom assessment that is aligned with what has been learned, sets clear expectations that are communicated in advance, and leads to understanding and meeting

EXHIBIT 10.1. EXAMPLE OF CLASSROOM ASSESSMENT TASK.

Learning Targets:

- Experience teamwork through scientific exploration and dialogue
- Gain knowledge acquisition and ability to support scientifically based opinions
- Compare and contrast the structure (including protein structure), functions, reproductive success, and adaptations relative to a disease-causing virus
- Discuss immunity responses (both external and internal) as protective devices

Question for Group _____ for Panel Discussion:
In your opinion, could a minuscule, nonliving, WHO-eradicated virus wipe out humankind?

Investigation prior to the panel discussion should include some of the following facts:

⇨   What is this virus?
⇨   Significant Facts and Historical Events (Timeline)
- Egypt – 1100s B.C.–Pharaoh Ramses V
- China – around 265–313 A.D.
- Europe – around 580 A.D.
- South America – 1500s
- North America and other countries – 1500 to WHO eradication claims
- Current status and WHO emphasis
⇨   Support – Viral Understanding (Notebook entries)
- What is a virus?
- How does a virus cross over from nonliving to the living worlds?
- What do viruses look like?
- Why is it so hard to treat a viral infection?
- How do these entities differ from bacteria?

Source: McMunn, 1990.

students' individual needs as well as needs most of them have in common clearly can make learning more rewarding to more students.

Exhibit 10.1 shows one example of such a classroom assessment. This is a partial formative assessment that a teacher designed to allow students to learn about viruses and bacteria via guided instruction. Each group receives a different virus or bacteria to study and prepares for a panel discussion. In this discussion, each student must address a different question in the prompt and provide specific information from research activities. The teacher facilitates the groups and checks their progress. She also allows some class time for using the Internet or library, and time for conducting interviews with significant adults. The school journalism students are invited to class on the panel discussion days; they are charged with writing the information learned and sharing it with the whole school in their next paper. This type of formative assessment gives students some choice, puts the responsibility of the work on them, and challenges them to seek their own knowledge to share with their peers. This learning process is much more motivating for most students, since it allows the students to interact with each other rather than just sit, take notes, memorize facts, or take a test.

In our professional development workshops, we have found that most teachers are familiar with Maslow's (1970) hierarchy of needs, which posits that a person's most basic needs (physiological and safety needs) must be met before that person can move on to fulfilling higher needs such as needs for belongingness, esteem, and ultimately, self-actualization. Glasser (1986) links a similar set of human needs to student motivation in revealing ways. The needs he enumerates are to (1) survive and reproduce, (2) belong and love, (3) gain power, (4) be free, and (5) have fun. In Glasser's view, all are equally important and must be reasonably satisfied.

When asked, "What is the best part of school?" students will invariably answer, "My friends." This demonstrates fulfilling the strong need to belong and feel loved. The need to gain power, to feel that one is respected and worth listening to, is less likely to be satisfied in the school setting. Both students and teachers experience feelings of powerlessness, and this failure of the school to meet the need for power may cause serious student discipline problems. The need for freedom is also rarely fully met in the school setting. However, students seem to accept the need for school rules and regulations. The need for fun is also rarely a problem, since "few schools are grim; lack of fun is not a major flaw" (Brandt, 1988, p. 40).

Glasser points out that students who are working hard in school (the motivated students) are the ones who are getting their needs satisfied. They are also the ones who see school as a need-satisfying place. To assist nonmotivated students to adopt this school view, Glasser recommends the use of learning teams (Glasser, 1986, p. 81). When students work in teams

1. They gain a sense of belonging.

2. Belonging provides the initial motivation, but as the students achieve academic success, they begin to sense that knowledge is power.

3. Stronger students fulfill needs of power and friendship as they help weaker students.

4. Weaker students find that contributing effort to a team multiplies that effort, and therefore they feel more powerful.

5. Students begin to depend not just on the teacher, but on themselves, thereby increasing their own feelings of power and freedom.

By using learning teams teachers may help students meet their belonging, power, freedom (and fun!) needs.

Enhancing Student Motivation

If, like Alfie Kohn (1993, p. 198), teachers wish to emphasize *how students are motivated,* rather than *how motivated they are,* they will find that their teaching behaviors and classroom strategies will necessarily evolve in new directions. The first four sections of this book have been devoted to strategies that engage students in their own learning. We will review some of these strategies and offer several more here.

Meece and McColskey (1997) recommend that teachers use ideas presented in theories of motivation to implement changes in the classroom spheres of instruction, climate, and assessment. Such changes will enhance the "intrinsic motivation to learn" of students (p. 34). We will discuss making changes in teaching practice in all these classroom spheres in light of the Classroom Assessment Cycle.

The ultimate goals of the Classroom Assessment Cycle are to improve instruction and enhance student learning. In this part of Chapter Ten, we review the cycle but this time use student motivation as our focusing lens. In our previous chapters we noted that the Classroom Assessment Cycle seeks to accomplish its goals by accessing standards (clarifying targets), using quality tasks and assessments (collecting evidence), analyzing data (formulating inferences), and adopting quality instructional practices (modifying instruction). Now we attempt to reexamine the cycle by evaluating how the components of the cycle affect students' involvement in their own learning. Such involvement, according to the best practices of teaching discussed in Chapter Nine, is key to enhancing student learning. Motivational theories explicated at the beginning of this chapter have also indicated that such student involvement is mandatory if motivation to learn is to be enhanced. So these questions remain: How can we involve students in their own learning? How can we use the Classroom Assessment Cycle to support student motivation and evoke student interest in learning?

Changes in Instruction That Enhance Student Motivation

Meece and McColskey (1997) identify three dimensions of instruction that have an impact on student motivation and involvement in learning: (1) "appropriate difficulty levels of work assignments," (2) "relevance and meaningfulness of instruction," and (3) "diversity, variety, and novelty of learning opportunities" (pp. 34–47).

Most of these dimensions have been discussed in previous chapters. For example, appropriateness and feasibility of tasks was featured in Chapter Six, "Designing Quality Assessment Tasks," which directly referenced the quadrant of the Classroom Assessment Cycle that states "evidence is collected in a variety of ways." To promote student involvement in their own learning, assessment tasks must be carefully designed. Chapter Six listed the attributes of such carefully designed tasks. They must be aligned to learning targets, exhibit cognitive complexity, and promote deep understanding of concepts, as well as being developmentally appropriate and feasible to accomplish.

Two sample tasks may help explicate how the task itself can either involve students or fail to involve them. In the following two scenarios, the tenth grade science standard being addressed is, Appreciate the diversity of life.

• *Scenario One:* The teacher requires the students to memorize all the following levels within the animal, plant, and moneran kingdoms: phylum, class, order, and family.

• *Scenario Two*: Student groups of four students each are given a set of twenty cards containing specific organisms from three different kingdoms. Each individual student must choose five animals from the card set and research these animals. The research should address body structure, appendages, eating and defense mechanisms, habitat, reproduction, and prevalence. After the research is performed, students share their findings with the group. The group then creates a concept web showing similarities, differences, and connections between and among organisms in the three kingdoms.

The task in Scenario Two better exemplifies the quality attributes of tasks than the one described in Scenario One. Both place the responsibility for learning on the student, but the second is clearly more motivating (as well as more cognitively challenging, more inclusive, more supporting of deep understanding, more feasible, and more interesting to students) than the first. Therefore, by using the quality attributes of good task design, student interest can be evoked and student motivation enhanced.

Performance-based tasks (a subset of constructed-response assessment) that use authentic problems that involve students in collecting data and analyzing it and engage students over time can also have positive effects on student motivation, according to Meece and McColskey (1997). They state that students "report greater interest in tasks that are cognitively demanding and ambiguous" (p. 26). In Chapter Nine, within the quadrant of the Classroom Assessment Cycle in which "instructional plans and modifications are carried out," educating the whole child was introduced as a best practice of teaching, and problem-based learning was suggested as one instructional strategy that supported this practice. Problem-based scenarios place students in real-life roles and therefore enhance the relevance of the concepts presented. Again, refer to Exhibit 10.1 as an example of such a problem-based, real-life task in which students must work together to formulate solutions.

Diversity of learning experiences has been iterated and reiterated throughout this text. Diversities of assessments were emphasized throughout Part Two (Chapters Three, Four, and Five) and diversities of instructional strategies were particularly discussed in Chapter Nine. One strategy for enhancing the diversity, variety, and novelty of learning opportunities is the use of the scientific learning cycle (Marek & Cavallo, 1997), based on the work of Piaget (Piaget & Inhelder, 1956). This cycle has three components: exploration, terminology, and concept application. Figure 10.1 graphically displays this cycle.

FIGURE 10.1. SCIENTIFIC LEARNING CYCLE.

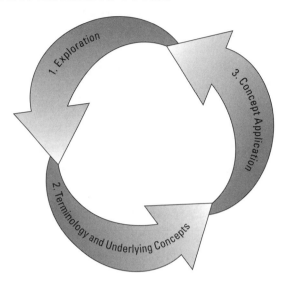

In the exploration stage, information is presented to students in such a way as to cause a loss of equilibrium (comfort with present knowledge). The students then feel a need to ease the disequilibrium, so they become motivated to learn. One example of the use of the scientific learning cycle comes from a chemistry class.

In chemistry class, students are required to understand, write, and make applications with chemical reactions. Exhibit 10.2 provides an example of the use of the scientific learning cycle in this chemistry class, where students are working to learn about chemical reactions. The exploration portion of the cycle was enacted by giving students a laboratory exercise to perform. They were asked to mix droplets of different chemicals together and record their observations on a form. They were also asked to hypothesize about what was happening when the chemicals mixed. The terminology acquisition portion of the cycle involved having students write out questions of "need to know" about the reactions. This gave the teacher some diagnostic information and helped pinpoint basic concepts and vocabulary needed to forward student learning of reactions. Then students were provided with definitions of terms needed to understand the

EXHIBIT 10.2. EXAMPLE OF THE USE OF THE SCIENTIFIC LEARNING CYCLE IN CHEMISTRY.

1 – Exploration Activity			2 – Questions	3 – Concept Application Activity	
Chemicals Mixed	Spot Number	Observations Made	Need to Know to Complete...	Reaction Formula	What Happened in This Reaction?
Hydrochloric acid and Sodium Hydroxide	1	Solid forms in liquid	How to write a reaction. What is the solid?		
Hydrochloric acid and	2	Turns the clear liquid to	Why did the liquid change		

Source: McMunn, 1992.

observed chemical reactions. These terms included *precipitate, ionic bonding, covalent bonding,* and so forth. Within this Piagetian step, students were able to partially regain equilibrium and begin to understand the concepts underlying chemical reactions.

Finally, once the students understood some underlying concepts, they moved to the final stage of the cycle, concept application. Here students were asked to complete a chart, giving correct chemical formulas and writing chemical reaction equations for the observed reactions. In the equations, they had to indicate whether a precipitate was formed or a gas was given off. They also had to account for any color changes observed.

When using the scientific learning cycle, the first step is clearly the most important for motivation. The students must be presented with gaps or holes in their knowledge structures in order to motivate them to learn new material. If the teacher simply presents all the information needed, students will not perceive a need to actively participate in the learning process.

Changes in Classroom Climate That Enhance Student Motivation

When it comes to making adaptations that make the classroom climate more motivating for students, Meece and McColskey (1997) recommend (p. 34):

- Holding high expectations for all students
- Fostering student autonomy and choice
- Promoting cooperation and teamwork rather than individual competition
- Knowing the students
- Improving classroom management and discipline

Again, most of these concepts were covered in previous chapters. For example, our discussion of standards and benchmarks introduced the idea of high expectations in Part One, "Clarifying Learning Targets." We covered the topics of fostering student autonomy and choice, promoting cooperation and teamwork, and knowing the students in Chapter Nine. In Chapter Eight we discussed analyzing student data and stressed the importance of knowing our students and delving into their thinking processes. The figures, charts, and tables included in Chapter Eight provide examples of how we can gain better pictures of our students. In Chapter Three, within our explanations of skill targets, we discussed why it is important for students to work in teams. Again, in this chapter, when presenting Glasser's motivation theories, we again emphasized the use of learning teams. All the factors emphasized throughout this book lead us to believe that quality, formative learning processes established in our Classroom Assessment Cycle are motivating factors that are key to student learning.

However, thus far, classroom management and discipline have not been introduced in this book. Teachers need data in order to understand how classroom routines relating to management and discipline can affect student motivation. The best way to collect these data is to talk with students! The following sample survey (Table 10.1) was designed to help teachers with such data collection. This survey covers not only the classroom climate but also classroom assessment and instruction. We suggest that the teacher take the survey before administering it to students. Then the teacher can compare his answers with the students' answers. The process will be enlightening and will identify many areas that need to be addressed, as it is rare to find that teachers and students are in complete agreement.

Fraser and Fisher's study on classroom climate instruments in the *Journal of Research in Science Teaching* suggests a "potential usefulness of teachers employing classroom environment instruments to provide meaningful information about their classrooms" (1986, p. 401). Since students are more involved in the classroom they can observe more of the typical behavior of the classroom teacher than can an outside observer. We warn teachers to remember that many personality factors may influence student perception, such as whether they like the teacher or not.

TABLE 10.1. CLASSROOM MOTIVATION SURVEY FOR TEACHERS AND STUDENTS.

Statement	Most of Time	Some of Time	Never Occurs
Classroom Environment			
1. Students are aware of the rules in this classroom.			
2. Students participate in establishing the rules in this classroom.			
3. The teacher asks for feedback on topics of student interest.			
4. Students are allowed to choose their own projects.			
5. The teacher expects all students to achieve in this classroom.			
6. Students get lots of opportunities to work with each other in this classroom.			
7. The teacher makes changes in lessons and activities based on input from students.			
8. The teacher knows my name and something personal about me.			
9. Students feel comfortable when talking with the teacher about assignments or classroom activities.			
10. Students feel comfortable enough to talk with the teacher about their problems.			
11. The teacher takes time in class to talk with individual students about classwork.			
12. Students are treated with respect in this class.			
13. Students are expected to respect each other in this classroom.			
14. Punishment and rewards are handled in a fair manner.			
15. The teacher appears friendly and enthusiastic.			
Please add any comment about the classroom environment:			
Classroom Assessment			
16. The teacher explains how an assignment will be graded before students begin work.			
17. Assignments are usually clear so everyone knows what to do.			
18. Deadlines for assignments are reasonable.			
19. Students are asked to assess their own work.			
20. Students are asked to assess the work of their peers and give feedback for improvement.			
21. The teacher gives good feedback so students know what they need to do to improve their grades.			
22. Feedback tools, such as scoring guides, rubrics, and checklists are used in this classroom.			
23. In this class learning is more important than the grade you make.			
24. Students are allowed to redo their work prior to receiving a grade.			
25. The teacher does not mind if everyone gets an "A" on an assignment.			
Please add any comment about classroom assessment practices:			
Classroom Instruction			
26. Classroom activities are not the same every day.			
27. Learning is fun in this classroom.			
28. Students understand the purpose of assignments in this classroom.			
29. Class activities encourage students to use their creativity.			
30. Assignments appear to be relevant to real life situations.			
31. Assignments may be complex, but the work can be shared among peers.			
32. Students feel comfortable working in groups in this classroom.			
33. Assignments are challenging, but "do-able."			
34. The teacher provides needed support or help to students on classwork.			
35. The teacher uses a variety of activities in this classroom.			
36. Classroom activities are interesting to students.			
37. Some assignments are given that allow more than one right answer.			
38. Students see connections between the work done in this class and other classes at the school.			
39. Students are given enough time to learn something.			
40. Students complete their homework assignments for this class.			
Please add any comments about classroom activities:			

Susan used the Classroom Motivation Survey in her high school science classes. The dimensions having the greatest disparity were numbers 7 (The teacher makes changes in lessons and activities based on input from students), 23 (In this class learning is more important than the grades you make), and 29 (Class activities encourage students to use their creativity). Although Susan had marked "most of the time" for all three of these, the students were more likely to choose "some of the time" or "never occurs." The adaptations Susan made in her classes, from the data she analyzed, included

- Explicitly telling students how and why an assignment or activity changed from how it was previously presented or taught

- Teaching students the terms *formative* and *summative* and using these terms to describe classroom assessments to emphasize the amount of time spent on each assessment purpose

- Incorporating more projects into class work and giving students more choices about how they could demonstrate learning of concepts in these projects

Changes in Assessment Practices That Enhance Student Motivation

The final category described by Meece and McColskey (1997) and the one most central to this text is making adaptations that make classroom assessment more motivating for students. Meece and McColskey recommend that teachers offer

- Clear goals and expectations
- Multiple methods of assessment
- Feedback for improvement
- Opportunities to improve
- Good methods of evaluating and reporting student progress

Clear goals and expectations are central to the discussion of rubrics in Chapter Seven, and multiple methods of assessment were emphasized in Part One. The remaining dimensions from the list above are topics relating to giving students appropriate feedback, as discussed in Chapter Nine and also later in Chapter Eleven.

The Critique of the Assessment Environment survey found in Table 10.2 targets assessment issues and may help teachers ascertain areas of potential improvement. As with the previous survey (Table 10.1), we suggest that both the teacher and the students answer the questions in order to gather evidence in multiple ways and thus get a clearer picture of what is actually occurring in the classroom.

Once teachers collect and analyze the data (answers to the questions), an action plan can be formulated to improve classroom assessment and thereby enhance student motivation within the assessment dimension.

TABLE 10.2. CRITIQUE OF THE ASSESSMENT ENVIRONMENT.

Statement: Assessments in this Classroom:	*Most of Time*	*Some of Time*	*Never Occurs*
1. Assess students on clear learning targets.			
2. Have clear, relevant, and meaningful context that engages students to perform.			
3. Go beyond simple recall of facts.			
4. Are easily managed.			
5. Give clear criteria to students prior to scoring the responses, product, or performance.			
6. Allow students an opportunity to self-assess or revise work.			
7. Allow students an opportunity to peer assess and help each other improve.			
8. Are seen as a way to learn.			
9. Integrate other subject areas.			
10. Model effective classroom instruction.			
11. Reveal levels of proficiency (that answers may be more than right or wrong).			
12. Are used by the teacher to improve and adjust instructional strategies.			
13. Provide clear and concise instructions to students.			
14. Are interesting to do.			
15. Align to what the state, district, or school values in student learning (pre-established learning targets).			
16. Are designed as free as possible of cultural, ethnic, or gender stereotypes.			
17. Allow adequate time for completion.			
18. Are worth doing.			
19. Have an appropriate level of difficulty.			
20. Allow students to know how a grade will be figured and reported.			

What actions should be taken to improve assessments in this classroom based on the ratings above?

Source: Butler, 1998.

Addressing Motivational Needs

This chapter began by stating that one teacher responsibility is to encourage the will to engage by creating motivating learning opportunities for students. The intention of discussing motivation theories and studies and providing examples of motivating practices has been to prepare teachers to meet this responsibility. The remainder of this chapter provides a recommended process by which teachers can address the motivation and assessment needs of their students.

Through reflective activities, teachers try to identify the central problem of motivation in the classroom. Then they collect data to verify or nullify the concern. (The two sample surveys found in Tables 10.1 and 10.2 may be useful in this endeavor.) Teachers then continue analyzing the collected data and attempt to determine which of the three indicator categories (instruction, climate, or assessment) is most affected. The next step is to explore and prioritize strategies for improvement that might be used to address the dimensions in which change is desired (strategies of the kinds discussed throughout this book). Finally, teachers formulate an action plan that lists the chosen priorities and strategies and sets out a timeline for putting them into action. Teachers will then be well on their way to creating that roomful of motivated students everyone covets.

Here is a summary of these steps:

1. Identify the problem
2. Collect and analyze data around the problem
3. Determine indicator categories
4. Explore and prioritize strategies to work on the problem
5. Constantly action plan

A facilitated process of dialogue for teachers to meet with colleagues to discuss their progress on these steps would be beneficial. A classroom teacher may first perform steps 1–5 and then ask a team of interested colleagues to meet to seek guidance or feedback on his classroom practices based on the information collected. This process could also be used for a whole school wanting to work on motivation.

This chapter has focused our attention on the Classroom Assessment Cycle through learning factors that are external to the cycle but that strongly influence its functions. The external factor that we particularly examined was the importance of a classroom environment that promotes learning through describing and enhancing student motivation. In the chapter, we examined definitions of motivation, studied motivational theories, and explored ties between motivation and the Classroom Assessment Cycle. Finally, we introduced instruments and a process that can be used by teachers to critique and improve their own classroom learning environments.

Building upon our previous studies of the Classroom Assessment Cycle and motivation, Chapter 11 expands this chapter's section "Changes in Assessment Practices That Enhance Student Motivation" by examining the concept of grading.

Related Assessment Factors

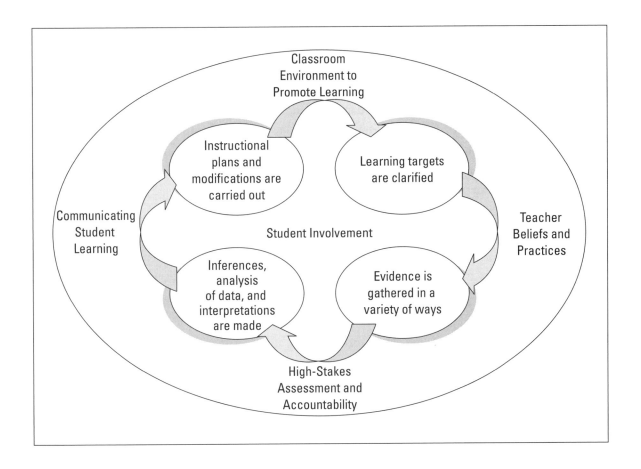

Part Five (Chapters Eleven and Twelve) continues to address factors that influence the Classroom Assessment Cycle, ones that have a great impact on teacher thinking and on practices related to assessment—practices often embedded in memories of how we as students were assessed. We have already looked at teachers' personal beliefs about assessment and strategies for creating a positive classroom environment to promote learning. The two chapters in this section examine techniques for effectively communicating student achievement to stakeholders and methods for bridging the gap between classroom assessment and high-stakes testing issues and accountability.

The issues presented here move our focus beyond the classroom and sometimes beyond the purview of the teacher. For example, teachers usually control how grades are determined in the classroom, but the way that grades are reported is often directed by district and state mandates. Thus we are exploring assessment issues that many educators have no control over and that often leave them feeling frustrated or overwhelmed.

In Chapter Eleven, "Rethinking Grading Practices," we address the communication of student achievement. Once classroom assessment practices change and begin to promote an emphasis on learning rather than on grading, teachers need to know how to translate the assessment results into a grade that reflects achievement and that can be understood by all stakeholders (students, parents, the school staff, the community, and so forth). Some grading issues that may arise involve finding appropriate ways to score student work to reflect the learning of targets (standards) and to determine on-grade-level proficiency; designing grade books that reflect best practices of grading; and making a distinction between formative work and summative work in calculating grades.

Chapter Twelve, "Challenges of High-Stakes Testing," deals with a powerful constituent of assessment knowledge. Large-scale standardized testing with important consequences for schools and students can be a positive driving force that helps teachers and schools become accountable and helps them begin to focus on what students need to learn and how they should be assessed. However, testing results are sometimes not communicated well to educators or communicated so poorly that inaccurate information about testing and accountability may filter down to classrooms. Such miscues may actually create conditions that either promote teaching to the test or promote quick-fix programs. These measures often encourage or establish short-term learning goals rather than fostering the long-term goals for students that support deep knowledge and understanding or lifelong learning habits. Both the advantages and the disadvantages of high-stakes testing are explored in this chapter.

Rethinking Grading Practices

After working with teachers on grading practices and viewing multiple examples of gradebook pages, we have determined that gradebooks in schools mirror checkbooks. Consumers meticulously enter the amounts of checks, deposits, debits, and credits, and carefully subtract the figures, keeping a running total of available assets. At the end of the month, this total is checked against the bank's figures in an activity called balancing the checkbook. What the consumer tends to overlook, however, is the meaning of the information compiled in the checkbook. For example, few consumers know the percentages of their income spent on gifts, medicines, utility bills, or groceries. They are usually unable to ascertain whether they are losing or gaining ground each month as far as expenses versus income is concerned (unless a negative balance occurs each month). Although much time and care are spent on the record-keeping process, very little time is spent on meaning-making activities. The teacher, like the consumer, is a meticulous bookkeeper. However, too few teachers reflect on the consequences of grading (to students, parents, or themselves) or reflect on the subjective decisions that result in the apparently objective grades they assign to students.

Thinking intelligently about grading involves having some insight into the history of grading, reviewing educational research delineating positive and negative impacts of grading on students, and reflecting on one's own grading practices. So this chapter addresses these questions:

- What is the history of grading practices?
- What grading practices are counterproductive, and what are the negative effects of grading in general?
- What are the characteristics of a productive grading plan?
- How can a gradebook be organized to support a productive grading plan?

The History of Grading Practices

Grading is a relatively new development in the history of education, but one that has been the target of much discussion and controversy since its inception (see Guskey, 1996a; Kirschenbaum, Napier, & Simon, 1971). Grading by percentages did not start in this country until after the late 1800s, when high schools, then increasing in number, began using percentage grades rather than progress reports in order to better compare the performances of individuals in a class. By 1919, colleges were screening applicants by their high school grades. In the 1920s and 1930s schools were moving away from a hundred-point scale (percentages) and using instead a three-point scale (excellent, average, or poor) or a five-point scale (excellent = A, good = B, average = C, poor = D, failing = F). Grading on a curve increased in popularity, using a normal distribution curve for students in a class. (Teacher comments on student appearance, motivation, citizenship, and conduct began to appear on report cards too.) The 1930s also saw the development of the standardized test.

At the same time, as early as 1910, educators were questioning the efficacy and the wisdom of giving grades. A classic study by Starch and Elliot in 1912 demonstrated variability in grading practices among 142 high schools. The study examined reliability of percentage grading practices in English and math (Brookhart, 2004). Teachers from each school graded the same English paper, and the grades awarded for the paper varied by as much as forty-seven percentage points. Starch and Elliott's 1912 reprise of this study, this time using a geometry paper, revealed even higher variability among the grades given (a 67 point difference). In 1933, educator Warren Middleton, who was charged with "leading a committee that would revise his school's grading and reporting system" (Guskey, 1996a, p. 13), lamented: "At first, the task of investigating the literature seemed to be a rather hopeless one. What a mass and a mess it all was! Could order be brought out of such chaos? Could points of agreement among American educators concerning the perplexing grading problem actually be discovered?" (quoted in Guskey, 1996a, p. 13). As controversy over grading systems continued in the 1930s, some schools abolished grading and went to pass/fail systems with a mastery approach. A study in the 1950s (Kirschenbaum, Napier, and Simon, 1971) showed that individual comments from the teacher on student papers increased student achievement on subsequent tests, thus emphasizing the need to go beyond just issuing grades.

Nevertheless, between 1940 and 1960, approximately 80 percent of schools began using the five-point scale. Late in the 1960s some colleges moved to eliminate grades and go to pass-fail coursework. It seems, from looking at the history of grading, that challenges to grading practices began almost as soon as they were adopted. Grading issues resurfaced in the 1980s and continue today.

Brookhart (1994) conducted a comprehensive review of nineteen studies on teachers' grading practices and found that paper-and-pencil tests and written evidence contribute mostly to grades, teachers vary in their understanding of the purposes of grades (and often include nonachievement factors in grades), and teacher practices are not consistent with recommendations from measurement specialists. Brookhart (2004) also stresses that teacher education in measurement and assessment is lacking.

Therefore, Starch and Elliot's studies were only the first to point out weaknesses in grading practices. And the "mass and mess" of grading referred to by Middleton is still present today. Arguments still rage within the current literature over the variability of grading practices, the methods of grading to use with standards-based curricula, the utility of grading in promoting student achievement, the use of zero scores in figuring student grades, the affective consequences of grading, the difficulty in understanding and communicating the meaning of grades, and the procedures for grading students with special needs.

Teachers who are informed assessors keep an eye on these grading controversies by reading recent literature and educational research findings. The following is a brief overview of recent developments pertinent to grading practices, intended to aid in this process of creating informed assessors.

Four factors that have led researchers to vigorously confront various changes in grading and reporting practices in recent years are

1. The growing emphasis on standards and performance-based assessment

2. Public doubt as to efficacy of schools and school systems, asking for additional and better information on learning and quality of education for students (the call for accountability)

3. Advances in technology that allow individualized student record-keeping, with multiple records stored for each student

4. Knowledge that a gap in our knowledge base and practice exists (Guskey & Bailey, 2001).

Other agents that have caused educators to refocus on grading and reporting issues are the popularity of constructivist theories of learning and the influence of brain-based research and of Gardner's Theory of Multiple Intelligences (O'Connor, 1999). In addition, the changes in the world economy are being cited as a major influence on the type of assessment needed in schools: "Educators consider themselves to be in 'the success business,' ensuring that students have real opportunity available to them and that the economy has sufficient skilled and knowledgeable people to continue to function efficiently and effectively. These economic changes, coupled with new understandings about learning, are leading to significant changes in the ways children are taught and the ways in which they are assessed" (O'Connor, 1999, p. 6).

Out of such analysis and questioning has come a set of grading practices that are distinct from the traditional methods of grading. It is to the learner's advantage that we keep the new set of factors in mind when thinking about grading. The distinction between traditional grading practices and these newer methods are displayed in Table 11.1.

TABLE 11.1. COMPARISON OF TRADITIONAL AND NEW GRADING PRACTICES.

Traditional Grading	*New Grading*
Norm referenced	Criterion referenced
Summative only	Mix of formative and summative
"Secret" practices	Practices shared with students
Attitude, effort, absences included	Grade focused on achievement
Use of averages	Other indicators of central tendency used

Source: Butler, 2004.

In the following sections, practices from these grading systems are discussed in terms of their counterproductive and productive results, according to recommendations derived from current assessment research.

Grading Practices That Are Counterproductive, and the Negative Effects of Grading

Research calling for changes in assessment practices emphasizes that all grading practices should enhance learning. Here are seven practices, derived from Canady and Hotchkiss (1989, p. 68) and O'Connor (1999), that tend to do the opposite; these can impede learning. We aligned these seven practices into three broad issues: issues in calculating grades, issues in aligning grades and instruction, and issues in grading that discourage effort. We conclude this section with researchers' comments on negative effects of grading.

Issues in Calculating Grades

Wide variations in the ways grades are calculated mean that looking at only the grade itself, an A or B or C, does not tell one as much as many people assume. The variations may encompass use of different grading scales, different grading policies, calculation of final scores in different ways, and discrepancies in the use of zero scores.

Practice 1: Using Different Grading Scales or Policies Across Classes, Schools, or Districts. O'Connor (1999, p. 25) looked at five different rating scales used throughout North America and found, "An A can mean anything from 80 percent to 95 percent, a failing grade can be anywhere between 49 percent and 74 percent. What do these variations mean? For example, is a 49 percent [in one district] the same as 74 percent [in another district]? There is no way of knowing this by comparing marked student work from both jurisdictions, but the wide variation makes one wonder about the meaning of grades."

Similarly, a recent research report involving 110 secondary science teachers in three different Massachusetts counties revealed seventeen different approaches to assigning grades, ranging from giving examinations at the end of the grading period, to using periodic oral examinations, tests, or quizzes, to assessing student work habits (Feldman, Alibrandi, & Kropf, 1998). Even within the same school, different teachers may have different policies regarding late work, make-up work, and dropping grades. This variation in policies results in confusion for the students about what grades mean as they move from class to class and hear an ever-changing litany of grading practices.

Practice 2: Using Averaging to Figure Final Grades. When the teacher records *all* grades and calculates the final grade as an average of these, that "average" may not accurately reflect the student's overall achievement level. Speaking statistically, "Because of the imprecision of grading and the absence of uniform intervals between grades, grades are not interval data. Grades are ordinal! And, since grades are ordinal, the best summary of grades—and therefore the grade that should appear on the report card—is the median, not the mean" (Wright, 1994, p. 724). The *mean* is, of course, the statistical average of all the grades. Wright is advocating the use of the *median* instead, the grade at which half the grades are higher and half are lower. The median is obtained by listing all the grades in descending order. When there are an odd number of grades, the median is the grade that occurs in the center of the list, with an equal number of grades below it and above it. When there are even numbers of grades, the two grades in the center are averaged (added and divided by two) to obtain the median.

How do these two methods of central tendency affect student grades, especially when a student has had an "off" day? Consider the following test scores for Jeff:

92, 94, 93, 67, 98, 91, 90

Jeff earned the 67 test score the day after his parents separated. A strict averaging of these scores would give Jeff a final grade of 89. But placing the scores in descending order

98,

94,

93,

92,

91,

90,

67

and then figuring the median gives Jeff a final grade of 92. Which grade more closely approximates Jeff's achievement in the class? Of course, this final grade is also affected by the quality of the assessments and by the learning it represents.

Practice 3: Using Averages That Include Scores of Zero. "Zeros have a devastating effect on students' grade-point averages. For example, assume that a student has the following numerical grades: 90, 92, 88, 90, 91, 89, and 91. The student's average grade is 90.1. Add a single zero and the average drops to 78.9" (Canady & Hotchkiss, 1989, p. 69). To counteract such devastating effects, not just on the grade but on the student's interest in learning, consider these three practical solutions (McMillan, 1999). First, teachers can record a grade corresponding to the bottom of the grading scale rather than recording a zero. For example, if an F begins at 69, the teacher may record 69 for any missing work. Alternatively, teachers can record zeros, but "use them only for assignments that count little toward the final grade. That is, if homework is 10 percent of the final grade and there are 10 homework assignments, each assignment counts as only 1 percent of the final grade. A student would have to get many homework zeros to have an appreciable impact on the final grade" (McMillan, 1999, p. 5). Finally, teachers might place an "effort" grade as well as an achievement grade on the report card. Zeros, given for incomplete assignments, would count toward the effort grade but not toward the grade on student achievement. Of course, a teacher seeing a pattern of missing work has a responsibility to investigate. Such a perceived pattern should activate a data analysis process and eventually culminate in an instructional modification.

Issues in Aligning Grades and Instruction

One of the major themes of this book has been alignment. In Part One, we dissected curriculum standards into embedded learning targets in order to match these targets to appropriate assessment methods in Part Two. We continued the alignment theme in Parts Three and Four by emphasizing the need for instruction to support (match with) both the curriculum and assessments. Here, in Part Five, we find a new need for alignment. We must now ensure that our grading practices support the curriculum, the assessments, and the instruction.

Practice 4: Putting the Cart Before the Horse by Testing Before Teaching. Too often, teachers do not realize until they are grading a test that students have not learned the assigned material. In this case, the assessment is blatantly unfair. Students must be given time to assimilate new materials and they must have time to practice new skills before being "tested." The cart that is coming before the horse is the summative assessment cart, which is preceding the formative assessment horse.

Pop quizzes often fall into this category of premature testing and may be "simply punitive measures that teachers employ when they suspect that their students have not learned the material. . . . Such tests will change the distribution of grades for the marking period. However, unless our primary focus is sorting and selecting rather than teaching and learning, we must question whether such practices represent the best use of teachers' and students' time" (Canady & Hotchkiss, 1989, p. 70).

Practice 5: Choosing Instructional Activities That Fail to Prepare Students for the Type of Assessment Used. For example, teachers may ask only factual, lower-order questions during classroom instruction yet include higher-order questions on a test. Or students may be asked to demonstrate a skill in class while the teacher observes yet be required to answer detailed written questions about the skill on an exam. In both cases, the method of instruction does not allow students to practice the skills they will need for the assessment. As we emphasized earlier, when learning improvement is the overall goal, planning instruction begins with identifying the standards and benchmarks and learning targets that students will be asked to achieve. One helpful way to think of this is as "the backward design process": "Rather than creating assessments near the conclusion of a unit of study (or relying on the tests provided by textbook publishers, which may not completely or appropriately assess *our* standards), backward design calls for us to operationalize our goals or standards in terms of assessment evidence as we *begin* to plan a unit or course. It reminds us to begin with the question, What would we accept as evidence that students have attained the desired understandings and proficiencies—before proceeding to plan teaching and learning experiences?" (Wiggins & McTighe, 1998, p. 8).

Clearly, a match must be made between method of instruction and method of assessment if teachers hope to foster student success and formulate grades that are reflective of learning.

Issues in Grading That Discourage Effort

Grading practices applied inflexibly may effectively backfire; students may find that a grading system makes future efforts fruitless. When a student receives a sufficient number of failing grades, a sense of hopelessness can become evident in his or her behavior in the classroom. In this instance, grading practices are actually having deleterious effects on student motivation. As Covington's (1984) work, described in Chapter Nine, reminds us, repeated performance failures lead to decreased feelings of self-worth. To "protect their sense of worth or personal value" (Covington, 1984, p. 5), students must opt out by decreasing their efforts. Consider the following two nonmotivating practices:

Practice 6: Communicating Doubt That Students Can Succeed. Teachers communicate doubt when they tell students halfway through the semester that their grades are too low to earn a passing grade for that semester. Student effort then becomes a moot point. Teachers using a fixed percentage scale method (for example a method where tests count 33 percent, homework counts 33 percent, and class work counts 34 percent) or a total point method (final grades are assigned based on the percentage of total possible points for the course that the student has accumulated, such as 250 out of 270 = 93 percent) may find themselves in a precarious assessment position. Students are often clever enough to extrapolate their final grade from current records. Those students who clearly see no way to succeed are rarely motivated to try.

Methods we have already discussed can help teachers avoid this serious problem. In advocating a standards-based grading method, where the major concern is whether the student ultimately can meet a standard, McColskey and Busick (1994), for example, recommend weighting later work more heavily than earlier work in order to solve this problem. Discussing assigning grades in mathematics communication, they point out that early scores for this skill "may not present as accurate a picture of student ability to communicate in mathematics as scores at the end of the grading period. So, it could well be argued that if parents are to be provided an accurate picture of their child's achievement level, only the mathematics communication scores for the journal entries at the end of the grading period should be considered" (McColskey & Busick, 1994, p. 12). These authors also recommend grading work only after students have had sufficient time to practice a skill, rather than recording grades on practice work. This recommendation reinforces the need that formative assessments come before summative ones.

Practice 7: Penalizing Risk-Takers.   Students who sign up for advanced classes and then find that such classes are too challenging rarely have a viable option for change. They must stay in the class and continue to garner low grades, or they may opt to move to a lower-level class, *with their present low average as baggage.* Such options send a message to students that it is safer to stay in lower level classes. One strategy for encouraging educational risk taking is to offer "provisional placements without penalties." This "might encourage students to risk trying more challenging work without jeopardizing their grade-point averages" (Canady & Hotchkiss, 1989, p. 71).

Negative Effects of Grading

In critiquing grading, some researchers go far beyond recommending changes to existing practices and seek broader changes in grading systems, and some even recommend discontinuing the practice of giving grades in schools. Here is a listing of the major problems that need to be addressed, as they have been expressed by a number of educational researchers:

Grades Are Unable to Predict Future Success

- "Neither college nor high school grade point average is a cogent predictor of success after school" (Edwards & Edwards, 1999, p. 260).

- "Ironically, grades don't define people in the real world outside of schools. . . . [E]veryone can think of someone who wasn't school smart (in other words, didn't get good grades), but who became extremely successful, exhibiting intelligence, even becoming leaders in their field once they left school" (Strickland & Strickland, 1998, p. 131).

Grades Are Subjective

- "Grades aren't valid, reliable, or objective" (Kohn, 1999, p. 40).

- "Are grades an explanation of product? progress? effort? achievement? growth? Each of these is a part of what we assess and evaluate in our classes and each has an impact on the learning process and what is learned, but a single grade obviously can't report all these things" (Strickland & Strickland, 1998, p. 130).

- "When subjectivity translates into bias . . . negative consequences can result. Teachers' perceptions of students' behavior can significantly influence their judgments of scholastic performance. . . . Even the neatness of students' handwriting can significantly affect a teacher's judgment" (Guskey, 1994, p. 16).

Grading Undermines the Learning Process

- "[W]hen extrinsic rewards, like grades, are used to reinforce learning, children become conditioned to them. They exhibit considerable interest in what will appear on examinations but do not really care about what is learned" (Edwards & Edwards, 1999, p. 261).

- "While it's not impossible for a student to be concerned about getting high marks and also to like what he or she is doing, the practical reality is that these two ways of thinking generally pull in opposite directions. Some research has explicitly demonstrated that a 'grade orientation' and a 'learning orientation' are inversely related" (Kohn, 1999, p. 39).

Grading Disrupts Relationships

- "Grades spoil teachers' relationships with students. . . . Grades spoil students' relationships with each other. . . . Rewards [grades] . . . disrupt relationships in very particular ways that are demonstrably linked to learning, productivity, and the development of responsibility" (Kohn, 1993, pp. 40, 54).

- "In school, students are segregated in terms of grades received. That practice breeds intolerance, thus diminishing trust and interfering with communication between different groups of students" (Edwards & Edwards, 1999, p. 261).

- "Grading on the curve pits students against one another in a competition for the few rewards (high grades) distributed by the teacher. Under these conditions, students readily see that helping others will threaten their own chances for success" (Guskey, 1994, p. 16).

Grading Promotes Cheating

- "Grades reduce a student's sense of control over his or her own fate, and cheating is seen as an attractive way to achieve more control and reduce the risk of failure" (Edwards & Edwards, 1999, p. 261).

- "Researchers have found that the more students are led to focus on getting good grades, the more likely they are to cheat, even if they themselves regard cheating as wrong" (Kohn, 1999, p. 40).

Characteristics of a Productive Grading Plan

Teachers may not feel empowered to cure these grading problems (enumerated above) by implementing a sweeping change such as the abolishment of letter or percentage grades on report cards. Many teachers feel that they must grade because it is part of school policy. However, teachers can look for ways to restructure their grading practices in an attempt to counteract the possible negative effects of grading. To aid them in such restructuring, Exhibit 11.1 may be helpful. This figure provides a checklist of grading practices designed to counteract the counterproductive practices discussed earlier in this chapter. We will first buttress these grading practices that support learning with relevant research (some of which has been previously introduced in our "counterproductive practices" section) and then, in the last section of this chapter, provide some practical advice to teachers on the implementation of these practices.

Grades Are Strictly Tied to Student Achievement of Curricular Standards

O'Connor (2002, p. 39) particularly emphasizes this grading practice, stating, "In order for grades to reflect standards directly and not just by chance, grades must be based directly on standards." This standards-based grading implies that student work habits, attendance, class participation, and effort should be reported, but *should not* be used to figure a grade for student achievement. O'Connor (2002, p. 40) believes that factors such as "student ability, effort, attitude, behavior, participation, and attendance," if included in grades, makes them "almost meaningless for their main purpose—communication." Stiggins (1997) echoes this sentiment, and Friedman (1998, p. 78) goes so far as to state: "I believe that attitude, effort, ability, behavior, and the like should not affect grades at all, because grades should reflect the level of student achievement in the course. If there is an interest in non-achievement traits, the report card should have a place where this information can be shared, separate from the course grade. If teachers are allowed to mix something like attitude with course grades, there is a real danger that grades will be strongly influenced by teacher opinions as opposed to work that can be graded objectively."

EXHIBIT 11.1. CHECKLIST OF GRADING PRACTICES THAT SUPPORT LEARNING.

1. Grades are strictly tied to student achievement of curricular standards.

   ❏ Dimensions such as student behavior, attendance, or effort are reported separately.

2. Grades are meaningful, in that they are derived from quality assessment tasks that

   ❏ Are clear in assessment purposes

   ❏ Promote metacognition

   ❏ Align to learning targets and instructional strategies

   ❏ Are cognitively challenging

   ❏ Are age- and grade-level appropriate, as well as feasible

   ❏ Give clear teacher expectations that are shared with students prior to the work being attempted

3. Grades are figured from summative assessments whereby

   ❏ Students receive timely and useful feedback through the use of rubrics on formative assessments

   ❏ Teachers activate prior knowledge with diagnostic assessments and use the results to plan instruction

4. Zeros for missing work do not overly penalize students and

   ❏ May be reported under effort categories rather than used in calculating academic grades

   ❏ The lowest grade on the grading scale can be substituted for zeros

5. Grading policies are shared with students and with parents at the beginning of the year.

6. Grading policies are standardized within the school and district where

   ❏ Issues such as make-up work, late work, and missing work are addressed in these policies

7. Grades reflect students' current achievement level where

   ❏ Grades are not a compendium showing the path the student took to learn

   ❏ Every assignment attempted by the student is not used in figuring the grade; the grade may be figured on only the most recent achievement data

8. Teachers use statistical measures that most clearly convey current achievement levels.

   ❏ Teachers consider using the mode or the median instead of the mean.

Source: Butler and McMunn, 2004.

Like the previous researchers, Wiggins (1998, p. 12) recommends that grades be "linked directly to credible and important state or national standards for assessing performance on authentic tasks." In this manner, grades can "provide accurate, quality information about what students have learned, what they can do, and whether their learning status is in line with expectations for that level" (Guskey, 1996b, p. 20).

Grades Are Meaningful and Derived from Quality Assessment Tasks

Stiggins (2001b, p. 16) addresses the need for grades to be based on high-quality assessments by particularly emphasizing that such assessments should have clear learning targets. "How are teachers to provide dependable information about student achievement if targets are not clearly defined?" he asks. O'Connor (2002, p. 79) reiterates the need for quality assessments based upon standards and recommends that teachers "use criterion-referenced . . . performance standards that are public, based on expert knowledge, clearly stated in words or numbers, and supported by exemplars or models." Brookhart (2004, p. 52) goes even further in advocating quality assessment practices as the underpinning of grades, stating, "The performance tasks you ask students to do, or the test questions you ask them to answer, must allow students to exhibit understanding or mastery of whatever concepts or skills you are looking for." Thus, Brookhart, like Stiggins and O'Connor, emphasizes the concept that grades must be aligned with learning targets. She further recommends that grades be based upon cognitively challenging assessments and notes that "one of the most common errors in classroom test construction occurs when a question seems to tap higher-order thinking, but in fact taps recall of predigested information" (Brookhart, 2004, p. 52). Perhaps Guskey and Bailey (2001, p. 46) best summarize the need for grades based on quality assessments. They write, "Evaluation experts stress that if you are going to make important decisions about students that have broad implication, such as the decisions involved in grading, then you must have good evidence. . . . In the absence of good evidence, even the most detailed and sophisticated grading and reporting system is useless."

Grades Are Figured from Summative Assessments

Ken O'Connor states, "Formative assessment should be used primarily to give feedback to students . . . on the progress of learning, whereas summative assessments are used to make judgments about the amount of learning and so are included in grades." He further elucidates that in high schools "this may be the single most important guideline because many secondary teachers have a strong tendency toward putting a number on everything students do and putting everything into the grade" (O'Connor, 2002, p. 109). Brookhart (2004, p. 70) takes the view, "In classroom practice, some assessments serve both formative and summative functions." She believes that a variety of assessments must be included in grades to give a "fuller and more reliable picture of student achievement." We agree with this precept and with Brookhart's

(2004, p. 10) statement that "the grade students get for an assignment should be the closest possible estimate you can make about their real achievement on whatever the assignment is supposed to measure."

Like Brookhart, we feel that a preponderance of evidence is needed and that students' final grades should never be based upon a single grade, or even on less than five grades. We feel that teachers should provide many opportunities for students to demonstrate their progress toward curricular goals. When teachers "gather grading information from a range of sources . . . . [it] allows students to demonstrate their competence in the subject in a variety of ways" (Friedman & Troug, 1999, p. 35). We also agree with Brookhart that some tasks may have formative and summative functions. For example, a constructed response assessment item such as a theme paper can be both formative (in the draft stages) and summative (the final copy). However, we stand with O'Connor in that he would only "count" the final copy, and not use any of the formative assessments of the paper in figuring the final grade.

Zeros for Missing Work Do Not Overly Penalize Students

The actual computation of the grade should also take into account the cautions discussed earlier about the devastating effect of zeros on students' grades (McMillan, 1999). O'Connor (2002, p. 151) lists a number of serious problems with the use of zeros: "The effect of such extreme scores, especially when coupled with the practice of averaging; the lack of proportionality between 0 and 50–70 as the passing score compared with the much smaller differentials between the other score points in the grading scale; the inaccurate communication that results from the use of zeros; and the ineffectiveness of zeros as responsibility-creating mechanisms."

In agreement with McMillan and O'Connor are Guskey and Bailey (2001), who identify the use of zeros as one of the most questionable grading practices. Guskey (1996a, p. 21), writing in 1996 in the *ASCD Yearbook,* also noted, "Assigning a score of zero to work that is late or missed or neglected does not accurately depict student's learning. . . . Students who receive a single zero have little chance of success because such an extreme score skews the average."

Grading Policies Are Shared with Students and Parents

The purpose of grades is to communicate information about student achievement (O'Connor, 2002; Brookhart, 2004; Guskey and Bailey, 2001; Nitko, 2004; Marzano, 2000). This information is communicated to all stakeholders, including students, parents, other teachers, guidance counselors, school administrators, postsecondary institutions, and employers in the community (Nitko, 2004). Nitko notes that communicating student achievement information to parents is particularly problematic and challenging. "Some research shows that parents' and teachers' understanding of what report card grades mean are often far apart. For example, parents may see grades as reflecting pure achievement [when they actually contain nonacademic factors]" (Nitko, 2004, p. 331). To ensure that parents and teachers have a common understanding of the meaning of grades, Marzano (2000) recommends outlining the grading policies in a letter to parents. This letter will list topics, skills, and abilities to be taught during the year and explain how final grades are derived. Such a letter might ensure that the communication purpose of grading is honored by providing "high quality information to interested persons in a form they can understand clearly and use effectively" (Guskey and Bailey, 2001).

Grading Policies Are Standardized

Guskey and Bailey (2001, p. 1) advance the view that grading policies throughout the United States are widely divergent. "Most teachers," they report, "try hard to develop grading policies and reporting methods that are accurate and fair. Nevertheless, the policies and methods they use tend to vary widely from one teacher to another, even among those who teach at the same grade level within the same school." O'Connor, as reported earlier, researched grading scales across North America and found results similar to those of Guskey and Bailey—wide divergence. These researchers have helped us define the problem (no consistency in grading policies), but what are some solutions?

O'Connor (2002, p. 34) states that one solution to the inconsistency would be to anchor grades with "marked student work" from all jurisdictions. This method is also advocated by Brookhart (2004), who states that such anchor papers are used to train raters for large-scale assessments. These raters must be supplied with anchor papers from each level of performance, however, if they are to consistently score student work.

Although the anchor paper method of ensuring consistency might be feasible within a school (teachers of same subjects could gather and score student work together to establish inter-rater reliability), it is too cumbersome a method to use in establishing consistency across districts, states, or nations. What, then, can be done?

Guskey and Bailey (2001, p. 53) suggest that districts adopt a "multifaceted reporting system" because reporting systems must serve multiple purposes and no single reporting system can serve all purposes well. Such a multifaceted reporting system "might include a report card, standardized assessment reports, planned phone calls to parents, monthly progress reports, school open-houses, newsletters to parents, portfolios or exhibits of student work, and student-led conferences." Through the use of such multiple sources, the district adopting this system could minimize consistency errors and "communicate multiple types of information to multiple audiences in multiple formats" (Guskey & Bailey, 2001, p. 2). Such multifaceted systems, then, would enhance the reliability of the assessment evidence reported.

Grades Reflect Students' Current Achievement Levels

Students participate in many activities throughout a grading period. The teacher must differentiate beforehand which activities will "count" and which will not. Frisbie and Waltman (1992) suggest thinking in terms of three levels of activities. The first and broadest level is evaluation, which includes almost all the activities done by students. For evaluation activities, students may eventually receive grades, but some may be assessed only by informal means. For example, the first draft of a paper might be peer-reviewed by another student. Therefore, feedback on student performance was obtained for this activity. However, the peer assessment would not be included in the final grade for the class.

The next activity level is reporting. Activities in the reporting set are activities that generate entries in the gradebook. Still, however, not all the reporting entries will figure into the final grade. The last and narrowest level of activities, then, is the "grading" category. Here, only those activities that are used to compute the final grade are included.

Teachers may also wish to consider Guskey's (1996b, p. 19) recommendation that they look at "learning criteria" when considering what activities will count toward a final grade. Guskey divides learning criteria into product, process, and progress criteria. Table 11.2 provides an overview of these three criteria.

These three categories of criteria focus on the teacher's perceptions about the grading process. For example, "product criteria are favored by advocates of performance-based approaches to teaching and learning" (p. 19). Therefore, teachers using a product orientation to grading are primarily focused on student achievement (what students know and are able to do). In contrast, "process criteria are emphasized by educators who believe product criteria do not provide a complete picture of student learning. From their perspective, grading and reporting should reflect not just the final results, but *how* students got there" (p. 19). Teachers who consider student effort and attendance as grading parameters would have a process orientation then. Progress criteria "are used by educators who believe it is most important to consider how much students have gained from their learning experiences. . . . Teachers who use progress criteria look at *how far* students have come, rather than where they are" (p. 19).

If the grading is designed to show only the most current achievement levels, then teachers may consider adopting Guskey's product criteria and Frisbie and Waltman's grading level of activities. Teachers use statistical measures that clearly convey current achievement levels.

Stiggins (1997) recommends using the most current information rather than the average of all scores, on the grounds that what matters is whether the student demonstrates mastery of all learning targets on a comprehensive final exam. "The key grading question is this: Which piece of information provides the most accurate depiction of the student's real achievement at the end of the grading period—the final exam score or that score averaged with all five unit tests?" Indeed, "If students demonstrate achievement at any time that, in effect, renders past assessment information inaccurate, then you must drop the former assessment from the record and replace it with the new. To do otherwise is to misrepresent that achievement" (Stiggins, 1997, p. 431).

TABLE 11.2. CHARACTERISTICS OF A PRODUCTIVE GRADING PLAN: UNIT OF STUDY ON SCIENCE MEASUREMENT.

Questions to ask . . .	Product	Process	Progress
What are the purposes for the scores?	Achievement to the learning targets addressed.	Nonachievement factors, such as effort, participations, etc.	Improvements or gains noted in learning.
What are the standards and learning targets?	Looking at the bigger picture, what are the "chunks" in learning that the term addresses?	Is teamwork or effort going to be assessed as part of an effort grade? How will it be done?	From a diagnostic assessment what do students need to learn? Are they making gains?
What scores are recorded (formative and summative, if given)?	If formative scores are given then what will they tell the learner? What do they tell the teachers?	Showing if the students were good team players or participated is good but needs to be reported separately.	If students are not progressing or they are not meeting the targets then redoing the work is a good strategy.
What summative scores are recorded in grade book?	Only scores that reflect student learning of the target.	None for practice related to learning.	Scores that best reflect student learning of targets.
What scores are used to determine the final grade from grade book?	Scores the teacher and student feel best reflect learning.	None, but can be reported separately on a report card.	Scores that teacher and student feel best reflect learning.

Source: Summarized from Guskey and Bailey, 2001, and O'Connor, 1999.

Others do not go so far as recommending that previous grades be disregarded, but they do suggest weighting later work more heavily than earlier work (McColskey & Busick, 1994). O'Connor (2002, p. 145) advocates using the median rather than the mean to calculate grades because "the use of the median has the greatest impact when performance is highly variable. Thus, students who perform at a consistently high level or at a consistently low level will see little or no difference in their final grades regardless of which method of central tendency is used." Using the mean would thus help the student who simply didn't "get it" (learn the concepts) when concepts were first presented, but who eventually gained an understanding and improved his performance. Marshalling support for the discontinuation of averaging and advocating for use of the mean, Guskey (1996b, p. 21) writes, "Averaging falls far short of providing an accurate description of what students have learned. For example, students often say, 'I have to get a B on the final to pass this course.' But, does this make sense? If a final examination is truly comprehensive and students' scores accurately reflect what they have learned, should a B level of performance [on the exam] translate to a D for the course grade? If the purpose of grading and reporting is to provide an accurate description of what students have learned, then averaging must be considered inadequate and inappropriate."

Organizing a Gradebook to Support a Productive Grading Plan

If teachers wish to adopt grading practices that support learning, they must first examine their own grading practices and be prepared to make changes. They will also need to revamp their present record-keeping methods in order to facilitate the changes they plan to make. In this last section of Chapter Eleven, we supply some practical suggestions for transforming a gradebook into a powerful tool that supports a productive grading plan.

Examining Present Grading Practices

To most closely examine current grading practices, a teacher needs to access a complete gradebook, such as the one from the previous school year. In examining this gradebook, the worksheet from Exhibit 11.2 may be helpful. The questions in this worksheet help the teacher determine

Organizational structure of the gradebook

Types of assessment data recorded (diagnostic, formative, summative)

Categories of grades used to figure interim course grades

Categories of grades used to figure final course grades

Weights for different types of assignments

Grading scale used (if numerical grades convert to letter grades)

How grades of zero are used

Components of the grade (achievement, nonachievement items)

Percentage of students' making As, Bs, Cs, and so forth.

Planning for Change

Once the gradebook has been examined, the teacher must decide whether present practices are aligned with the grading practices that support learning. A review of Exhibit 11.1 may aid the teacher in making such an assessment. If this assessment

EXHIBIT 11.2. EXAMINING CURRENT GRADING PRACTICES.

Questions to aid in examination of the present grade book

Is the grade book organized around

☐ Standards?

☐ Topics or units?

☐ Types of assignments (quizzes, tests, homework)?

☐ Assessment purposes (diagnostic, formative, summative)?

Are different weights indicated?

☐ Do some grades count "twice?"

☐ Are grades multiplied by factors or percentages?

What types of assignments are found in the grade book, and how much does each "count"?

	Interim Grade	Final Grade
☐ Homework	_____%	_____%
☐ Participation	_____%	_____%
☐ Group work	_____%	_____%
☐ Tardiness	_____%	_____%
☐ Classroom behavior	_____%	_____%
☐ Attendance	_____%	_____%
☐ Projects	_____%	_____%
☐ Class assignments	_____%	_____%
☐ Culminating exams	_____%	_____%
☐ Other (explain)	_____%	_____%
☐ Other (explain)	_____%	_____%

Formative grades in the grade book:

☐ Are indicated by_____

☐ Count toward interim course grade

☐ Count toward final course grade

Summative grades in the grade book:

☐ Are indicated by_____

☐ Count toward interim course grade

☐ Count toward final course grade

Diagnostic grades in the grade book:

☐ Are indicated by_____

☐ Count toward interim course grade

☐ Count toward final course grade

Final course grade, percentages of students earning

A _____%   D _____%

B _____%   F _____%

C _____%

Numerical grading scale point ranges

A _____pts to _____ pts   D _____ pts to _____pts

B _____pts to _____ pts   F _____ pts to _____pts

C _____pts to _____ pts

Zero scores

☐ Absent

☐ Present and used to figure interim course grades

☐ Present and used to figure final course grades

reveals that present practices are not aligned with recommended grading practices, the teacher must make a list of items that may need to be rethought or reworked to bring about this alignment. This, then, becomes the prescriptive list for change. A sample list might include items such as:

- Discontinue use of zero grades

- Keep nonachievement grades separate from achievement ones

- Only use summative assessments to figure grades

Once the teacher compiles this prescriptive list, the next step is to reorganize the gradebook to facilitate record-keeping for the new grading practices.

Reorganizing the Gradebook

The changes indicated in the list above will necessitate a new record-keeping scheme. The portion of the gradebook shown in Exhibit 11.3 provides an exemplar of one way a gradebook could be transformed to facilitate these changes.

EXHIBIT 11.3. GRADEBOOK FORMAT FOR FORMATIVE, DIAGNOSTIC, AND SUMMATIVE SCORES.

H	G	F	E	D	C	B	A	Name	1	2	3	4	5	6	7	8	9	10
								Jenny										
			o	NS	NS	4	NS		95	50	88							
			T							Redo								
										90								
								Report ⇒										
			✓	NS	NS	2	NS	**Melody**	65	83	85							
			Redo						Redo	Redo								
			4						85	92	85							
								Report ⇒										

#	F/D – Assignments	Score Key	#	Summative Assignments
A	Pre-lab assessment of tools	1–4 – Rubric score	1	Tools test (fill in blank)
B	Unit conversion worksheet	NS – Not scored	2	Unit Conversion Test (open ended)
C	Unit conversion homework	0–100 – Percent		Unit Conversion Test (redo score)
D	Unit conversion redo work	✓/o – Complete/not	3	Organizing Data Test (open ended)
E	Homework on data organization	T – Good team player	4	?

In Exhibit 11.3, note the following:

- Formative, diagnostic, and summative grades are recorded separately

- Students do not earn zero scores, but are directed to "redo" assignments

- Nonachievement scores (such as "team player") are recorded on the formative-diagnostic side of the gradebook and therefore are not used to figure interim or final course grades

By reorganizing the gradebook, this teacher has been able to enact changes in her grading practices that bring them more in line with those recommended by current researchers. One best practice of grading that this gradebook does not yet reflect is that of weighting most recent grades more than earlier ones in order to produce overall grades that reflect the student's current achievement level. This teacher may also need to create a grading policy letter that can be distributed to students and parents and may need to work with other teachers at her school to standardize grading policies.

———————

This chapter has been integral in explicating one of the factors (grading) influencing classroom assessment that occur outside the Classroom Assessment Cycle. Chapter Twelve explores another of these outside factors: the high-stakes test.

Challenges of High-Stakes Assessment

12

As we mentioned in Chapter One, tests are classified as high stakes when the results are used to mandate actions that affect stakeholders in education or simply when the public perceives the tests to be of high importance. Such high-stakes tests may affect all educational stakeholders, often in negative ways. As in all classroom assessment, a single assessment cannot provide all the information that is needed about student learning, and therefore it is unfair to make important placement decisions based on only one piece of information. The following scenario uses the analogy of a dentist to emphasize the often unfair ways in which high-stakes assessment data are used.

The Dentist: An Assessment Story

My dentist is great! He sends me reminders so I don't forget checkups. He uses the latest techniques based on research. He never hurts me, and I've got all my teeth, so when I ran into him the other day, I was eager to see if he'd heard about the new state program. I knew he'd think it was great.

"Did you hear about the new state program to measure the effectiveness of dentists with their young patients?" I said.

"No," he said. He didn't seem too thrilled. "How will they do that?"

"It's quite simple," I said. "They will just count the number of cavities each patient has at age ten, fourteen, and eighteen and average that to determine the dentist's rating. Dentists will be rated as excellent, good, average, below average, and unsatisfactory. That way parents will know which are the best dentists. It will also encourage the less effective dentists to get better," I said. "Poor dentists who don't improve could lose their licenses to practice."

"That's terrible," he said.

"What? That's not a good attitude," I said. "Don't you think we should try to improve children's dental health in this state?"

"Sure I do," he said, "but that's not a fair way to determine who is practicing good dentistry."

"Why not?" I said. "It makes perfect sense to me."

"Well, it's so obvious," he said. "Don't you see that dentists don't all work with the same clientele; so much depends on things we can't control? For example," he said, "I work in a rural area with a high percentage of patients from deprived homes, while some of my colleagues work in upper middle class neighborhoods. Many of the parents I work with don't bring their children to see me until there is some kind of problem, and I don't get to do much preventive work. Also," he said, "many of the parents I serve let their kids eat way too much candy from an early age, unlike more educated parents who understand the relationship between sugar and decay. To top it all off," he added, "so many of my clients have well water that is untreated and has no fluoride in it. Do you have any idea how much difference early use of fluoride can make?"

"It sounds like you're making excuses," I said. I couldn't believe my dentist would be so defensive. He does a great job.

"I think you are overreacting," I said. "'Complaining, excuse making, and stonewalling won't improve dental health'. . . I am quoting from a leading member of the DOC," I noted.

"What's the DOC?" he asked.

"It's the Dental Oversight Committee," I said, "a group made up of mostly laypersons to make sure dentistry in this state gets improved."

"Spare me," he said. "I can't believe this. Reasonable people won't buy it," he said hopefully.

The program sounded reasonable to me, so I asked, "How else would you measure good dentistry?"

"Come watch me work," he said. "Observe my processes."

"That's too complicated and time consuming," I said. "Cavities are the bottom line, and you can't argue with the bottom line. It's an absolute measure."

"That's what I'm afraid my parents and prospective patients will think. This can't be happening," he said despairingly.

"Now, now," I said, "don't despair. The state will help you some."

"How?" he said.

"If you're rated poorly, they'll send a dentist who is rated excellent to help straighten you out," I said brightly.

"You mean," he said, "they'll send a dentist with a wealthy clientele to show me how to work on severe juvenile dental problems with which I have probably had much more experience? Big help."

"There you go again," I said. "You aren't acting professionally at all."

"You don't get it," he said. "Doing this would be like grading schools and teachers on an average score on a test of children's progress without regard to influences outside the school, the home, the community served, and stuff like that. Why would they do something so unfair to dentists? No one would ever think of doing that to schools."

I just shook my head sadly, but he had brightened. "I'm going to write my representatives and senator," he said. "I'll use the school analogy—surely they will see the point."

He walked off with that look of hope mixed with fear and suppressed anger that I see in the mirror so often lately.

Source: Adapted from John Taylor's SchoolTalk Column, Lancaster County School District, 300 South Catawba Street, Lancaster, South Carolina, 29720. Ph.: 803-286-6972. Fax: 803-286-4865

The dentist described in this story illustrates the feelings of frustration many educators are currently expressing in the present climate of school accountability. Such accountability has become a basic concept in public education since the publication of *A Nation at Risk* (National Commission on Excellence in Education, 1983). This report highlighted declining student achievement in America's schools and fueled a whirlwind of educational reforms. The resulting educational reform movement cast a critical eye upon the nation's educators. As reforms were adopted and money allocated for education, policymakers, businessmen, state and local education agencies, and parents wanted accountability, "proof that their investment in education produce[d] higher levels of achievement for all students" (Archbald & Newmann, 1988, p. 7).

When Darling-Hammond and Ascher (1991) studied big city school systems to determine where accountability for performance lies and how that accountability is assigned, they found five types of what they call *accountability mechanisms:* (1) political accountability mechanisms arise because school board members, state school superintendents, and legislators must stand for election at regular intervals; (2) legal accountability mechanisms often are born when state governing agencies enact laws or policies, which may be subsequently challenged in the courts; (3) bureaucratic mechanisms arise when regional, state, and district educational agencies set regulations to ensure that schools meet accreditation standards; (4) professional mechanisms come into play when teachers are required to take special course work, pass exams, or perform other activities to qualify for licensure; and (5) market mechanisms arise as parents or students choose to attend particular programs or schools in response to individual needs. These processes are complex, and Darling-Hammond and Ascher suggest that "policymakers often try to achieve accountability by the apparently easiest strategy: monitoring students' test scores and sometimes linking teacher or school rewards and sanctions to such measures" (p. 4).

This view certainly outlines the primary advantage of using standardized testing for accountability purposes: the relative ease with which such testing programs can be implemented (Archbald & Newmann, 1988), as opposed to the more complex forms of assessment described in this text. Another distinct advantage, according to Darling-Hammond and Ascher (1991), is that standardized testing allows simple comparisons to be made between students, schools, districts, states, and nations. In addition, testing has great power to influence the curriculum taught in America's schools (Kohn, 2000). For example, testing can identify curriculum areas in need of improvement, help focus instruction on skills, and serve as a lever for introduction of new curricular materials (Haney & Madaus, 1986). Darling-Hammond and Ascher (1991) also point out that testing programs can affect student and teacher performance and behaviors. Tests can motivate students to learn important material and provide teachers with diagnostic information needed to improve their instruction. A final advantage of standardized testing is that such programs can help communities hold teachers and schools accountable for the learning of their charges (Haney & Madaus, 1986) and, indeed, help expel incompetent teachers (Kohn, 2000).

Nevertheless, governments and communities may be expecting more from large-scale, standardized, high-stakes testing than it is capable of producing. The impetus in this chapter is to reinforce the utility and value of frequent and varied classroom assessment by pointing out the dangers inherent in depending on only one factor, such as standardized, high-stakes testing, in determining student achievement. Standardized test scores should be regarded as only one of the important elements in decision making about student progress. Remember that the use of multiple measures is necessary to form a full and accurate picture of student achievement. It is imperative that teachers understand both the advantages, perceived and real, and the disadvantages, both obvious and hidden, of the reliance on standardized testing that has grown out of the present emphasis on accountability in the larger environment. Teachers should be able to speak knowledgeably to parents, the public, and governing bodies about accountability issues and be prepared to educate these groups about the varied kinds of assessment that are needed if assessment and evaluation are to fulfill the functions of accurately determining how much learning is occurring, what kinds of learning are occurring, and what can be done to improve instruction.

Thus the remainder of this chapter focuses on three questions:

- What are the purposes behind large-scale standardized testing?
- What are the criticisms of large-scale standardized testing?
- What strategies are used by teachers and schools when faced with high-stakes tests that have an impact on student learning?

The Purposes Behind Large-Scale Standardized Testing

According to Cannell (1987), there is no state in the union not testing its elementary students with some type of high-stakes test. As discussed in Chapter One, the term *standardized* means that these large-scale tests use uniform procedures for administration and scoring. *High-stakes* means the results mandate a particular action, such as graduation. Like all assessments, these large-scale tests may be norm-referenced or criterion-referenced and they may focus on aptitude or achievement (also discussed in Chapter One). However, the issue that matters here is that all standardized test results are used in a decision-making process. These decisions are related to the stated purpose of the testing, which is typically one or several of the following:

- To enhance good educational practice
- To reduce the use of harmful or wasteful educational practices

- To create internal mechanisms in a system to identify, diagnose, and change courses of action that do not lead to learning (Darling-Hammond & Ascher, 1991)

- To diagnose student strengths and weaknesses

- To evaluate teachers

- To indicate the general health of education within a system (Haney & Madaus, 1986)

- To make a diploma meaningful by defining minimum competencies of high school graduates

- To identify students who need remediation

- To ensure that teachers are actually teaching desired skills or competencies

- To aid employers in identifying those students who have relevant workplace skills

- To encourage students to acquire particular skills or competencies (Lazarus, 1981)

- To select the most promising students for colleges

- To recognize excellence in students, teachers, schools, and systems (Archbald & Newmann, 1988)

- To "measure school and school district performance to help teachers and principals identify weaknesses and changes in instructional practices" (Guide to President Bush's FY 2006 Education Agenda, 2005) www.ed.gov/about /overview/budget/budget06/nclb/indes/htms

- To ensure "All children receive the quality education they deserve" (Guide to President Bush's FY 2006 Education Agenda, 2005) http://www.ed.gov/nclb /landing.jhtml?src=pb

These testing purposes can be categorized by the "kind of function they serve . . . : instructional, guidance, administrative, or research" (Mehrens & Lehmann, 1987, p. 12). Diagnosis of student strengths and weaknesses is an instructional purpose of testing. The teacher could use these test results to inform his own practice and to tailor education to the particular needs of the students.

An employer who asks job applicants to take a placement test has a guidance purpose in mind. The school district that looks to evaluate programs, teachers, or systems on various measures has an administrative purpose for that test. In the broad sense, all these functions are also research, but more narrowly, individuals or organizations seeking comparative data to test hypotheses or identify broad trends may be said to have a research purpose. For example, the scores of the most promising students in one decade might be compared to those of the most promising students in another decade to determine whether this student category is changing in any way.

Many national organizations and groups support a well-designed system of assessment and accountability when the criteria include some of the following:

- A clear test purpose that is scientifically validated and that uses the most appropriate method for testing (NCTM, 2000; Carpenter, 2001; Greene, Winters, & Forster, 2003)

- Multiple sources of assessment information to make decisions about student learning (NCTM, 2000)

- Use of the assessment information to advance student learning and inform instruction (Commission on Instructionally Supportive Assessment, 2001)

- Tests aligned to curriculum standards (Carpenter, 2001; NCTM, 2000; Commission on Instructionally Supportive Assessment, 2001)

Regardless of the purpose of high-stakes testing, if test results are to be used in decision making, they must be understandable, reliable, and accurate. When controversies over standardized testing arise they are typically focused on criticisms that the test scores fail to meet one or more of these criteria.

Criticisms of Large-Scale Standardized Testing

Reviews of large-scale assessment studies emphasize that when researchers scrutinize testing, most contend that results of such testing (if used properly) can be very helpful (Sadowski, 2000). In this section, however, we review some of the problems associated with improper performance. We address problems concerning how large-scale test results are reported, how these tests employ problematic statistical concepts, and how these tests are constructed. It is our contention that any criticisms presented here are a powerful contribution to the case for carrying out *classroom assessment* as we have been describing it in this book.

Issues in the Reporting of Test Scores

Many authors in this field argue that the public and parents, in particular, either misinterpret the meaning of standardized test scores or fail to understand the rubric, or scoring guide, used. It is not surprising, however, that people are confused about the meaning of test results. Testing is now an industry and that industry has engendered its own complex vocabulary. To understand the scores, one must understand that vocabulary. Here is a basic introduction that illustrates why teachers should delve further into this topic. We use the multiple-choice test scores for a single student, Superboy, as an example.

Consider the *raw scores* for Superboy found in Table 12.1. By themselves these scores have little meaning. One cannot tell, for example, how Superboy compared against other superheroes. Also, one should hesitate to assume that Superboy answered more questions correctly in the Strength vs. Locomotive category than he did in the other two categories, as the number of questions in each category is not known. For example, the test may have asked only sixteen questions about Leaping Tall Buildings, in which case Superboy got them all right.

For these reasons, *derived scores* for Superboy might be more informative. Derived scores might take the form of percentages. Percentage scores are figured by dividing the number of correct items by the total number of items and then multiplying the answer by a hundred. Assume that the Leaping Tall Buildings category had twenty questions. Therefore, Superboy's derived percentage score would be $(16/20 \times 100) = 80$ percent for this category. Percentage scores for the other categories can be figured the same way, once the total number of items in each category is known (see Table 12.2).

With a percentage score and the scores of the other students, one can easily compare performances within a category. For example, if the Incredible Hulk received 90 percent in the Leaping Tall Buildings category, then the Hulk answered more of the questions correctly and performed better than Superboy in this category.

One might also consider Superboy's percentile rank or his grade equivalent score (Table 12.3). A *percentile* is "the point on the distribution below which a certain percentage of the scores fall. A percentile rank gives a person's relative position or the percentage of students' scores falling below that individual's obtained score" (Mehrens & Lehmann, 1987, p. 113).

TABLE 12.1. RAW SCORES.

Student	*Leaping Tall Buildings*	*Speed vs. Bullet*	*Strength vs. Locomotive*
Superboy	16	33	42

TABLE 12.2. DERIVED PERCENTAGE SCORES.

Student	*Leaping Tall Buildings*	*Speed vs. Bullet*	*Strength vs. Locomotive*
Superboy	80%	92%	88%

TABLE 12.3. PERCENTILE RANKS.

Student	*Leaping Tall Buildings*	*Speed vs. Bullet*	*Strength vs. Locomotive*
Superboy	98	99	99

These data indicate that in the Leaping Tall Buildings category, Superboy performed as well as or better than 98 percent of the students who took the test. Note that Superboy's percentile rank is different from his derived percentage score. Superboy got only 80 percent of the questions right on this section, but that performance placed him in the top 2 percent of superheroes. One of the most common errors found in interpreting test results is confusing percentage scores with percentile ranks. "Parents in particular are likely to erroneously equate a percentile rank of 82 with getting 82 percent of the items correct or getting 82 percent of the possible points" (Payne, 1997, p. 411). Percentile rankings are helpful in determining where a student is strongest and weakest in comparison to other students. Obviously, Superboy needs to work on Leaping Tall Buildings, as this was his lowest area of achievement.

Standardized test results may also be reported in *grade equivalents*. Assume that Superboy was in the seventh grade when he took this standardized exam. Table 12.4 shows his grade equivalents in each category.

What do these scores actually mean? First, assume that Superboy's scores are being compared against those of a norm group consisting of superheroes in grades seven, eight, nine, ten, eleven, and twelve. In this norm group were three superheroes just beginning the seventh grade and their raw scores for Leaping Tall Buildings were 8, 9, and 10. The median (middle) score for the seventh grade superheroes, then, was 9. If Superboy had scored a 9, he would have a grade equivalent of 7.0. Superboy's grade equivalent, however, is 11.2. This means he achieved the median performance of superheroes in the second month of the eleventh grade. It is important to understand, however, that this means Superboy performed Leaping Tall Buildings as well as the average student in the second month of eleventh grade would have performed *on the seventh grade criteria* used on the test. Therefore, this result does not mean that Superboy can actually leap tall buildings as well as an eleventh grader. Like the percentile rankings, these scores make it easy to compare Superboy's relative performance on different portions of the exam and to compare Superboy's performance to that of other seventh grade superheroes.

This small sample of testing vocabulary is only the tip of the iceberg. An in-depth study of standardized assessment would garner many more terms, such as nominal scales, ordinal scales, interval scales, ratio scales, mental age scores, scaled scores, stanines, normal curve equivalents, and profiles (Mehrens & Lehmann, 1987; Payne, 1997). No wonder consumers of test scores are confused! Without guidance, the public has little chance of understanding the numbers on a test report.

TABLE 12.4. GRADE EQUIVALENTS.

Student	Leaping Tall Buildings	Speed vs. Bullet	Strength vs. Locomotive
Superboy	11.2	12.8	12.9

Issues in Statistical Methods

Even more controversial than the scores themselves are the means of deriving them. To truly understand the meaning of the score, one must understand some of the statistical measures used in testing and have some knowledge of the test content.

Consider percentile rankings once more; they reflect test design as well as student performance:

> Standardized tests are designed so the scores of any representative population of students will be normally (bell-shaped) distributed—that is, 68 percent of the scores will always fall between a certain score above and a certain score below the mean. To achieve these properties, developers of standardized tests write and try out several questions on students. The questions selected for the final test are those that about half the students get right. Questions that most students get right or wrong are not used, because if just about everyone gets a question right or wrong that question does not help to rank students from high to low. . . . To achieve a normal curve, the developers deliberately choose certain items to ensure that at least half the students will always score below average [Archbald & Newmann, 1988, pp. 53–54].

So if a student scores below average on a test (below the fiftieth percentile), it may be because the test was designed to create this score! Or as Kohn (2000, p. 318) puts it: "Exactly 10 percent of test takers will score in the top 10 percent, and half will always fall below the median. This is not a function of failing schools; it is a function of the meaning of the word *median.*" Therefore, even though percentile rankings make it easier to compare students' performances one to another, the true meaning of the performance may still be murky.

Another criticism of standardized testing related to statistics addresses the tendency for individual student scores to be aggregated to create a school profile. For one thing, this aggregated score will not reveal any differences that exist among various student groupings (see, for example, Archbald and Newmann, 1988, p. 58). In addition, this profile is typically compared to other school profiles, but the usefulness of this comparison may be limited because "schools may differ in test performance for reasons having little to do with program quality . . . a school serving lower-income students can have a markedly greater educational effect on its students than a school serving more affluent families, yet still show lower test scores" (Archbald & Newmann, 1988, p. 59). Darling-Hammond and Ascher (1991, p. 7) concur:

> Although school-based analysis can provide rich data, for some educational issues the school is either too large or too small a unit for analysis. In schools with tracks and other educational groupings, it is important to know not only whether a school offers calculus, for example, but which and how many students can take this course, and what the other math course options are. In the same vein, while a school may contain computers, their use and availability may differ depending on the track. To answer questions of equity, a school's resources must be compared to those of other schools in the district and in other districts.

So the context of the school is vastly important in making comparisons school to school, school to district, district to district, state to state, and nation to nation. Reports of test scores, however, rarely include school context information. This leads to further statistical misconceptions reported in the media and taken for truth by the public.

In short, due to the complexity of statistical methods involved in calculating scores, the layperson has little hope of interpreting test results accurately and meaningfully. Indeed, even as testing continues to increase in the United States, "many parents are unfamiliar with the names of the tests, don't understand what test scores mean, and, more critically, don't know what is measured by their state's educational assessment" (Carter, 2000, p. 2).

Issues in Test Construction

The confusion over the interpretation of results is often exacerbated by ignorance concerning the content of the exams. Consider one major implication of the method we described earlier of selecting questions for norm-referenced standardized exams. Questions that all (or no) students answer correctly do not find their way onto these exams. This means that they rarely deal with the central or most important content teachers have emphasized in classes, as most students would tend to get such content-related questions correct. Kohn (2000, p. 319) reports that norm-referenced tests "are therefore likely to require knowledge that is not taught in schools—thereby heightening [the effect of] socioeconomic factors that are highly correlated to out-of-school learning—because the primary objective is to distinguish one student from another." Such out-of-school learning includes, for example, "learning stemming from the linguistic environment of the home, and the student's exposure to reading opportunities, numerical problem-solving opportunities, and other sources of information (movies, TV, museums, magazines, parental conversation and explanations, learning games)" (Archbald & Newmann, 1988, p. 59). Therefore this manner of selecting questions raises concerns about the fairness of the tests.

A related concern is the evidence that large-scale standardized testing is having the unexpected result of raising dropout rates among minority students. McNeil (2000, p. 730) reports that in Texas during 1978, "more than 60 percent of black students and almost 60 percent of Latinos graduated." However, by 1990, "after four years of the Perot-era standardization reforms, graduation rates for blacks, Latinos, and whites had all dropped. . . . [And] fewer than 50 percent of all black and Latino ninth-graders make it to graduation." It has also been argued that high-stakes testing "has been the primary instrument that justifies keeping minority children in lower end tracks and for explaining their eventual failure" (Ohanian & Ruiz, 2000, p. 290) and that "the tests are designed for a 'general' population and usually ignore minority or underrepresented groups" (Strickland & Strickland, 1998, p. 206).

The fact that content selected for exams seems to unfairly profit one group to the detriment of others is not the only criticism associated with the construction of standardized tests. Many authors (Archbald & Newmann, 1988; Kohn, 2000; Bond, 1996; Beard, 1986) lament the superficial nature of standardized exam content. They imply that the test questions are, in effect, a mile wide and an inch deep. They cover a vast array of disciplines, but consist mainly of recall or factual questions and tests of low-level skills and do not test understanding of concepts or of interrelationships between disciplines. Norm-referenced tests and minimum competency exams in particular have come under attack.

What educational "meat" are the standardized tests missing? Davey (1992, p. 3) recommends, "Students should demonstrate whether they can organize their thoughts, analyze information, and formulate arguments." Kohn (2000, p. 318) concurs that certain "mental operations, such as organizing information and constructing an argument," are what is largely missing from these tests. Traditional testing also neglects "the kinds of competence expressed in authentic 'real life' situations beyond school—speaking, writing, reading, and solving mechanical, biological, or civic problems" (Archbald and Newmann, 1988, p. 69).

In fact, it seems that an emphasis on standardized testing can impede excellence rather than enhance it. Darling-Hammond and Ascher (1991) find that scores on assessments of higher-order thinking skills have declined in virtually all subject areas since 1970, perhaps because the "narrow information on the test comes to substitute for a substantive curriculum in the schools" (McNeil, 2000, p. 730). For instance, McNeil's study of Texas schools preparing for the Texas Assessment of Academic Skills showed the use of test-preparatory materials "that have virtually no value beyond practicing for the tests. The scores go up in these classrooms, but academic quality goes down" (p. 730). Among the issues McNeil found in the area of reading, for example, were that "Reading samples are material students are meant to forget the minute they mark their answers" (p. 731) and that although more students were passing the reading tests, teachers were reporting that fewer students were actual readers. Ohanian and Ruiz (2000, p. 291) offer anecdotal support for the latter finding with his description of a superintendent of schools posing for a picture in support of high-stakes testing: "He shows young children a poster delineating what is important in reading: title, author, illustrator, objective. We adults may read for wonder, for wit, to be transported to another place, to experience other people's feelings. Children must read to find a machine-scorable objective."

Such a focus on teaching to ensure good test results means, "to some extent at least, a high test score reflects not knowledge or intelligence, but good test taking skills. If students' scores can indeed be raised by teaching them tricks or by cramming them full of carefully chosen information at the last minute, this should be seen not as an endorsement of such methods but as a devastating revelation about how little we have to learn from the results of these tests" (Kohn, 2000, p. 321).

Other Issues

Educators and others have raised a number of additional problems associated with large-scale standardized testing. Here are two of particular concern.

Seeing Students Who Are Poor Performers as Liabilities. One school superintendent has observed that "as a direct result of high-stakes testing, When a low-performing child walks into the classroom, instead of being seen as a challenge, or an opportunity for improvement, for the first time since I've been in education, teachers are seeing [him or her] as a liability" Kohn (2000, p. 322). In effect, then, high-stakes testing may pit teachers against students if the testing environment means teachers must strive to maintain high test scores if they are to retain their jobs or to qualify for raises.

Making It Harder to Retain Teachers. High-stakes testing may also have a harmful effect on retention of teachers. Having to shoulder the "blame" for all of education's ills may, indeed, cause teachers to rethink their career choices, especially when those who mandate and design these tests are shaping the curriculum that teachers must teach and be judged for teaching (see, for example, Gallagher, 2000; McNeil, 2000).

When we look at all the information available, it is easy to understand why the current high-stakes testing environment in America is so controversial. It is certain that with Bush's NCLB plans, high-stakes assessment will be around for some time. So what should we do to deal with the issues at the school and classroom levels?

High-Stakes Tests That Affect Student Learning: Strategies Used by Teachers and Schools

Educators tell us they are sometimes torn between a focus on strategies to get test scores up quickly (score increases that may not represent real student learning gains) and strategies that support a high-quality learning environment for every classroom. From our experience, classroom teachers and schools are often pressured to implement short-term, "quick-fix" strategies designed to "get test scores up so students' chances of passing high-stakes tests improve" (McColskey and McMunn, 2000). In this last section of Chapter Twelve, we explore both short-term and long-term strategies used by educators caught in the high-stakes testing arena.

Exploring Short-Term Strategies

This pressure may come from leaders at the district or school level who may not realize the importance of evaluating high-stakes improvement strategies to see whether they benefit student motivation, learning, and development over time. This lack of evaluation may communicate primarily a short-term, "get the scores up at any cost" approach to learning.

Some concerns teachers report about high-stakes testing are "the neglect of subjects, topics, outcomes not tested; the overuse of instructional materials that mimic state test items; and reduction of the pool of tested students through tactics such as discouraging certain students from taking higher level courses" (McColskey & McMunn, 2000, p. 116).

Is it possible to continue the commitment to organizational and instructional reform even within a high-stakes state testing environment? A former superintendent and assistant superintendent of Elizabeth City-Pasquotank School District in North Carolina collaborated with SERVE in 1995 on a publication about that district's efforts to build a professional commitment to quality learning. The superintendent concluded "that while focusing on improving practice and quality will result in long-term improvement, short-term survival requires some attention be given to preparing students to perform on the type of state accountability tests administered. Our approach has been to include not only test scores but also research-based instructional practices as the focus of dialogue with teachers and administrators to build a culture of inquiry" (McColskey and McMunn, 2000, p. 116).

Visit many educational conference showrooms, talk to educators, or surf the Internet and one will find a vast array of resources that claim to improve test scores dramatically. Examples of these short term strategies include

- Test workbooks or computer programs that mimic high-stakes test formats or questions
- Less emphasis on non-tested subjects and performance types of assessments
- School rewards for increasing student scores
- Holding pep rally-like student sessions to stress testing importance, preparation for the test day, and test-taking skills
- Using class time to practice or prepare for testing
- Choosing workshops for teachers from vendors that promise improved test scores as results

There are other short-term strategies not listed here, but looking over the above bulleted list, one should note that most of these strategies deal with getting students ready and motivated for the test. What is lacking is the emphasis on learning. We realize from our work as teachers and assessors that familiarity with the testing format is important. Students must be prepared for the formats they will experience on high-stakes tests. However, we recommend such preparation be done as part of instruction, in a continuous cycle of classroom assessment rather than as an isolated test-prep event.

Jones, Jones, Hardin, and others (1999) reported on the time elementary educators in North Carolina spent on such test prep events or on test practice in a study of

470 teachers. Their survey results showed that 80 percent of the teachers reported that students spent more than 20 percent of their total instructional time practicing for state tests, more than 28 percent reported that students spent more than 60 percent of instructional time practicing for tests, and more than 70 percent reported that students were spending more time practicing on tests than in the past.

Popham (1995, p. 238) explains, "If students in their regular classroom instruction are allowed to deal only with the explicit item format used on a test, they will be far less likely to generalize what they have learned. Test scores may rise, but comparable content mastery may not."

Like Popham, we believe that testing improvement strategies may improve test scores in the short term, but these strategies may not affect student learning in the long term. This is why we emphasize the use of continuous classroom assessment, rather than asking teachers to depend upon large-scale testing to enhance student achievement.

We realize, however, that high-stakes testing is not going away. We also realize that, when used appropriately, this type of testing can provide useful information, so we suggest that school leaders encourage school faculty to discuss test preparation strategies and identify the pros and cons of each, and "to develop a reasonable set of educationally defensible strategies with a positive impact on students. Then ask, Are they defensible?" (McColskey & McMunn, 2000, p. 117). We would encourage teachers to request that their leaders look at the research and hold faculty discussions related to the short-term fixes presented in this portion of Chapter Twelve. In other words, faculties must decide on priorities for instruction. Do we want to teach the test or actually test the learning?

Exploring Long-Term Strategies

Where does this leave teachers? If we are truly serious about designing a supportive and effective learning environment aimed at student learning, we must revisit the Classroom Assessment Cycle and consider more long-term strategies dealing with high-stakes testing that enhance student learning.

Understanding the key role formative assessment plays in developing students' confidence and depth of knowledge and using information from classroom assessment to inform needed modifications in teaching strategies is key to helping students progress. As reported in the Introduction, Black and Wiliam reviewed 250 articles by researchers in several countries and unmistakably concluded, "improving formative assessment raises standards" (2004, p. 9). Therefore, a powerful strategy for improving learning is to enhance formative assessment practices. This strategy may not show quick results but may, in fact, keep the students progressing toward greater achievement over time.

As stated earlier, high-stakes testing results can provide useful information to teachers. Examining and analyzing high-stakes test results and using these results appropriately is key to helping all students improve. A long-term strategy might include unpacking patterns of performance on state tests. This means not just looking at all students who did poorly in comprehension and setting up groups for specific instruction in this area, but actually unpacking the patterns of performance for *individual* students. Buly and Valencia (2002) studied the percentages of students who failed state reading tests dealing with meaning (comprehension and vocabulary), fluency (rate and expression), and word identification. Though the high-stakes results originally showed that the failing students had similar needs, an additional cluster analysis of the data showed that individual student needs were quite different. Buly and Valencia noted that 18 percent of the students were *automatic word callers,* which meant that they read quickly and accurately but did not comprehend what they read. Another group was identified as *slow word callers,* and 17 percent of the students failed in comprehension because they read so slowly. The strategies needed to help these two groups improve are very different. By thoroughly unpacking the high-stakes data, however, it was possible to determine individual student needs. This unpacking of data is the type of data analysis of test information that is needed in order to help all (individual) students.

Developing teacher and school capacity for implementing long-term strategies to work on instructional reform is difficult. Holding collegial conversations around some of the following questions may help begin this process:

1. What strategies are we using to improve test scores in this school?

2. Are these strategies effective?

3. If not these strategies, then what strategies should we use to help improve our school test scores and the learning for all of our students?

4. Can we defend the strategies we use to parents and students?

5. What will these strategies help us do?

6. How will we know whether the strategies are being implemented in an appropriate and useful manner?

7. If we use these strategies, where do we hope to be in two, three, or five years?

8. How will we measure our success?

Classroom assessment offers another source of information about student achievement, one that can reveal much about student learning that high-stakes tests can miss. Table 12.5 summarizes differences between the classroom assessments and high-stakes testing. We hope that teachers will find these points useful in marshalling arguments

TABLE 12.5. CHARACTERISTICS OF CLASSROOM ASSESSMENT VERSUS HIGH-STAKES TESTING.

Characteristic	Classroom Assessment	High-Stakes Testing
Implementation	Time-consuming	Relatively efficient
Purpose	Diagnose individual student progress	Comparison of achievement student-to-student, school-to-school, district-to-district, state-to-state, nation-to-nation
Format	Diverse, calls for creation of student products	Most often multiple choice
Level of questions or activities	High order (analysis, synthesis, evaluation)	Low order (recall or application)
Reporting	Focuses on what individual students know and are able to do	Uses numerical scores, derived by complex statistical methods; aggregates student scores so that individual performance is secondary to group performance

in support of classroom assessment as a major strategy to help improve high-stakes testing.

It is appropriate to close this chapter on high-stakes, large-scale assessment with the comments of Marilyn Cochran-Smith, editor of the *Journal of Teacher Education*. In her editorial from the September–October 2000 issue, Cochran-Smith reminds readers that "high stakes" is a term borrowed from gambling.

> The term is used to indicate the potential for both great losses and great wins when one makes the choice to play at the big-money table. Unfortunately, much of the heated debate about high-stakes tests assumes that, like the best of poker games, test results are based solely on the skill demonstrated in a fair game played at a table to which everybody has had the same invitation and at which everybody has the same chance of drawing a winning hand. Test takers caught in the high-stakes national testing movement have had no choice about whether they will play in the big-money game.

Teachers, as players in the high-stakes game, should choose to act in accordance with their ethics and conscience, setting as their goal the best possible educational experience for students.

Conclusion:
An Appeal for Change

As the end of this book draws near, we should review our intentions to judge the effectiveness of this book in conveying the intended concepts. The major goal of *A Teacher's Guide to Classroom Assessment: Understanding and Using Assessment to Improve Student Learning* is captured within the title. The book is intended as a reflective tool for teachers that will enhance their understanding of classroom assessment and promote the implementation of classroom assessment best practices. We have endeavored to assemble a compendium of information on classroom assessment, provide a holistic view of classroom assessment, support assertions about classroom assessment with current research, and disturb the complacency of teachers about their own classroom assessment practices.

From personal experience, we know that having one's complacency disturbed results in an unpleasant, highly emotional state. Our own experiences have taught us that teachers who have been challenged to implement changes or innovations often feel overwhelmed, inadequate to the task, and frustrated. If these feelings can be overcome, however, perturbations of everyday routines can lead to profound growth.

At the end of a long book, it is often useful to view a summary of topics covered and reflect on the concepts introduced. As you read the remainder of the Conclusion, please record your own reflections concerning the topics reviewed. These reflections can then be used as an index of text ideas that provoked the greatest personal responses.

The Introduction and Chapter One disclosed the rationale for the book, provided an overview of topics covered, and introduced the assessment language used throughout this guide. The first section of this book introduced and closely examined the Classroom Assessment Cycle (Figure C.1). This cycle was then used as the organizing focus of Parts One through Four (Chapters Two through Ten).

Beginning in Chapter Nine, important assessment constituents influencing the Classroom Assessment Cycle were introduced. These constituents included teacher

FIGURE C.1. CLASSROOM ASSESSMENT CYCLE.

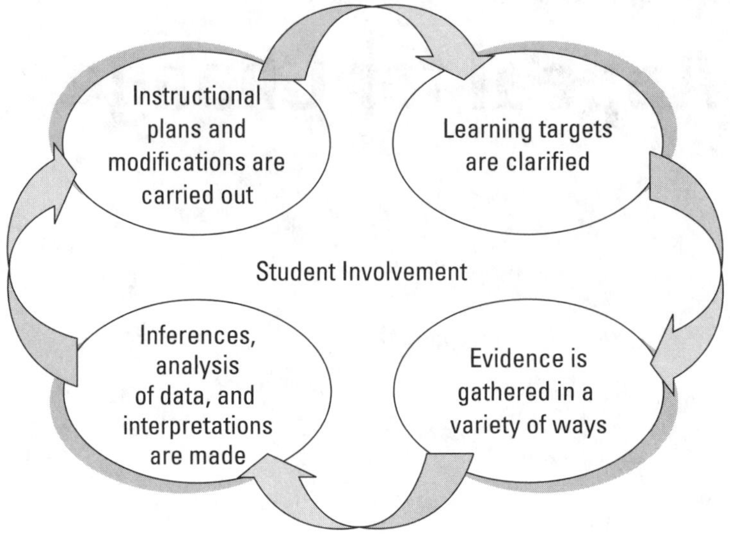

beliefs and practices, classroom environments promoting learning, communication of student achievement, and high-stakes testing and accountability. Figure C.2 portrays how the Classroom Assessment Cycle floats within the sea of these influential constituents. Chapters Nine and Ten, as well as the two chapters in Part Five (Chapters Eleven and Twelve) reviewed concepts related to these factors.

To promote reflection on the topics covered within this guide, we created Table C.1. This table lists the most vital information presented within each section of the book, chapter by chapter. Some of the ideas listed here are controversial; some appear to be common sense. However, all capture the essence of what we are attempting to convey to teachers.

All the concepts in all the chapters have encouraged teachers to examine their own assessment practices, with enhancing student achievement as the ultimate goal of this examination. It can be a powerful experience for one teacher to reflect, research, and revise his or her own teaching practice. However, a focus only on individual teacher change can never achieve more far-reaching, systemic change. Just as it takes more than one person to perform "the wave," more than one teacher must change in order for there to be positive impact on all the students in a system. All the parts of the system (teachers, students, administrators, support staff) must agree and recognize the need for change so that a coordinated effort can occur. Without this buy-in from all, change will be slow and will cause confusion among the different parts of the school population who do not understand the need for the change. In order to change assessment practices, schools and districts must be supportive and encourage the change. In addition, there is a need to look at the whole system to see how each part fits into the "big picture."

FIGURE C.2. CLASSROOM ASSESSMENT CYCLE SHOWING EXTERNAL AND INTERNAL FACTORS.

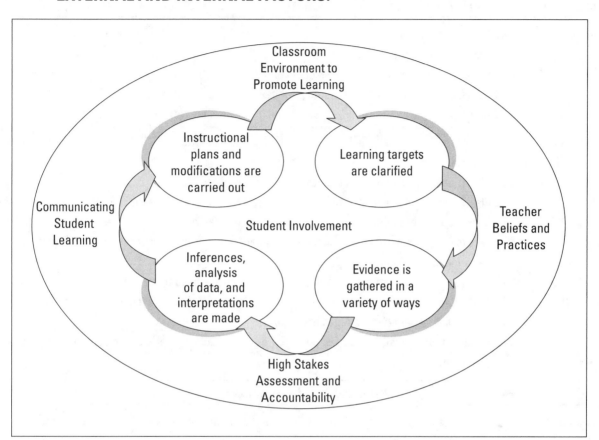

The big picture in assessment encompasses classrooms in which the beliefs and practices of the teacher support

- Clarifying learning targets for students
- Collecting high-quality student achievement data
- Analyzing assessment data and formulating sound conclusions from this analysis
- Modifying instruction to match the learning needs of the students

In order to implement this big picture, both personal and systemic changes are needed. Although changing may be difficult, the rewards will be reaped in enhanced student achievement and in personal growth. These changes will be made slowly as educators must plan, experiment, gather evidence, reflect, modify, and revisit ideas. While educators are moving along this route to assessment change, they must realize they will never finalize their work or reach an endpoint, since the destination is always more change. Therefore, change should be viewed as a continuous process of growth.

TABLE C.1. SUMMARY OF CHAPTER CONCEPTS.

Chapter Title	Important Concepts
Introduction	❑ Research demonstrates that student achievement is increased by the use of quality classroom assessment practices ❑ The purpose of formative assessment is to provide feedback to students about their progress ❑ Assessment literacy is not often taught in teacher preparation programs ❑ Assessment practices are influenced by factors within and factors outside the classroom
Chapter 1: Understanding the Varieties of Assessment	❑ There is a place for all types of assessments in the classroom; the key is to use a variety of assessment types ❑ Classroom assessment is an ongoing process ❑ Classroom assessments can be diagnostic, formative, or summative in purpose ❑ Classroom assessments can be categorized as selected or constructed-response assessments; constructed-response assessment can be further subdivided into product and performance assessments ❑ Standardized tests are high stakes when the results are used to mandate actions ❑ Norm-referenced tests are used to classify students; criterion-referenced tests measure how well a student has achieved a standard ❑ Aptitude tests measure capacity, potential, or ability; achievement tests measure the effect of learning
Part 1: Clarifying Learning Targets	
Chapter 2: Unpacking Standards and Benchmarks	❑ Standards are statements of what should be taught; benchmarks explain what students must do to meet these standards ❑ Curriculum must adapt to world changes ❑ There is no hope of students achieving learning targets if everyone in the classroom (teacher and students) do not have a clear understanding of what students should know and be able to do ❑ Curriculum must be "unpacked" to help teachers understand what they are being asked to teach to students
Chapter 3: Defining Student Expectations	❑ The five learning targets are Knowledge and Understanding, Reasoning, Performance Skills, ❑ Product Development, and Dispositional targets ❑ Teachers should plan assessments before they plan instruction ❑ Teachers can no longer rely on the textbook for the sequence and pacing of a course; selecting text information and planning the sequence of instruction has become a giant task for teachers

Chapter Title	Important Concepts

Part 2: Gathering Assessment Evidences

Chapter Title	Important Concepts
Chapter 4: Understanding and Selecting Assessment Methods	❏ By using multiple and diverse sources, teachers can be sure they have ample evidence to accurately assess student performance ❏ Constructed response assessment is the direct, systemic observation of actual student performance according to pre-established criteria. ❏ Questioning, teacher observations, and student/teacher dialogues are general methods that can be used to assess student learning ❏ Examples of simple product assessments include short answer sentences or paragraphs, graphic organizers, graphs, tables, and matrices ❏ Examples of performance assessments include oral presentations, demonstrations, enactments, debates, and panel discussions
Chapter 5: Written Product, Portfolio, and Project Assessments	❏ Examples of more complex product assessments include logs, journals, notebooks, portfolios, and projects. ❏ Portfolios may be classified by their purposes, as best works, memorabilia, growth, or proficiency portfolios ❏ All assessment types must be carefully designed to align with curricular learning targets
Chapter 6: Designing Quality Classroom Assessment Tasks	❏ Instructional tasks and assessment tasks often overlap ❏ High-quality assessment tasks have clear assessment purposes, are aligned with learning targets and instruction, promote metacognition, are cognitively challenging, are developmentally appropriate and feasible, and are engaging to students
Chapter 7: Creating Useful Scoring Guides	❏ Holistic rubrics provide students with only one score; analytical rubrics provide scores for several criteria ❏ Analytical rubrics provide feedback to students on their strengths and weaknesses ❏ High-quality rubrics use criteria appropriate to the task, contain descriptions of performance level written in language the students can understand, utilize a format appropriate to the assessment purpose, and contain easily understood score conversion guides

Part 3: Working with Assessment Data

Chapter Title	Important Concepts
Chapter 8: Tracking and Analyzing Results	❏ Data analysis is an iterative process that involves looking for patterns, making inferences, testing these inferences, and then formulating conclusions ❏ Good conclusions about student learning cannot be made unless 1) there is an understanding of the purpose of the assessment, 2) the evidence collected is sound, and 3) there is sufficient evidence upon which to base good decisions ❏ Assessment data can diagnose what teachers are teaching and prescribe how teaching needs to be improved ❏ For assessment data to be useful, it must be accessible. This necessitates an organizational scheme.

TABLE C.1. SUMMARY OF CHAPTER CONCEPTS. (Cont'd.)

Chapter Title	Important Concepts
Part 4: Linking Assessment and Instruction	
Chapter 9: Revising Feedback and Instructional Plans	❑ Teachers' assessment beliefs and practices bear directly on the ability of teachers to implement new assessment strategies ❑ Teaching best practices include a learner-centered environment, teacher-as-reflective practitioner, students-as-reflective practitioners, and education of the whole person ❑ Modified instructional plans help address any achievement gaps uncovered in the data analysis process ❑ Instructional strategies must be aligned with curricular learning targets and with assessment methods ❑ Differentiating instruction means simply reacting responsively to students' learning needs
Chapter 10: Using Assessment to Motivate Students	❑ It is the teacher's responsibility to encourage students' "will to engage" in learning ❑ Motivation is a learned competence ❑ Infusing diversity and variety into instruction positively impacts student motivation
Part 5: Factors Influencing Classroom Assessment	
Chapter 11: Rethinking Grading Practices	❑ Grading practices have been controversial since grades first began to appear ❑ Counterproductive grading practices encompass issues in calculating grades, in aligning grades and instruction, and in grading that discourages effort ❑ Productive grading plans contain grades that are tied to curricular standards, derived from quality assessment tasks, figured from summative assessments, contain no grades of zero, and reflect students' current levels of achievement
Chapter 12: Challenges of High-Stakes Assessment	❑ Criticisms of large scale standardized testing include how results are reported, how statistical concepts are employed in these results, and how the tests are constructed ❑ The public often misinterprets the meaning of such standardized test scores ❑ The use of a single test score should never be the sole piece of assessment evidence for student achievement

Although assessment changes will be difficult to achieve and hard to implement, we hope that the concepts presented here have both persuaded readers of the need for change and motivated individuals to implement new practices. The students will benefit, as effective assessment practices always lead to enhanced student achievement.

Go forth, and spread the word through the examples you set for your students, colleagues, and others on how you use classroom assessment to improve student learning. Good luck!

Appendix: Reflection and Discussion Questions

In this appendix, we present questions designed to prompt teacher reflection about and discussion of classroom assessment issues. The Introduction and the various chapters of this text may assist you in formulating educated answers to some of the questions, but most of the questions have no one right answer. They are designed to stimulate critical thinking and conversations that lead to changes in assessment practices.

These questions are appropriate for both veteran and preservice teachers. They may aid veteran teachers to identify or uncover teacher beliefs and practices, influence their assessment practices, or aid them in reflecting on their current practices. The questions may help preservice teachers formulate high-quality assessment practices before entering the classroom.

Introduction

1. Think about your own classroom assessment processes and reflect on how they lead to student learning. Do they?

2. Are the authors suggesting that every assessment designed be based on the Classroom Assessment Cycle? Explain your thinking.

3. Do you have a "Len" story (a story of a student who was unable to show his or her understanding of your subject until your changed your assessment practices)? If so, what made the difference for this student's learning?

4. How would you explain the Assessment Iceberg (Figure I.1)?

5. Think about your school district. Is there an emphasis on classroom assessment? If not, how could you encourage this? If so, is the approach effective?

6. Looking at the Classroom Assessment Cycle, what quadrant would you begin with when planning for effective assessment for learning? Why?

7. Which quadrant of the Classroom Assessment Cycle would you have the most difficulties with, either in understanding it or knowing what to do with students in order to complete the quadrant? Why?

8. Looking at Figure I.3, why do the authors feel that teachers have less control over items in the outer perimeter?

9. Why is change so difficult for teachers? What are the things you might change about your current practice to improve your use of quality assessments?

10. What comes first for change to occur—a change in practice or in belief, or change based on student impact?

Chapter One

1. How do you define assessment? Do your classroom practices model this definition?

2. Think back upon your own learning experiences. Was assessment used to help you learn or was it used to give you a grade?

3. When would you use diagnostic assessment in your practice? How do you use formative and summative assessment information in your classroom?

4. Would having a class dye Easter eggs be an instructional assessment event or an activity? What is the difference between an assessment and an activity?

5. Can you think of a classroom assessment you use that is clearly authentic for the students? How do you know?

6. What information would you gain about a student from each of the three types of assessments (selected, constructed, and authentic) displayed in Exhibit 1.1?

7. Does *every* assessment need to be of high quality? Explain.

8. What are some examples of high-stakes tests used in your classroom or school?

9. When would norm referenced and criterion referenced tests be standardized or high-stakes or both?

10. What are the positive and negative aspects of minimum competency testing?

11. How would you go about assessing your tests to decide whether they are relevant, reliable, and valid?

Chapter Two

1. What are the "big rocks" that guide your planning in the classroom? Could your students identify these?

2. What language is used in your school or district for learning targets? Are these stated as standards, competencies, objectives, goals, or other names?

3. Why would curriculum be an entry point to a complete instructional experience for students? Could we start with instruction or assessment? How would that be different?

4. Students often ask teachers, Why do I need to know this? They are striving to understand the relevance of concepts to their own lives. Like these students, ask yourself, Why do I need to know about global shifts and their impact on curriculum? Why is this significant information?

5. How has the curriculum changed since you have been in education? What was it like when you were a student? What has affected how school offerings were determined over the years?

6. What are some things you like about the curriculum you presently teach or about any curriculum you experienced in the past? Are there parts you dislike?

7. *Unpack* means "taking things out of boxes or cases." Why is *unpack* a relevant term to use in regard to learning targets?

8. Locate a curriculum framework for your school or district and note how the document is organized. What strands are present?

9. Take a learning target you value for students and unpack it in such a way as to determine exactly what you want students to know and be able to do.

10. Competent assessment involves aligning the assessment with the learning targets. Give an example from your classroom or from your own experiences as a student when the learning target and the assessment used to measure student achievement of that target were misaligned.

Chapter Three

1. Highlight an example of each type of learning target (knowledge and understanding, reasoning, performance skills, product development, and dispositional targets) in your curriculum.

2. What is one kind of assessment you might use to determine students' achievement in the reasoning category?

3. Find a standard from your standard course of study or curriculum framework that spirals across the grade levels.

Chapter Four

1. For which learning targets do you collect multiple and varied assessments to reveal levels of student understanding?

2. When would a selected-response assessment be most efficient or effective? Which types of learning targets would closely align with selected-response assessment?

3. How do you use the information you collect during student observations (whether informal or formal)?

4. Do you consider questions as assessments? Why or why not?

5. Prior to teaching a lesson, prepare a list of questions to use that would evoke higher-order thinking. What impact did these questions have on student learning? How do you know?

6. The authors realize that constructed-response assessment is not new to the classroom. What is often missing in constructed-response assessments you have created or used?

7. How have you used diagrams or illustrations as assessments?

8. Do you use graphic organizers (Venn Diagrams, concept maps, webs) in your classroom? If so, do you use them as formative assessments or as diagnostic tools?

9. One important thing to emphasize with students is that data tables represent a way to organize data, whereas graphs are actually picture representations of that data. How do you use tables or graphs in your teaching?

10. Senior projects may target high school students, but many elementary and middle schools are using portfolio exhibitions similarly. Does your school encourage the creation of such student performances or products? How?

Chapter Five

1. How could you use a log for assessing student thinking in your content area?

2. Do all journals need written responses from the teacher? How could you set up a review of journals with peer groups? Would you? Discuss advantages and disadvantages of peer-reviewed journal entries.

3. Should students be given a grade on a notebook? What would be the basis for the grade?

4. Have you ever created a portfolio? If so, was there a purpose for doing it or was it just busy work? How do you know?

5. Often portfolios are seen as extra work for the teacher. Is this true? If so, how could that extra burden be minimized?

6. Which of the portfolio design questions listed in Chapter Five prompted you to think more about using portfolios? Why?

7. What are some examples of projects you use with your students or projects you have personally experienced? What made these special or not so special to your learning? How do projects enhance learning?

Chapter Six

1. If tasks are simply defined as "what a student is asked to do," what are some of the tasks you ask students to do in your classroom?

2. How might you use the Planning Template (Exhibit 6.1) to reflect upon your own task selection or design process?

3. Do your students understand that the purpose of the tasks given to them to do is to improve their learning? Are they motivated to complete the tasks? Why or why not?

4. What are some of the tasks you were asked to perform as a student that seemed purposeful and exciting? Why did you remember these?

5. Do you need to consider all of the factors (refer to Exhibit 6.1 for a review of these) mentioned in this chapter for *every* task you give students to do? Why or why not?

Chapter Seven

1. Is it fair to the students to review all products they turn in and *then* decide on a scoring scheme? What do you do?

2. What are some advantages and disadvantages of using rubrics that you have experienced?

3. The authors recommend that you think more about the characteristics of a good rubric, what it should include, and how it will be used instead of just being able to identify a particular rubric format. So why should you learn to differentiate among rubric formats?

4. Have you ever created or used a task-specific rubric? If so, what was it used for?

5. Have you experienced using a holistic or analytical rubric or both? Which one do you find the most beneficial for you? For your students?

6. When would you use a checklist with your students, rather than a rubric?

7. Are your rubrics completely aligned with the learning targets, the assessment tasks, and the instruction? How do you know?

8. A teacher asks that her students write their names on the upper left-hand corner of every assignment before handing it in. This criterion is found on every rubric used in the classroom. Is this essential? Why or why not?

9. How have you used student exemplars in your classroom?

10. How would you encourage students to use the feedback they receive from a rubric? How would you use it?

11. What rationales, other than strict percentage scoring, can be used to justify point conversions to grades on a rubric?

12. Why would you want to assess a rubric, using such an instrument as the one found in Table 7.5?

Chapter Eight

1. When you look at the students in your classroom, do you see a group of students or individuals? Which view would St. Germain and Guillot and the authors emphasize?

2. Before inferences are made, what questions guide *your* analysis of assessment evidence?

3. Can good inferences of students' overall learning be based solely on one assessment? Does this occur?

4. How many sources of data are "enough" to make good inferences about a student's overall learning?

5. What are specific patterns of performance or trends in student thinking that you look for in your assessment evidence?

6. Collecting anecdotal information to look for patterns and trends in student learning can be time consuming. What tools could a teacher use to make this process easier in the classroom?

7. For selected-response summative tests or formative quizzes, a Scantron machine (scoring equipment for types of selected response questions) can help run an item analysis for teachers. How could this information be used to look at patterns and trends in student learning?

8. What types of portfolios would work best for organizing data on student performances (best works, memorabilia, growth, or proficiency portfolios)?

Chapter Nine

1. What does modifying instruction mean?

2. Where did most of the question marks fall on the self-checklist for promoting assessment learning (Exhibit 9.1)?

3. How might you use Table 9.1 and Exhibit 9.1 in a faculty meeting?

4. Are your assessment practices modeled on ways you were assessed as a student? What are the similarities and differences in your practice and those you have experienced?

5. What are three instructional strategies you often use? Are they effective? How do you know?

6. Look at the strategies listed in the Behavior section in Table 9.2. How many of these strategies do you feel you use well? Which ones would you avoid and why?

7. Look at the strategies listed in the Cognitive section in Table 9.2. How many of these strategies do you feel you use well? Which ones would you avoid and why?

8. Look at the strategies listed in the Application/Process section in Table 9.2. How many of these strategies do you feel you use well? Which ones would you avoid and why?

9. Look at the strategies listed in the Other Strategies section in Table 9.2. How many of these strategies do you feel you use well? Which ones would you avoid and why?

10. Think of strategies you use that could be added to the examples within the Behavior, Cognitive, and Application/Process strategies shown in Table 9.2.

11. Can you think of an example of "good" feedback you received that helped you learn something that was difficult for you? Why was that feedback so useful?

12. What is your definition of differentiated instruction? Is this something you do well? What makes your practice effective or not?

13. With the No Child Left Behind legislation, there is an emphasis on using research-based practices in the classroom. What are research-based practices? What are you doing to ensure that you are using these practices?

14. Is your classroom teacher or learner centered? What evidence do you have that supports your answer?

15. How do you keep updated on current trends and reform efforts in research? Does your school support teachers-as-learners?

16. How do you promote learning for the "whole" person in your practice?

Chapter Ten

1. How many of the characteristics of motivated and nonmotivated students listed at the beginning of Chapter Ten are linked to assessment?

2. What are some external motivating factors for your students?

3. Are external or internal factors more powerful in student motivation?

4. Why is it important to understand theories of motivation?

5. Reflecting on your prior learning experiences, did you like competitive environments? Why or why not?

6. As a student, what types of classroom assessments motivated you the most?

7. How do you set up a classroom climate that honors the student need to belong?

8. Often, when we review Glasser's proposed set of human needs relating to student motivation, the need to have fun is not received well by educators. Why do you think this is true?

9. What are some ways that you support motivation and evoke student interest in learning in your classroom?

10. Have you ever used the scientific learning cycle with your students? Is it only applicable to science?

11. Is the use of student teams a motivating factor for your students?

Chapter Eleven

1. How would you respond? "My daily work is not counted as a grade, so why should I do it?"

2. How would you respond? "Every teacher in this school does their own thing when grading classroom work and calculating grades to report to parents."

3. How would you respond? "How can my son get all As in this class and still score so low on the state test?"

4. How would you respond? "Once a grade goes into my grade book it never gets changed."

5. How would you respond? "Why don't all teachers use portfolios? Portfolios show what students can do, so grades are no surprise."

6. How would you respond? "My class misbehaved yesterday for a substitute. I'm going to give them a pop quiz today so they'll think twice about their behavior next time I'm absent."

7. How would you respond? "My colleagues get upset with me because all my students get good grades."

8. How would you respond? "I appreciate my son's physical education teacher. He grades kids on achievement of skills and other targets, not on 'dressing out.'"

9. How would you respond? "My daughter failed a course for this quarter. She forgot to hand in several homework assignments and was given zero scores. These zeros killed her B average."

10. How would you respond? "We've been studying decimals in math and we had a test. I did well on the decimal part but there were other things on the test that I did not know. So this caused my grade to drop."

11. How would you respond? "I only get feedback for my work after I turn it in."

12. How would you respond? "Our final scores are determined by averaging all our grades together. These include scores for participation and attendance."

13. How would you respond? "It seems as though all I do is grade."

14. How would you respond? "Everything counts as a grade in my class."

15. How would you respond? "The other fourth grade teachers gave at least ten As to students in their classes. I did not give any As this quarter. We have students of similar ability levels."

16. How would you respond? "I gave my students an extra grade for bringing in a signed paper."

17. How would you respond? "I'm not sure what it means for my child to get an A in reading."

18. How would you respond? "I'd like to give fewer grades, but I'm afraid my students won't do the work I need them to do without a grade."

Chapter Twelve

1. What do you think are the purposes for high-stakes assessment in general? For you? For your school?

2. What impact/s has No Child Left Behind (NCLB) had on views of high-stakes assessment? Are these positive or negative impacts?

3. What are some major criticisms of high-stakes assessment?

4. Do you know the differences in percentage scores, derived scores, percentile rank, and grade equivalent used in reporting test scores? Could you explain these to parents?

5. How are scores derived in your state for high-stakes students testing results?

6. High-stakes tests are here to stay. How can a classroom teacher prepare students for such a test without sacrificing curricular quality?

7. Are you familiar with some of the quick fixes discussed in Chapter Twelve? Have they been implemented at your school?

8. When data analysis is done on high-stakes results for your school, how are the data presented? Are the data helpful in diagnosing individual learning needs?

References

Ames, C. (1984). Competitive, cooperative, and individualistic goal structures: A cognitive-motivational analysis. In R. Ames & C. Ames (Eds.), *Research on motivation in education* (p. 189). Orlando, FL: Academic Press.

Ames, C. (1990, April). *The relationship of achievement goals to student motivation in classroom settings*. Paper presented at the annual meeting of the American Educational Research Association, Boston, MA.

Anderman, E. M., & Maehr, M. L. (1994). Motivation and schooling in the middle grades. *Review of Educational Research, 64*(1), 287–309.

Anderson, L., Krathwohl, D., Airasian, P., Cruikshank, K., Mayer, R., Pintrich, P., Raths, J., & Wittrock, M. (Eds.). (2001). *A taxonomy for learning, teaching, and assessing: A revision of Bloom's taxonomy of educational objectives.* (abridged ed.). New York: Addison Wesley Longman.

Apple, M. W. (1992). Educational reform and educational crisis. *Journal of Research in Science Teaching, 29*(8), 779–789.

Archbald, D. A., & Newmann, F. M. (1988). *Beyond standardized testing: Assessing authentic academic achievement in the secondary school.* (ERIC no. ED 301 587).

Arter, J. (2000). *Addendum to improving classroom assessment: A toolkit for professional developers.* Portland, OR: Northwest Regional Educational Laboratory, pp. 1–54.

Arter, J., & McTighe, J. (2001). *Scoring rubrics in the classroom.* Thousand Oaks, CA: Corwin Press.

Beard, J. G. (1986). *Minimum competency testing.* (ERIC no. ED 284 910).

Besvinick, S. L. (1988). Twenty years later: Reviving the reforms of the '60s. *Educational Leadership, 46*(1), 52.

Black, P., & Wiliam, D. (1998). Inside the black box: Raising standards through classroom assessment. *Phi Delta Kappan, 80*(2), 139–148.

Black, P., Harrison, C., Lee, C., Marshall, B., & Wiliam, D. (2004). Working inside the black box: Assessment for learning in the classroom. *Phi Delta Kappan, 86*(1), 8–21.

Bloom, B. (1984). The search for methods of group instruction as effective as one-to-one tutoring. *Educational Leadership. 41*(8), 4–17.

Bloom, B. S. (Ed.) (1956). *Taxonomy of educational objectives: The classification of educational goals: Handbook I, cognitive domain.* New York; Toronto: Longmans, Green.

Bond, L. A. (1996). *Norm- and criterion-referenced testing.* (ERIC no. ED 410 316).

Boud, D. (Ed.). (1985). *Problem-based learning in education for the professions.* Kensington, Australia: Higher Education Research and Development Society of Australia.

Brandt, R. (1988). On students' needs and team learning: A conversation with William Glasser. *Educational Leadership, 45*(6), 38–45.

Brewer, W. R., & Kallick, B. (1996). Technology's promise for reporting student learning. In *ASCD 1996 yearbook: Communicating student learning, 12*(186). Alexandria, VA: Association for Supervision and Curriculum Development.

Bridges, E. M., & Hallinger, P. (1991). *Problem-based learning in medical and managerial education.* Palo Alto, CA: Stanford University, School of Education. (ERIC no. ED 343 265).

Brookhart, S. (1994). Teachers' grading: Practice and theory. *Applied Measurement in Education, 7,* 279–301.

Brookhart, S. (2004). *Grading.* Upper Saddle River, New Jersey: Pearson Education.

Brophy, J. (1987). Synthesis of research on strategies for motivating students to learn. *Educational Leadership, 45*(6), 40–48.

Buly, M., & Valencia, S. (2002). Below the bar: Profiles of students who fail state reading assessments. *Educational Evaluation and Policy Analysis, 24*(33), 219–239.

Burke, K. (1994). *The mindful school: How to assess authentic learning.* Palatine, IL: IRI/Skylight Training and Publishing.

Butler, R. (1988). Enhancing and undermining intrinsic motivation: The effects of task-involving and ego-involving evaluation on interest and performance. *British Journal of Educational Psychology, 58,* 1–14.

Butler, S. M. (1997a*). Problem-based learning in a secondary science classroom.* Dissertation Abstracts International, 58 (02A), 4605. (University Microfilm No. AAD98–17308).

Butler, S. M. (1997b). Using science portfolios in a tenth-grade chemistry classroom. In J. Barton & A. Collins (Eds.), *Portfolio assessment: Handbook for educators.* Menlo Park, CA: Addison-Wesley Publishing Company.

Butler, S. M. (1999, September 16). Online group discussion. EMS475 available from courses.ncsu.edu/classes/ems475001/index.html.

Canady, R. L., & Hotchkiss, P. R. (1989). It's a good score! Just a bad grade. *Phi Delta Kappan, 71*(1), 68–71.

Cannell, J. J. (1987). Nationally normed educational achievement testing in America's public school: How all fifty states are above the national average. *Educational Measurement Issues and Practice, 7*(2), 5–9.

Carpenter, S. (2001). The high stakes of educational testing. *Monitor on Psychology. 32*(5). Available at www.apa.org/monitor/may01/edtesting.html.

Carter, G. R. (2000). Student testing: What do parents think? *Education Update, 42*(7), 2.

Cawelti, G., & Protheroe, N. (2001). *High student achievement: How six school districts changed into high-performance systems.* Arlington, VA: Educational Research Service, 1–104.

Clarkson, X. (1997). Using math portfolios in first-, second-, and third grade classrooms. In J. Barton & A. Collins (Eds.), *Portfolio assessment: Handbook for educators* (pp. 25–32). Menlo Park, CA: Addison-Wesley.

Cochran-Smith, M. (2000). Gambling on the future. *Journal of Teacher Education, 51*(4), 259–261.

Commission on Instructionally Supportive Assessment. (2001, October). *Building tests to support instruction and accountability: A guide for policymakers.* Available at www.aasa.org/issues_and_insights/assessment/Building_Tests.pdf.

Cordeiro, P., & Campbell, B. (1996). *Increasing the transfer of learning through problem-based learning in educational administration.* Plainville: University of Connecticut. (ERIC no. ED 396 434).

Corrigan, R. A. (1993). Responding to the crisis in science education. *Reforms in Science Education, K–12.* San Francisco: San Francisco State University. (ERIC no. ED 370 771).

Covington, M. V. (1984). The self-worth theory of achievement motivation: Findings and implications. *Elementary School Journal, 85*(1), 5–20.

Crooks, T. J. (1988). The impact of classroom evaluation on students. *Review of Educational Research, 58*(4), 438–481.

Darling-Hammond, L., & Ascher, C. (1991). *Accountability mechanisms in big city school systems.* (ERIC no. ED 334 311).

Davey, L. (1992). *The case for a national testing system.* (ERIC no. ED 410 239).

Davis, N. T., & Helly, M. (1995). Conflicting beliefs: A story of a chemistry teacher's struggle with change. *School Science and Mathematics, 95*(7), 45–50.

Edwards, C. H., & Edwards, L. (1999). Let's end the grading game. *Clearing House, 72*(5), 260–263.

Eisner, E. W. (1979). *The educational imagination.* New York: Macmillan.

Eisner, E. W., & Vallance, E. (1974). *Conflicting conceptions of curriculum.* Berkeley: McCutchan.

Ellis, A. K. (2004). *Exemplars of curriculum theory.* New York: Eye on Education.

Ewell, P. T. (1997). *Organizing for learning: A point of entry.* Draft prepared for discussion at the 1997 AAHE Summer Academy at Snowbird. National Center for Higher Education Management Systems (NCHEMS). Available at www.intime.uni.edu/model/learning/learn_summary.htm.

Feldman, A., Alibrandi, M., & Kropf, A. (1998). Grading with points: The determination of report card grades by high school science teachers. *School Science and Mathematics, 98*(3), 140–148.

Florida Department of Education. (1991). Course student performance standards, Chemistry I Honors. *Curriculum Framework.* Tallahassee, FL: Department of Education.

Florida Department of Education. (1996). *Sunshine state standards.* Tallahassee, FL: Florida Department of Education.

Foundation for Advancements in Science & Education. (Producer). (1993). *Good morning, Miss Toliver.* [Film]. (Available from FASE Productions, 4801 Wilshire Blvd., Suite 215, Los Angeles, CA 90010, 800–404–3273).

Fraser, B., & Fisher, D. (1986). Using short forms of classroom climate instruments to assess and improve classroom psychosocial environment. *Journal of Research in Science Teaching, 23,* 387–413.

Friedman, S. J. (1998). Grading teachers' grading policies. *National Association of Secondary Schools Principals Bulletin, 82*(597), 77–83.

Friedman, S. J., & Troug, A. L. (1999). Evaluation of high school teachers' written grading policies. *ERS Spectrum, 17*(3), 34–42.

Frisbie, D. A., & Waltman, K. K. (1992). Developing a personal grading plan. *Educational Issues: Measurement and Practice, 11*(3), 35–42.

Gallagher, C. (2000). A seat at the table: Teachers reclaiming assessment through rethinking accountability. *Phi Delta Kappan, 81*(7), 502–507.

Gallagher, S. A., Stepien, W. J., & Rosenthal, H. (1992). The effects of problem-based learning on problem solving. *Gifted Child Quarterly, 36,* 195–200.

Gallagher, S. A., Stepien, W. J., Sher, B. T., & Workman, D. (1995). Implementing problem-based learning in science classrooms. *School Science and Mathematics, 95,* 136–146.

Ginsburg, G., & Bronstein, P. (1993). Family factors related to children's intrinsic/extrinsic motivational orientation and academic performance. *Child Development, 64,* 1461–1474.

Glasser, W. (1986). *Choice theory in the classroom.* New York: HarperCollins.

Glatthorn, A., & Jailall, J. (2000). Curriculum for the new millennium. In R. S. Brandt (Ed.), *Education in a new era* (pp. 97–123). Alexandria, VA: Association for Supervision and Curriculum Development.

Greene, J. P., Winters, M., & Forster, G. (2003). Testing high stakes tests: Can we believe the results of accountability tests? *Manhattan Institute for Policy Research,* No. 33, Feb. 2003. Available at www.manhattan-institute.org/html/cr 33.htm.

Grundy, S. (1987). *Curriculum: Product or praxis?* Philadelphia: Falmer Press.

Guide to President Bush's FY 2006 Education Agenda. No child left behind: Expanding the promise. Retrieved February 2005 from www.ed.gov/about/overview/budget/budget06/nclb/indes/htms.

Guild, P. B. (1997). Where do the learning theories overlap? *Educational Leadership, 55*(1), 30–31.

Guskey, T. R. (1994). Making the grade: What benefits students? *Educational Leadership, 52*(2), 14–20.

Guskey, T. R. (1996a). Introduction. In T. R. Guskey (Ed.), *ASCD yearbook 1996: Communicating student learning.* Alexandria, VA: Association for Supervision and Curriculum Development.

Guskey, T. R. (1996b). Reporting on student learning: Lessons from the past—prescriptions for the future. In T. R. Guskey (Ed.), *ASCD yearbook 1996: Communicating student learning.* Alexandria, VA: Association for Supervision and Curriculum Development.

Guskey, T. R. (2000). *Evaluating professional development.* Thousand Oaks, CA: Corwin Press.

Guskey, T. R., and Bailey, J. (2001). *Developing grading and reporting systems for student learning.* Thousand Oaks, CA: Corwin Press.

Haney, W., & Madaus, G. (1986). *Effects of standardized testing and the future of the National Assessment of Educational Progress.* (ERIC no. ED 279 680).

Herman, J., & Dorr-Bremme, D. (1982). *Assessing students: Teachers' routine practices and reasoning.* Paper presented at AERA, New York, 1982.

Hills, J. R. (1991). Apathy concerning grading and testing. *Phi Delta Kappa, 72*(7), 540–545.

Howe, R. W. (1990). *Trends and issues in science education: Curriculum and instruction.* Washington, DC: Office of Educational Research and Improvement.

Impara, J. C., Plake, B. S., & Fager, J. J. (1993). Teachers' assessment background and attitudes toward testing. *Theory into Practice, 32*(2), 113–117.

Jones, G., Jones, B., Hardin, B., Chapman, L., Yarbrough, T., & Davis, M. (1999). The impact of high-stakes testing on teachers and students in North Carolina. *Phi Delta Kappan, 81*(3), 199–203.

Joyner, J., and McMunn, N. (2003). SERVE Regional Laboratory Performance Assessments in Math Project, Greensboro, NC. Unpublished.

Kendall, J. S., & Marzano, R. J. (2000). *Content knowledge: A compendium of standards and benchmarks for K–12 education.* Alexandria, VA: Association for Supervision and Curriculum Development.

Kirschenbaum, H., Napier, R., Simon, S. B. (1971). *Wad-ja-get? The grading game in American education.* New York: Hart.

Kohn, A. (1993). *Punished by rewards.* Boston: Houghton Mifflin Company.

Kohn, A. (1999). From degrading to de-grading. *High School Magazine, 6*(5), 38–43.

Kohn, A. (2000). Burnt at the high stakes. *Journal of Teacher Education, 51*(4), 315–327.

Krieger, J. (1989). ACS presents science education report to Congress. *Chemical and Engineering News, 67*(48), 54–55.

Kuhn, T. S. (1970). *The structure of scientific revolutions.* Chicago: University of Chicago Press.

Lakoff, G., & Johnson, M. (1980). *Metaphors we live by.* Chicago: University of Chicago Press.

Lawson, T. (2005, January 16). In Coach Carter's playbook. *Milwaukee Journal Sentinel.* Retrieved February 10, 2005, from www.jsonline.com/onwisconsin/movies/jan05/293039.asp?format=print.

Lazarus, M. (1981). *Goodbye to excellence: A critical look at minimum competency testing.* Boulder, CO: Westview Press.

Lewin, L., & Shoemaker, B. J. (1998). *Great performances: Creating classroom-based assessment tasks.* Arlington, VA: Association for Supervision and Curriculum Development.

Long, D. (1997). Using language arts portfolios in a fourth-and-fifth grade classroom. In J. Barton & A. Collins (Eds.), *Portfolio assessment: Handbook for educators* (pp. 33–42). Menlo Park, CA: Addison-Wesley.

Marek, E. A., and Cavallo, A.M.L. (1997). *The learning cycle: Elementary school science and beyond.* Portsmouth, NH: Heinemann.

Marshall, P. (1990). Metaphor as an instructional tool in encouraging student teacher reflection. *Theory into Practice: Metaphors We Learn By, 29*(2), 128–132.

Martin-Kniep, G. (1998). *Why am I doing this? Purposeful teaching through portfolio assessment.* Portsmouth, NH: Heinemann.

Marx, G. (1989). Educating for an unknown future. *Physics Education, 24*(3), 141–146.

Marzano, R. J. (2000). *Tranforming classroom grading.* Alexandria, VA: Association for Supervision and Curriculum Development.

Marzano, R. J., & Kendall, J. S. (1996). *Designing standards-based districts, schools, and classrooms.* Alexandria, VA: Association for Supervision and Curriculum Development.

Marzano, R. J., Pickering, D., & McTighe, J. (1993). *Assessing student outcomes: Performance assessment using the dimensions of learning model.* Alexandria, VA: Association for Supervision and Curriculum Development.

Marzano, R. J., Pickering, D., and Pollock, J. (2001). *Classroom instruction that works.* Alexandria, VA: Association for Supervision and Curriculum Development.

Maslow, A. (1970). *Maslow's hierarchy of human needs: Motivation and personality.* (2nd ed.). New York: Harper & Row.

Mastropieri, M. A., Scruggs, T. E., Bakken, J., & Brigham, E. J. (1992). A complex mnemonic strategy for teaching states and capitals: Comparing forward and backward associations. *Learning Disabilities Research Practice, 7,* 96–103.

McColskey, W., & Busick, K. (1994). Grading and reporting. In Regional Educational Laboratory Network Program on Science and Mathematics Alternative Assessment. *A Toolkit for Professional Developers: Alternative Assessment.* Portland, OR: Northwest Regional Educational Laboratory.

McColskey, W., and McMunn, N. (2000). Strategies for dealing with high-stakes state tests. *Phi Delta Kappan. 82*(2) pp., 115–120.

McColskey, W., & O'Sullivan, R. (1995). *How to assess student performance in science: Going beyond multiple-choice tests.* Greensboro, NC: SERVE.

McMillan, J. H. (1999). *Devastating effect of zero grades: What can be done?* Richmond: Virginia Commonwealth University. (ERIC no. ED. 428 136).

McMunn, N. (2000). Classroom Assessment: A driving force to improve learning. *Assessment Hotspots, 2*(1), 6.

McMunn, N., and Schenck, P. (1996). SERVE'S Creating effective student assessments handbook for participants. Bay District Schools Target Training. Unpublished training resource.

McMunn, N., Dunnivant, M., Williamson, J., & Reagan, H. (2004). *Competent assessment of reading: Toolkit for professional developers.* Greensboro, NC: SERVE Regional Educational Laboratory, University of North Carolina.

McMunn, N., McColskey, W., & O'Conner, K. (2000, April). Districts building teacher assessment capacity in classroom assessment. Paper presented at the American Educational Research Association Meeting, New Orleans, LA.

McMunn, N., Williamson, J., & Reagan, H. (2004). *Competent assessment of reading professional development model for teachers in grades 5–9.* Document resource in preparation. SERVE Regional Laboratory for the Research and Development Center, University of North Carolina, Greensboro.

McNeil, L. M. (2000). Creating new inequalities: Contradictions of reform. *Phi Delta Kappan, 81*(10), 729–734.

Meece, J., & McColskey, W. (1997). *Improving student motivation: A guide for teachers and school improvement teams.* Tallahassee, FL: SERVE.

Mehrens, W. A., & Lehmann, I. J. (1987). *Using standardized tests in education.* White Plains, NY: Longman.

Merrill, M. D., Drake, L. D., Lacy, M. J., Pratt, J. A., & the ID$_2$ Research Group. (1996). Reclaiming instructional design. *Educational Technology, 36*(5), 5–7.

Middleton, W. (1994). *Problem-based learning in workshops.* Adelaide, Australia: Griffith University, National Center for Vocational Education Research. (ERIC no. ED 380 542).

National Academies Press. (1993). Measuring up: Prototypes for mathematics assessment. Washington, DC: National Academies of Science.

National Commission on Excellence in Education. (1983). *A nation at risk: The imperative for educational reform.* Washington, DC: U.S. Department of Education.

National Council of Teachers of Mathematics. (2000). Position Paper: High-stakes testing. Retrieved October 18, 2004, from www.nctm.org/about/position_statements/highstakes.htm.

National Research Council. (1999). *National science education standards.* Washington, DC: National Academy Press.

Nitko, A. J. (2004). *Educational assessment of students.* (4th ed.). Upper Saddle River, NJ: Merrill/Prentice Hall.

Niyogi, N. S. (1995). *The intersection of instruction and assessment: The classroom.* Princeton, NJ: Educational Testing Service.

North Carolina Department of Public Instruction. (1995). *Course blueprint for biomedical technology.* Raleigh, NC: NCDPI.

North Carolina Department of Public Instruction. (1998). *Academic curriculum.* Retrieved September 21, 1998, from www.dpi.state.nc.us/curriculum/socialstudies/worldgeog.htm.

North Carolina Department of Public Instruction. (1999). *Classroom assessment: Linking instruction and assessment.* Raleigh, NC: Public Schools of North Carolina.

North Carolina Department of Public Instruction. (2000a). Closing the Achievement Gap: Views from Nine Schools. Website, retrieved June 15, 2000, from www.ncpublicschools.org/docs/schoolimprovement/closingthegap/reports/nineschools.pdf.

North Carolina Department of Public Instruction. (2000b). Website, available at www.dpi.state.nc.us/curriculum/science/scos/1999/19strands.

O'Connor, K. (1999). *The mindful school. How to grade for learning.* Arlington Heights, IL: SkyLight Training and Publishing.

O'Connor, K. (2002). *How to grade for learning: Linking grades to standards.* (2nd ed). Arlington Heights, IL: Skylight Training and Publishing.

Ohanian, S., & Ruiz, R. (2000). Agora: The impact of high-stakes testing. *Journal of Teacher Education, 51*(4), 289–292.

Parent Press. (Fall 2001). *Driving decisions with data.* Jackson, MS: Parents for Public Schools. Retrieved October 18, 2004, from www.parents4publicschools.com.

Payne, D. A. (1997). *Applied educational assessment.* Belmont, CA: Wadsworth.

Piaget, J., and Inhelder, B. (1956). *The child's conception of space.* New York: Routledge.

Plake, B. S., Impara, J. C., & Fager, J. J. (1993). Assessment competencies of teachers: A national survey. *Educational Measurement: Issues and Practice, 12*(4), 10–12, 39.

Popham, W. J. (1995). *Classroom assessment: What teachers need to know.* Needham Heights, MA: Allyn and Bacon.

Prather, J. P. (1993). Reform revisited: The trend toward constructivist learning. *Journal of Elementary Science Education, 5*(2), 52–70.

Prince William County Schools, Manassas, VA. Retrieved October 15, 2004, from www.pwcs.edu/curriculum/sol/flowshart1.html.

Protheroe, N. (2001). Improving teaching and learning with data-based decisions: Asking the right questions and acting on the answers. *ERS Spectrum, 19*(3), 4–9. Retrieved September 18, 2004, from www.ers.org/spectrum/sum01a.htm.

Regional Educational Laboratories. (1998). *Improving classroom assessment: A toolkit for professional developers (Toolkit98).* United States Department of Education, Office of Educational Research and Improvement. Portland, OR: Northwest Regional Educational Laboratory.

Roth, W. M. (1993). Construction sites: Science labs and classrooms. In K. Tobin (Ed.), *The practice of constructivism in science education* (pp. 145–170). Hillsdale, NJ: Lawrence Erlbaum.

Sadowski, M. (2000). Are high-stakes tests worth the wager? *Harvard Education Letter—Research On-line.* Retrieved March 7, 2005, from www.edletter.org/past/issues/2000-so/tests.shtml.

SERVE Regional Laboratory at University of North Carolina, Greensboro. (2003). *Senior project at SERVE: Examining the implementation and impact of Senior Project.* Greensboro, NC: SERVE.

Shafer, W. D. (1993). Assessment in teacher education. *Theory into Practice, 32*(2), 118–126.

Shavelson, R. J., & Ruize-Primo, M. (1998). On the assessment of science achievement conceptual underpinnings for the design of performance assessments: Report of year 2 activities. *CSE Technical Report 491.* UCLA, Los Angeles, CA: CRESST/Stanford University.

Starch, D., and Elliott, E. C. (1912). Reliability of the grading of high-school work in English. *School Review, 20,* 442–457.

Stiggins, R. (1997). *Student-centered classroom assessment.* Upper Saddle River, NJ: Merrill, Prentice-Hall.

Stiggins, R. (1998). *Classroom assessment for student success.* Annapolis Junction, MD: National Education Association.

Stiggins, R. (1999). Assessment, student confidence, and school success. *Phi Delta Kappan,* November, 191–198.

Stiggins, R., & Conklin, N. (1991). *In teachers' hands: Investigating the practice of classroom assessment.* Albany, NY: SUNY Press.

Stiggins, R. J. (2001a). *Student-involved classroom assessment* (3rd ed.). Upper Saddle River, NJ: Merrill Prentice-Hall.

Stiggins, R. J. (2001b, January.) The principal's leadership role in assessment. *NASSP Bulletin,* 13–26.

Strickland, K., & Strickland, J. (1998). *Reflections on assessment: Its purposes, methods, and effects on learning.* Portsmouth, NH: Boynton/Cook.

Tobias, S. (1993). *Overcoming math anxiety.* New York: Norton.

Tobin, K. (1990). Changing metaphors and beliefs: A master switch for teaching. *Theory into Practice: Metaphors We Learn By, 29*(2), 122–127.

Tobin, K., Briscoe, C., & Holman, J. (1990). Overcoming constraints to effective elementary science teaching. *Science Education, 74*(4), 409–420.

Tobin, K., & LaMaster, S. U. (1995). Relationships between metaphors, beliefs, and actions in a context of science curriculum change. *Journal of Research in Science Teaching, 32*(3), 225–242.

Tomlinson, C. A. (1999). *The differentiated classroom: Responding to the needs of all learners.* Alexandria, VA: Association for Supervision and Curriculum Development.

Tomlinson, C. A., & Allan, S. D. (2000). *Leadership for differentiating schools and classrooms.* Alexandria: VA: Association for Supervision and Curriculum Development.

Tomlinson, T. (1993). *Motivating students to learn.* Berkeley, CA: McCutchan.

U.S. Congress, Office of Technology Assessment. (1992). *Testing in America's schools: Asking the right questions.* OTA-SET-519. Washington, DC: U.S. Government Printing Office.

Westheimer, F. H. (1994). Deciding how much science is enough. *Journal of College Science Teaching, 23*(4), 203–206.

Wiggins, G. (1998). *Educative assessment.* San Francisco: Jossey-Bass.

Wiggins, G., & McTighe, J. (1998). *Understanding by design.* Alexandria, VA: Association for Supervision and Curriculum Development.

Williams, A. (1997). Lessons of middle-school experience using science portfolios in a sixth-grade classroom. In J. Barton & A. Collins (Eds.), *Portfolio assessment: Handbook for educators* (pp. 43–55). Menlo Park, CA: Addison-Wesley.

Williamson, J., McMunn, N., and Reagan, H. (2004). *Tools for providing feedback in reading: A reading assessment handbook for all teachers in grades 3–12.* Tallahassee, FL: SERVE Regional Laboratory.

Wise, S. L., Lukin, L. E., & Roos, L. L. (1991). Teacher beliefs about training in testing and measurement. *Journal of Teacher Education, 42*(1), 37–42.

Wright, R. G. (1994). Success for all: The median is the key. *Phi Delta Kappan, 75*(9), 723–725.

Yager, R. E., & Lutz, M. V. (1994). Integrated science: The importance of "how" versus "what." *School Science and Mathematics, 94*(7), 338–346.

Zhang, Z. (1997). *Assessment Practices Inventory: A multivariate analysis of teachers' perceived assessment competency.* Paper presented at National Council on Measurement in Education national conference, Chicago, 1997.

Index

Paraphrasing in Chapter Five from L. Lewin and B. J. Shoemaker, 1998, *Great Performances: Creating Classroom-Based Assessment Tasks,* Arlington, Virginia, p. 104. Reprinted by permission. The Association for Supervision and Curriculum Development is a worldwide community of educators advocating sound policies and sharing best practices to achieve the success of each learner. To learn more, visit ASCD at www.ascd.org.

Bulleted list in Chapter Five from *Portfolio Assessment: A Handbook for Educators,* 1997, Menlo Park, California: Addison-Wesley Publishing Company, Pearson Education. Used by courtesy of Pearson Education, Inc.

Bulleted list in Chapter Seven by Patricia Schenck, SERVE's unpublished training handbook on creating effective student assessment. Reprinted with permission.

Summarized and bulleted list in Chapter Nine from P. B. Guild (O'Rourke), Copyright © 1997. "Where Do the Learning Theories Overlap?" *Educational Leadership, 55*(1), 30–31. Reprinted with permission.

Explanatory text for Exhibit 9.1 from R. J. Stiggins, J. A. Arter, J. Chappuis, and S. Chappuis, *Classroom Assessment for Student Learning: Doing It Right—Using It Well.* Assessment Training Institute, 317 SW Alder, Suite 1200, Portland, Oregon, 97204. Figure 2.3, p. 51. Reprinted with permission.

Explanatory text for Table 9.2 from Prince William County Public Schools, Virginia. Website: http://www.pwcs.edu/curriculum/sol/flowchart.html.

Summaries in Chapter Ten from J. Meece and W. McColskey, 1997, *Improving Student Motivation: A Guide for Teachers and School Improvement Teams,* Tallahassee, Florida: SERVE. Reprinted with permission.

Excerpts in Chapter Ten from *Punished by Rewards* by Alfie Kohn. Copyright © 1993 by Alfie Kohn. Reprinted by permission of Houghton Mifflin Company. All rights reserved.

Bulleted list and summary text in Chapter Ten from *Choice Theory in the Classroom* by William Glasser, Inc., Joseph Paul Glasser, Alice Joan Glasser, and Martin Howard Glasser. Copyright © 1986, New York: HarperCollins Publishers, Inc. Reprinted with permission of HarperCollins Publishers.

Summarized text in Chapter Eleven from "It's a Good Score! Just a Bad Grade." By R. L. Canady and P. R. Hotchkiss, in *Phi Delta Kappan.* Copyright © 1989. Reprinted with permission from Robert Canady.

Text in Chapter Twelve from Wendy McColskey and Nancy McMunn, 2000, "Strategies with High-Stakes State Tests," *Phi Delta Kappan, 82*(2), 115–120.

Boxed text "The Dentist" was originally titled "Absolutely the Best Dentist." This assessment parody was written by John S. Taylor, then superintendent of the Lancaster County School District (South Carolina), who is now retired and living in Lancaster County.

The Heart of Teaching: Creating High-Impact Lessons for the Adolescent Learner

Audrey J. Sirota with Laura Ianacone Taschek

Paper   ISBN: 0-7879-7802-7

www.josseybass.com

"This is a must-have book for teachers in any content area, at any grade level—especially teachers of second-language learners. It provides specific, practical information and ideas using critical elements for developing language and higher-level thinking skills."

> —Maria Elena Garcia, school improvement administrator,
> Educational Service District 123, Pasco, Washington

The Heart of Teaching offers practical guidance in designing lessons and classroom activities that are powerfully effective for all types of students in grades 7–12, including those placed at risk of educational failure because of linguistic, socioeconomic, racial, and geographic factors. The approach is easily geared to standards and can be used to strengthen and enrich scripted lessons or mandated curricular units. With a strong emphasis on literacy, the book shows teachers how to assess a lesson plan and then how to design activities and exercises that can meaningfully engage all students, even those who have difficulty in school. The book also shows teachers how to use learning centers for differentiating lessons and for breaking the classroom into small, participatory settings.

The Heart of Teaching is richly furnished with model lessons, assessment rubrics, and other practical tools from real-life math, science, social studies, and English classrooms.

Audrey J. Sirota is a veteran teacher, educational consultant, trainer, and staff developer. She served with the Center for Research on Education, Diversity and Excellence (CREDE), where she conducted training programs for in-service and pre-service teachers and advised districts on staff development approaches.

Laura Ianacone Taschek teaches social studies at Lake Braddock Secondary School in Fairfax County, Virginia, where she also serves as a mentor teacher.

The Minds of Boys: Saving Our Sons from Falling Behind in School and Life

Michael Gurian and Kathy Stevens

Paper   ISBN: 0-7879-7761-6

www.josseybass.com

"Wonderfully readable. *The Minds of Boys* fills a great void for parents and educators by offering practical ways to change the developmental course for boys at risk. Gurian and Stevens show us that we don't have to surrender our boys to depression or school failure: an essential piece of school reform!"

—Robin Karr-Morse, author, *Ghosts from the Nursery*

In this fascinating and practical book, Michael Gurian—the author of the best-selling *The Wonder of Boys*—and Kathy Stevens show parents and teachers how to help our boys overcome their current classroom obstacles and failures. They offer clear-cut step-by-step guidance to help boys fulfill themselves, use their intelligence, work with their unique natural gifts, expand every bit of their potential, and ultimately succeed in life.

The Minds of Boys also presents a scientifically researched, field-tested program for helping boys learn the academic basics: reading, writing, math, and science. Drawing from the latest gender-based brain science and tested by the Gurian Institute and school districts across the United States, Canada, and Australia, the program speaks to specific differences in the way boys and girls learn, the best learning environment for boys' brains, how to help undermotivated and underperforming boys, how to use the arts and athletics to teach boys, how to teach and care for sensitive, aggressive, restless, or bored boys, and how to utilize the option of single-gender education at crucial periods of a boy's life.

Michael Gurian is the *New York Times* best-selling author of *The Wonder of Boys* and nineteen other books, including *A Fine Young Man, The Good Son, The Wonder of Girls,* and *Boys and Girls Learn Differently!* He is a pioneer in the fields of family development and education and has appeared on *Today, Good Morning America,* CNN, NPR, and in *The New York Times, USA Today, Time, Newsweek,* and elsewhere.

Kathy Stevens is the training director of the Gurian Institute and has worked in education, child development, and the nonprofit world for more than thirty years in programs as diverse as juvenile and adult corrections, teen pregnancy prevention, cultural competency training, domestic violence prevention, and women's issues.